THE INVINCIBLE IRON MAN
MY MONSTERS

IBLE IRON MAN VOL. 7: MY MONSTERS. Contains material originally published in magazine form as INVINCIBLE IRON MAN #500, #500.1 and #503; and IRON MAN ANNUAL #1. First printing 2011. Hardcover 978-0-7851-4836-4. Softcover ISBN# 978-0-7851-4837-1. Published by MARVEL WORLDWIDE, INC., a subsidiary of MARVEL ENTERTAINMENT, LLC. OFFICE OF PUBLICATION: 135 West 50th Street, New Y 10020. Copyright © 2010 and 2011 Marvel Characters, Inc. All rights reserved. Hardcover: $19.99 per copy in the U.S. and $21.99 in Canada (GST #R127032852). Softcover: $15.99 per copy in the U.S. .50 in Canada (GST #R127032852). Canadian Agreement #40668537. All characters featured in this issue and the distinctive names and likenesses thereof, and all related indicia are trademarks of Marvel ters, Inc. No similarity between any of the names, characters, persons, and/or institutions in this magazine with those of any living or dead person or institution is intended, and any such similarity which may purely coincidental. **Printed in the U.S.A.** ALAN FINE, EVP - Office of the President, Marvel Worldwide, Inc. and EVP & CMO Marvel Characters B.V.; DAN BUCKLEY, Publisher & President - Print, Animation & Divisions; JOE QUESADA, Chief Creative Officer; JIM SOKOLOWSKI, Chief Operating Officer; DAVID BOGART, SVP of Business Affairs & Talent Management; TOM BREVOORT, SVP of Publishing; C.B. CEBULSKI, Creator & Content Development; DAVID GABRIEL, SVP of Publishing Sales & Circulation; MICHAEL PASCIULLO, SVP of Brand Planning & Communications; JIM O'KEEFE, VP of Operations & Logistics; DAN xecutive Director of Publishing Technology; JUSTIN F. GABRIE, Director of Publishing & Editorial Operations; SUSAN CRESPI, Editorial Operations Manager; ALEX MORALES, Publishing Operations Manager; EE, Chairman Emeritus. For information regarding advertising in Marvel Comics or on Marvel.com, please contact John Dokes, SVP Integrated Sales and Marketing, at jdokes@marvel.com. For Marvel
ction inquiries please

IRON MAN

MY MONSTERS

WRITER: **MATT FRACTION**

ANNUAL #1
ARTIST: **CARMINE DI GIANDOMENICO**
COLORS: **MATTHEW WILSON**

ISSUE #500.1
ARTIST: **SALVADOR LARROCA**
COLORS: **FRANK D'ARMATA**

"HOW I MET YOUR MOTHER"
ARTIST: **HOWARD CHAYKIN**
COLORS: **EDGAR DELGADO**

ISSUE #500
ART & COLOR, IRON MAN & SPIDER-MAN:
SALVADOR LARROCA & FRANK D'ARMATA
ART & COLOR, GINNY STARK: **KANO**
ART & COLOR, HOWARD STARK II: **NATHAN FOX & JAVIER RODRIGUEZ**
ART & COLOR, TONY STARK & THE MANDARIN:
CARMINE DI GIANDOMENICO & MATTHEW WILSON

LETTERS: **VC'S JOE CARAMAGNA**
COVER ART: **SALVADOR LARROCA & FRANK D'ARMATA**
EDITOR: **ALEJANDRO ARBONA**
SENIOR EDITOR: **STEPHEN WACKER**

COLLECTION EDITOR: **JENNIFER GRÜNWALD**
EDITORIAL ASSISTANTS: **JAMES EMMETT & JOE HOCHSTEIN**
ASSISTANT EDITORS: **ALEX STARBUCK & NELSON RIBEIRO**
EDITOR, SPECIAL PROJECTS: **MARK D. BEAZLEY**
SENIOR EDITOR, SPECIAL PROJECTS: **JEFF YOUNGQUIST**
SENIOR VICE PRESIDENT OF SALES: **DAVID GABRIEL**
SVP OF BRAND PLANNING & COMMUNICATIONS: **MICHAEL PASCIULLO**

EDITOR IN CHIEF: **AXEL ALONSO**
CHIEF CREATIVE OFFICER: **JOE QUESADA**
PUBLISHER: **DAN BUCKLEY**

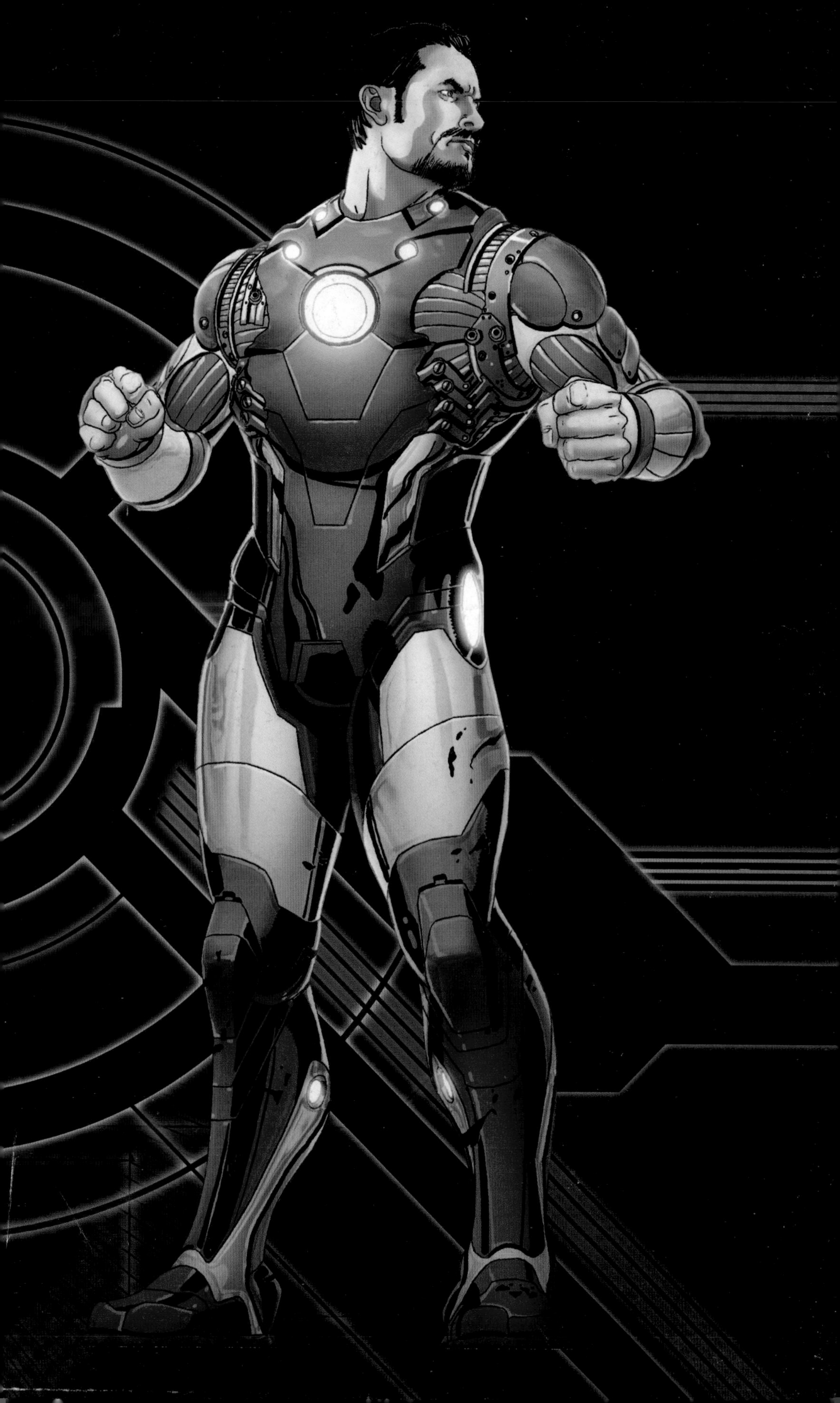

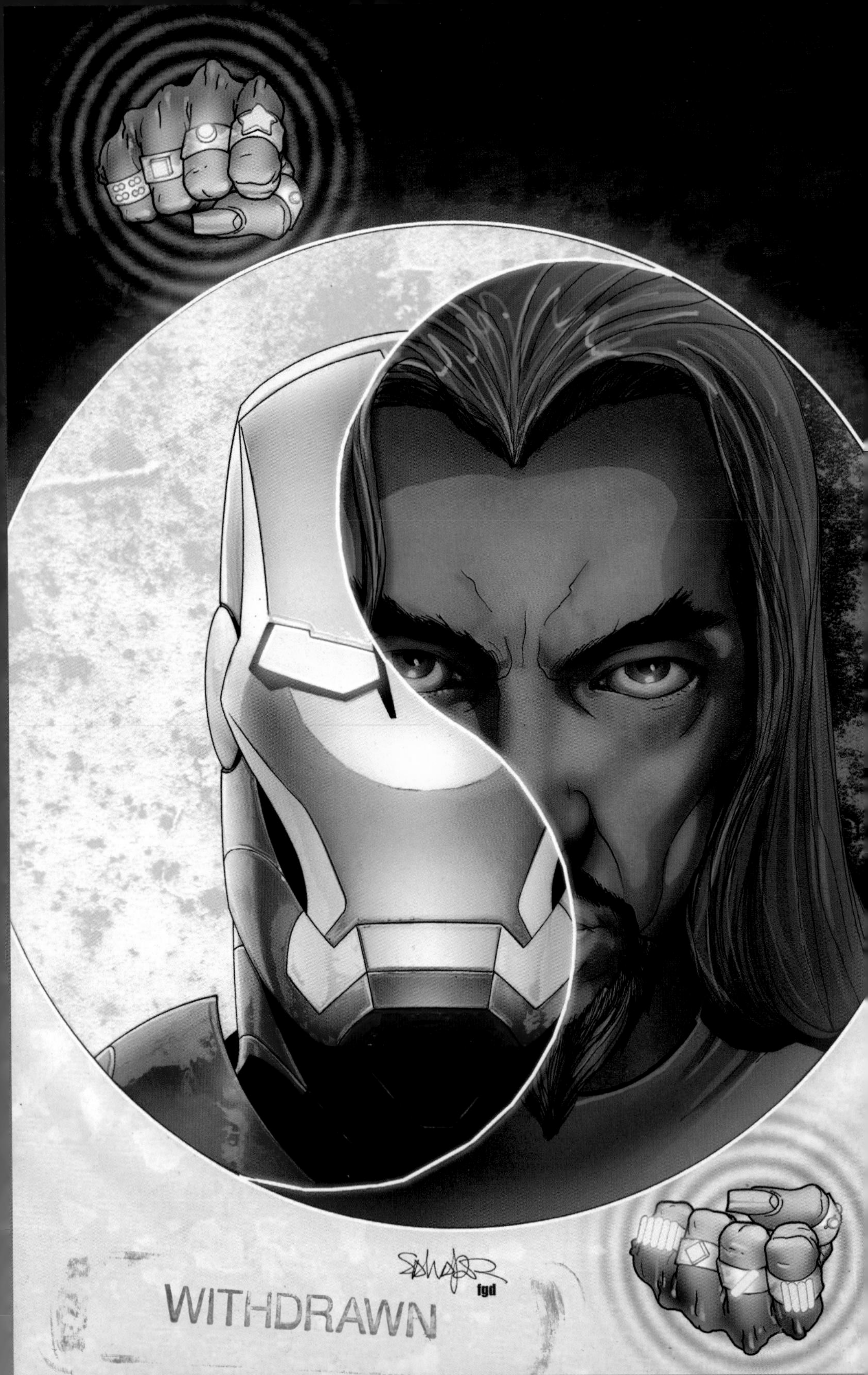
fgd
WITHDRAWN

ANNUAL 1 MANDARIN: THE STORY OF MY LIFE

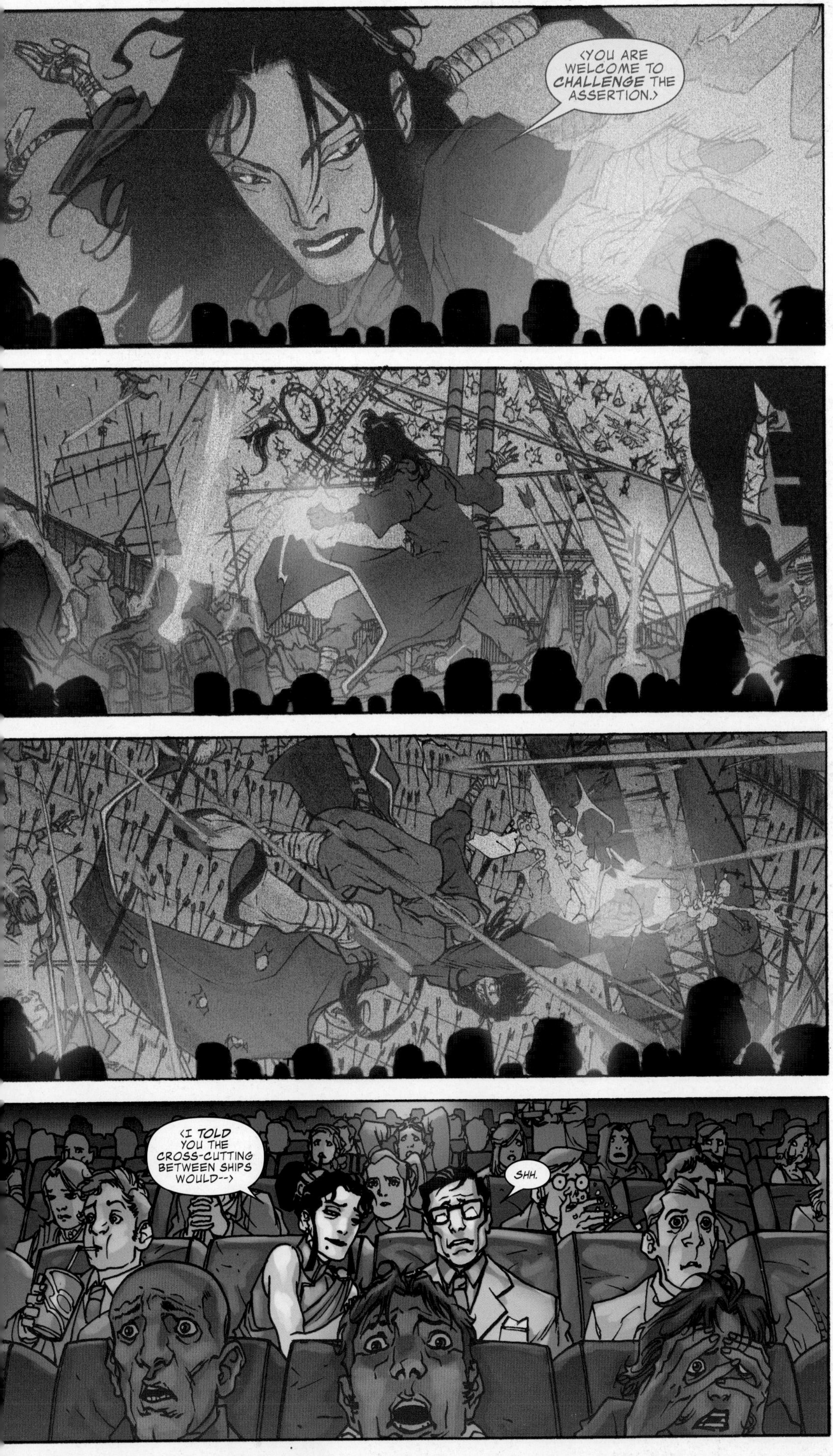

<YOU ARE WELCOME TO CHALLENGE THE ASSERTION.>
<I TOLD YOU THE CROSS-CUTTING BETWEEN SHIPS WOULD-->
SHH.

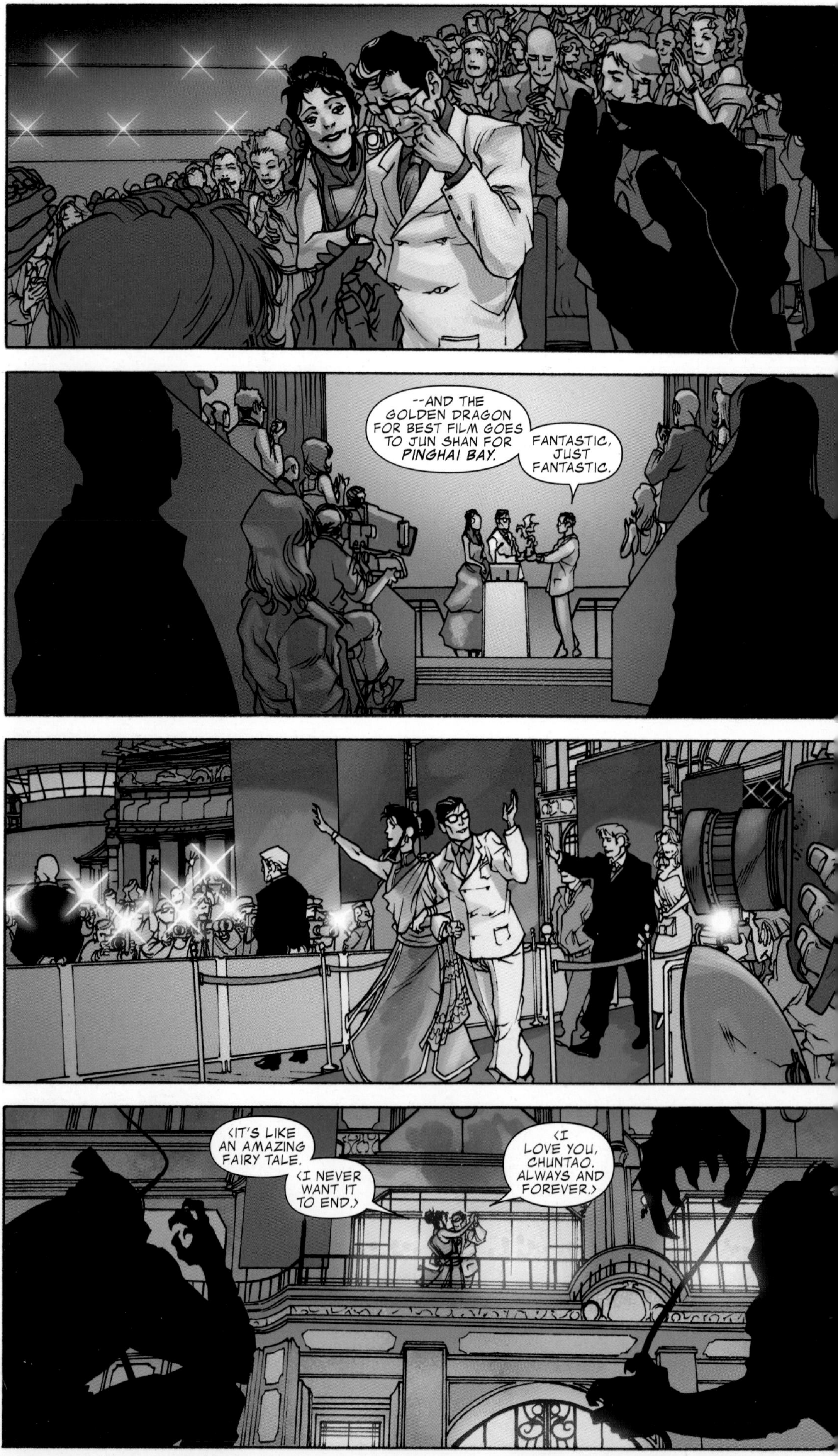
--AND THE GOLDEN DRAGON FOR BEST FILM GOES TO JUN SHAN FOR PINGHAI BAY.
FANTASTIC, JUST FANTASTIC.
<IT'S LIKE AN AMAZING FAIRY TALE.
<I NEVER WANT IT TO END.>
<I LOVE YOU, CHUNTAO. ALWAYS AND FOREVER.>

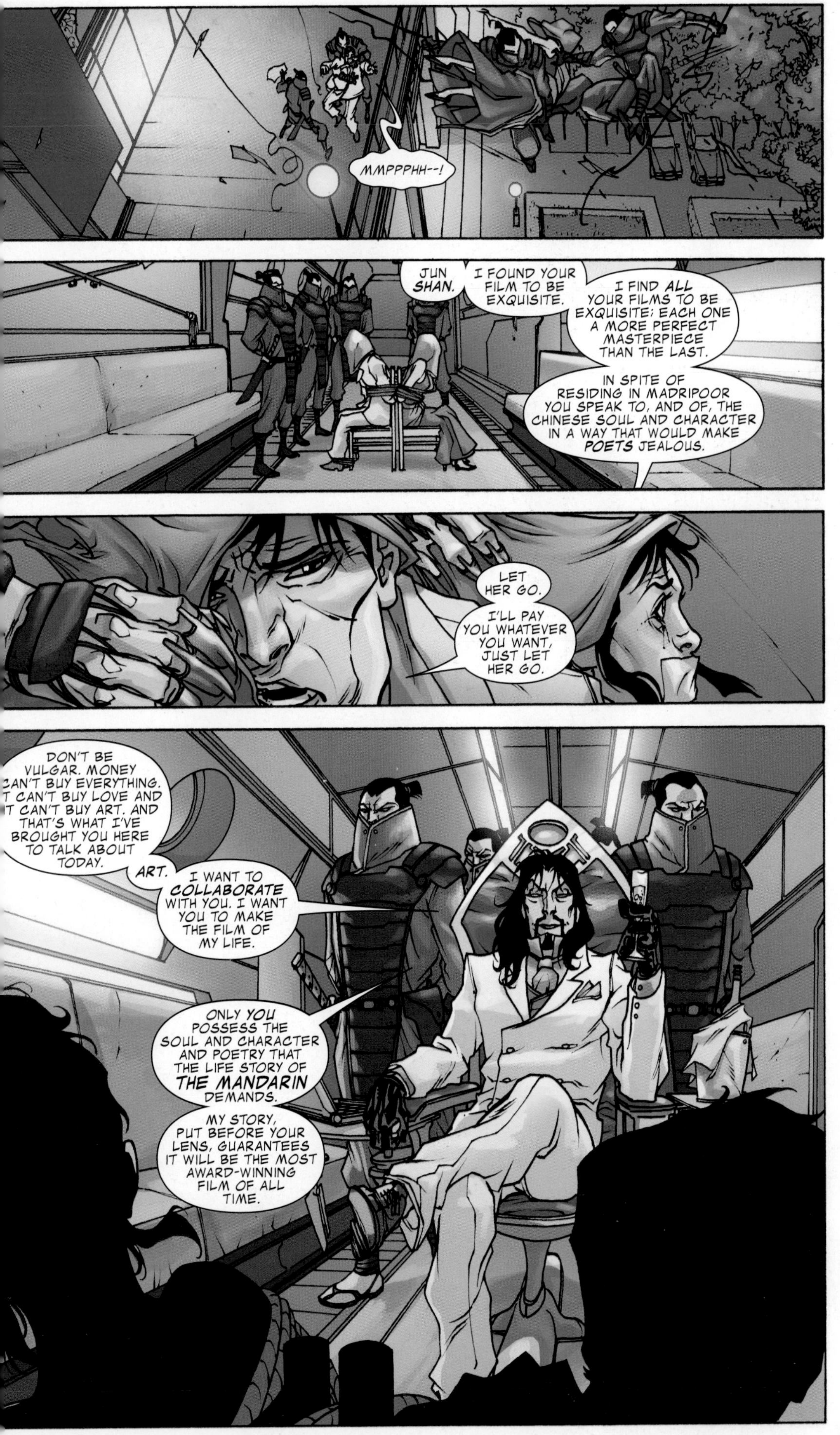

MMPPPHH--!
JUN SHAN.
I FOUND YOUR FILM TO BE EXQUISITE.
I FIND ALL YOUR FILMS TO BE EXQUISITE; EACH ONE A MORE PERFECT MASTERPIECE THAN THE LAST.
IN SPITE OF RESIDING IN MADRIPOOR YOU SPEAK TO, AND OF, THE CHINESE SOUL AND CHARACTER IN A WAY THAT WOULD MAKE POETS JEALOUS.
LET HER GO.
I'LL PAY YOU WHATEVER YOU WANT, JUST LET HER GO.
DON'T BE VULGAR. MONEY CAN'T BUY EVERYTHING. IT CAN'T BUY LOVE AND IT CAN'T BUY ART. AND THAT'S WHAT I'VE BROUGHT YOU HERE TO TALK ABOUT TODAY.
ART.
I WANT TO COLLABORATE WITH YOU. I WANT YOU TO MAKE THE FILM OF MY LIFE.
ONLY YOU POSSESS THE SOUL AND CHARACTER AND POETRY THAT THE LIFE STORY OF THE MANDARIN DEMANDS.
MY STORY, PUT BEFORE YOUR LENS, GUARANTEES IT WILL BE THE MOST AWARD-WINNING FILM OF ALL TIME.

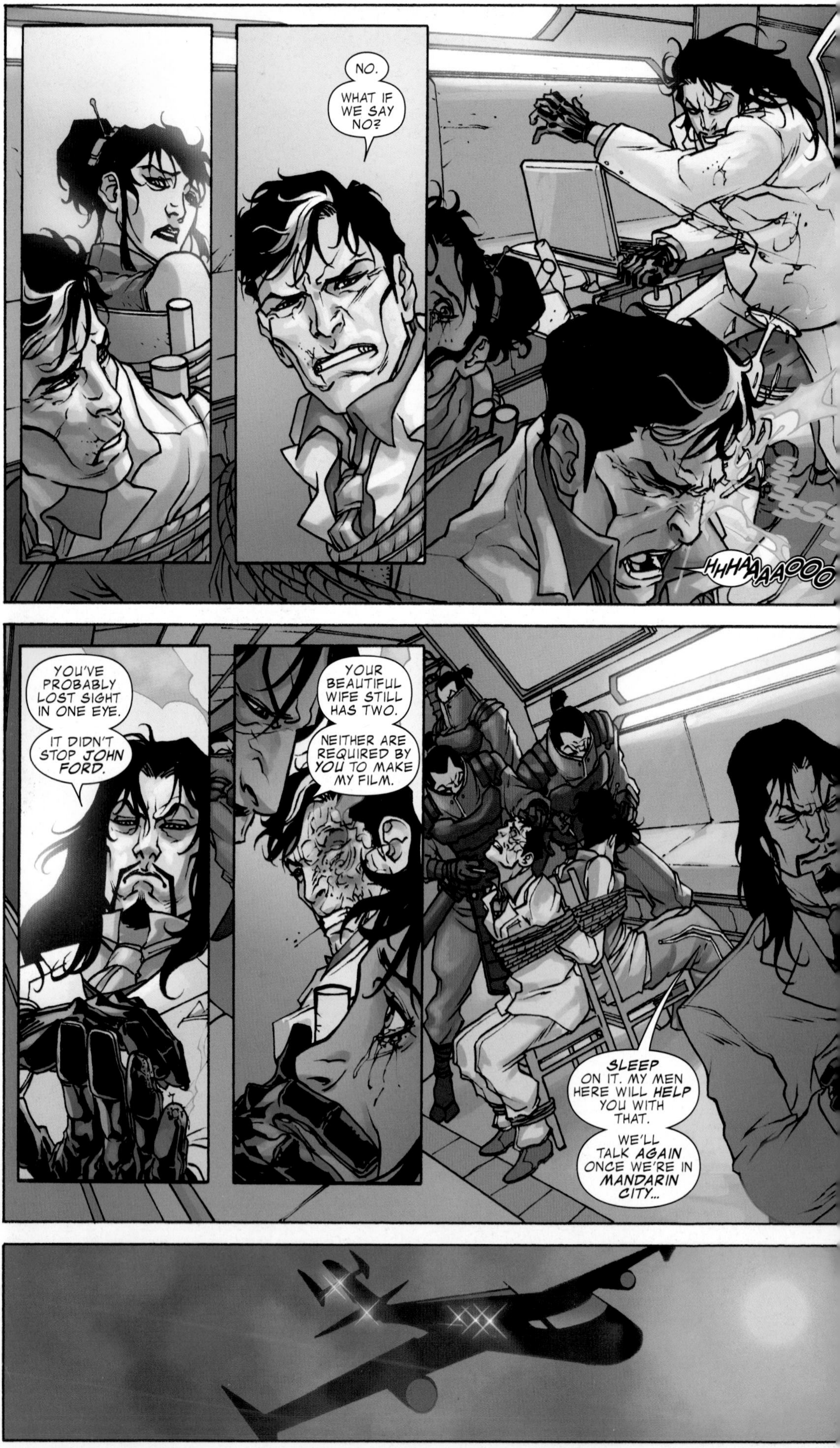
NO.
WHAT IF WE SAY NO?
HHHAAAAOOO
YOU'VE PROBABLY LOST SIGHT IN ONE EYE.
IT DIDN'T STOP **JOHN FORD**.
YOUR BEAUTIFUL WIFE STILL HAS TWO.
NEITHER ARE REQUIRED BY ***YOU*** TO MAKE MY FILM.
SLEEP ON IT. MY MEN HERE WILL ***HELP*** YOU WITH THAT.
WE'LL TALK ***AGAIN*** ONCE WE'RE IN ***MANDARIN CITY***...

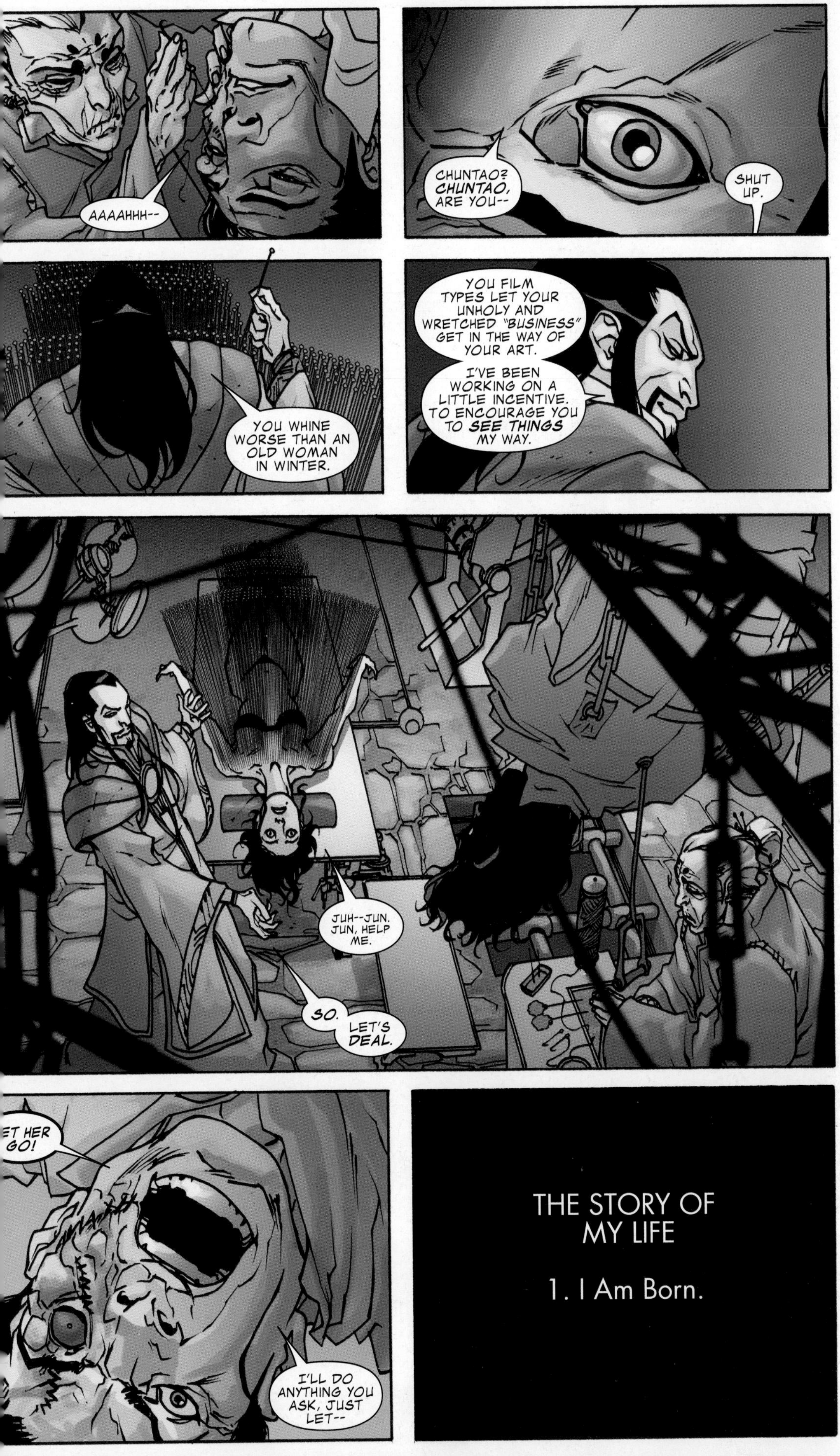
AAAAHHH--
CHUNTAO? CHUNTAO, ARE YOU--
SHUT UP.
YOU WHINE WORSE THAN AN OLD WOMAN IN WINTER.
YOU FILM TYPES LET YOUR UNHOLY AND WRETCHED "BUSINESS" GET IN THE WAY OF YOUR ART.
I'VE BEEN WORKING ON A LITTLE INCENTIVE. TO ENCOURAGE YOU TO SEE THINGS MY WAY.
JUH--JUN. JUN, HELP ME.
SO. LET'S DEAL.
ET HER GO!
I'LL DO ANYTHING YOU ASK, JUST LET--
THE STORY OF MY LIFE
1. I Am Born.

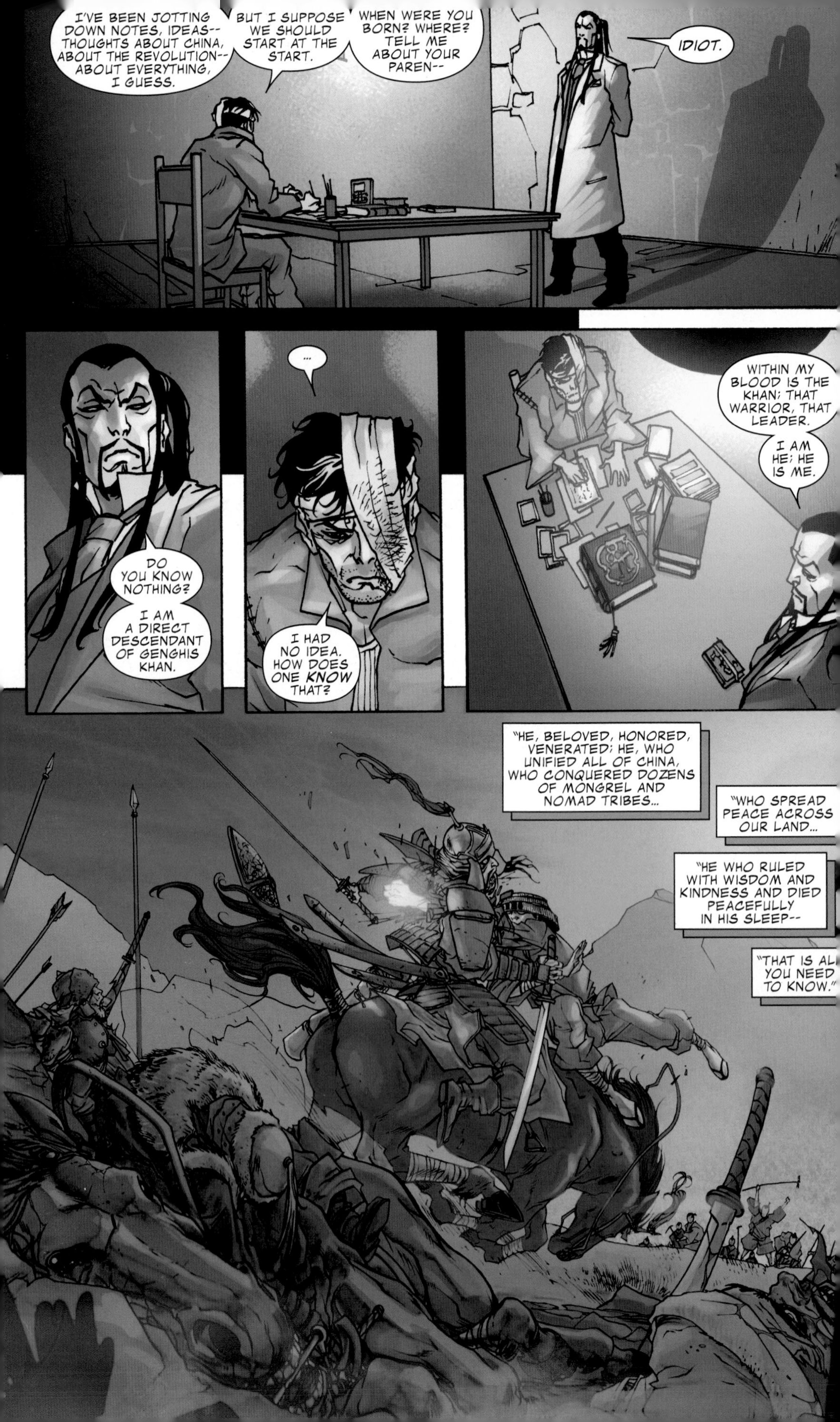
I'VE BEEN JOTTING DOWN NOTES, IDEAS-- THOUGHTS ABOUT CHINA, ABOUT THE REVOLUTION-- ABOUT EVERYTHING, I GUESS.
BUT I SUPPOSE WE SHOULD START AT THE START.
WHEN WERE YOU BORN? WHERE? TELL ME ABOUT YOUR PAREN--
IDIOT.
DO YOU KNOW NOTHING?
I AM A DIRECT DESCENDANT OF GENGHIS KHAN.
...
I HAD NO IDEA. HOW DOES ONE KNOW THAT?
WITHIN MY BLOOD IS THE KHAN; THAT WARRIOR, THAT LEADER.
I AM HE; HE IS ME.
"HE, BELOVED, HONORED, VENERATED; HE, WHO UNIFIED ALL OF CHINA, WHO CONQUERED DOZENS OF MONGREL AND NOMAD TRIBES...
"WHO SPREAD PEACE ACROSS OUR LAND...
"HE WHO RULED WITH WISDOM AND KINDNESS AND DIED PEACEFULLY IN HIS SLEEP--
"THAT IS ALL YOU NEED TO KNOW."

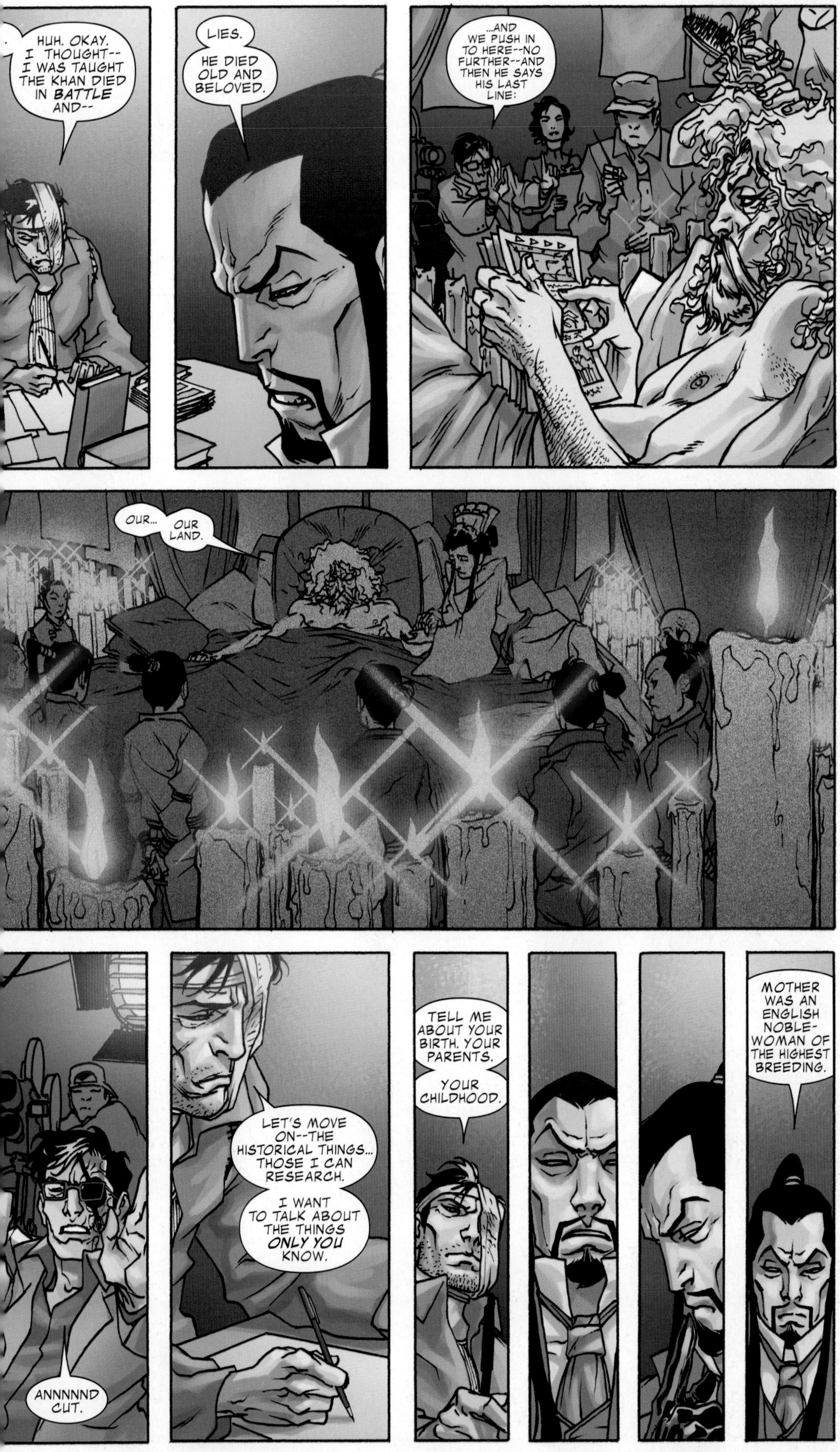

HUH. OKAY. I THOUGHT-- I WAS TAUGHT THE KHAN DIED IN BATTLE AND--
LIES.
HE DIED OLD AND BELOVED.
...AND WE PUSH IN TO HERE--NO FURTHER--AND THEN HE SAYS HIS LAST LINE:
OUR... OUR LAND.
ANNNNND CUT.
LET'S MOVE ON--THE HISTORICAL THINGS... THOSE I CAN RESEARCH.
I WANT TO TALK ABOUT THE THINGS ONLY YOU KNOW.
TELL ME ABOUT YOUR BIRTH. YOUR PARENTS.
YOUR CHILDHOOD.
MOTHER WAS AN ENGLISH NOBLE-WOMAN OF THE HIGHEST BREEDING.

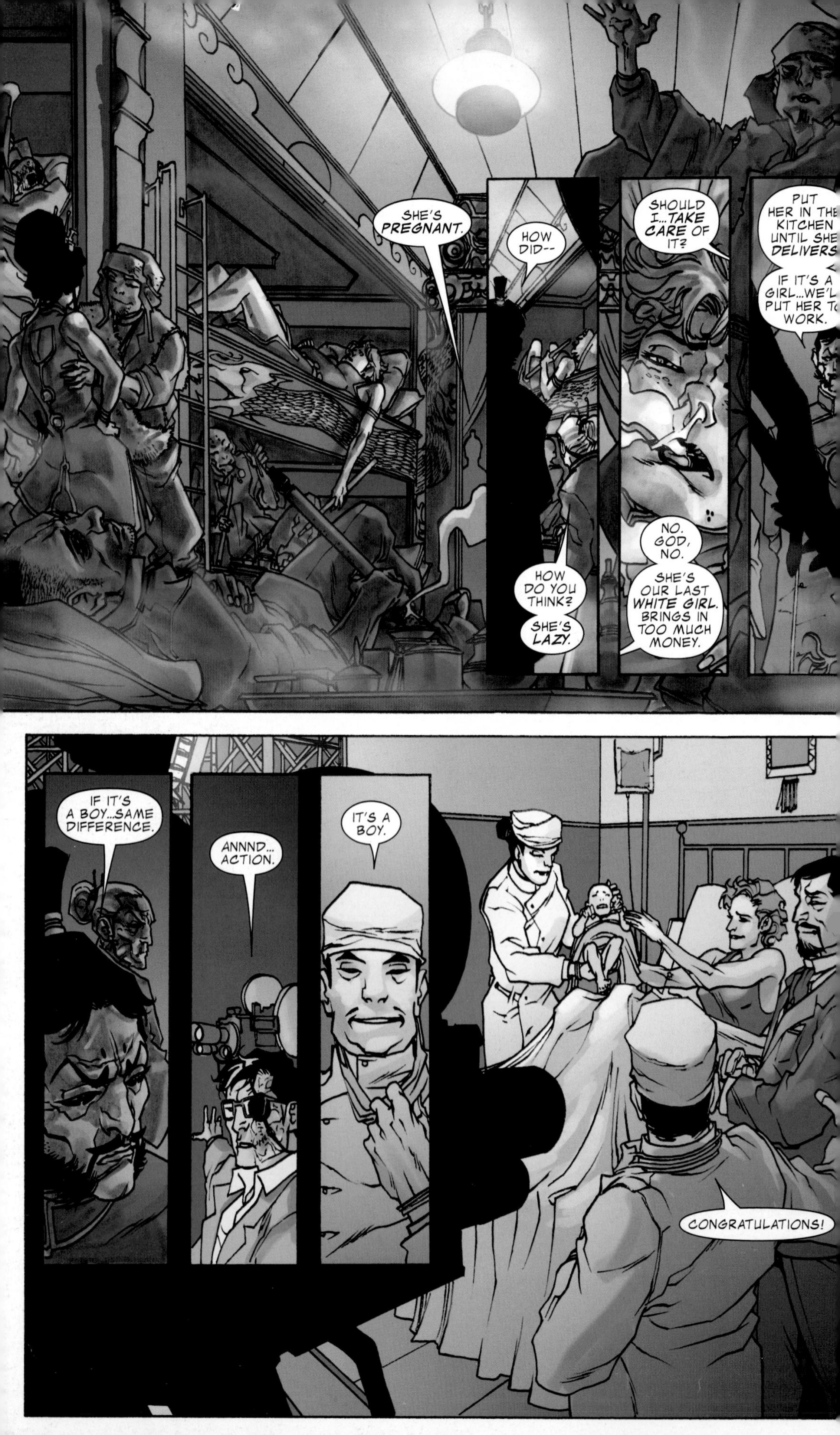
SHE'S PREGNANT.
HOW DID--
HOW DO YOU THINK?
SHE'S LAZY.
SHOULD I...TAKE CARE OF IT?
NO. GOD, NO.
SHE'S OUR LAST WHITE GIRL. BRINGS IN TOO MUCH MONEY.
PUT HER IN THE KITCHEN UNTIL SHE DELIVERS
IF IT'S A GIRL...WE'L PUT HER TO WORK.
IF IT'S A BOY...SAME DIFFERENCE.
ANNND... ACTION.
IT'S A BOY.
CONGRATULATIONS!

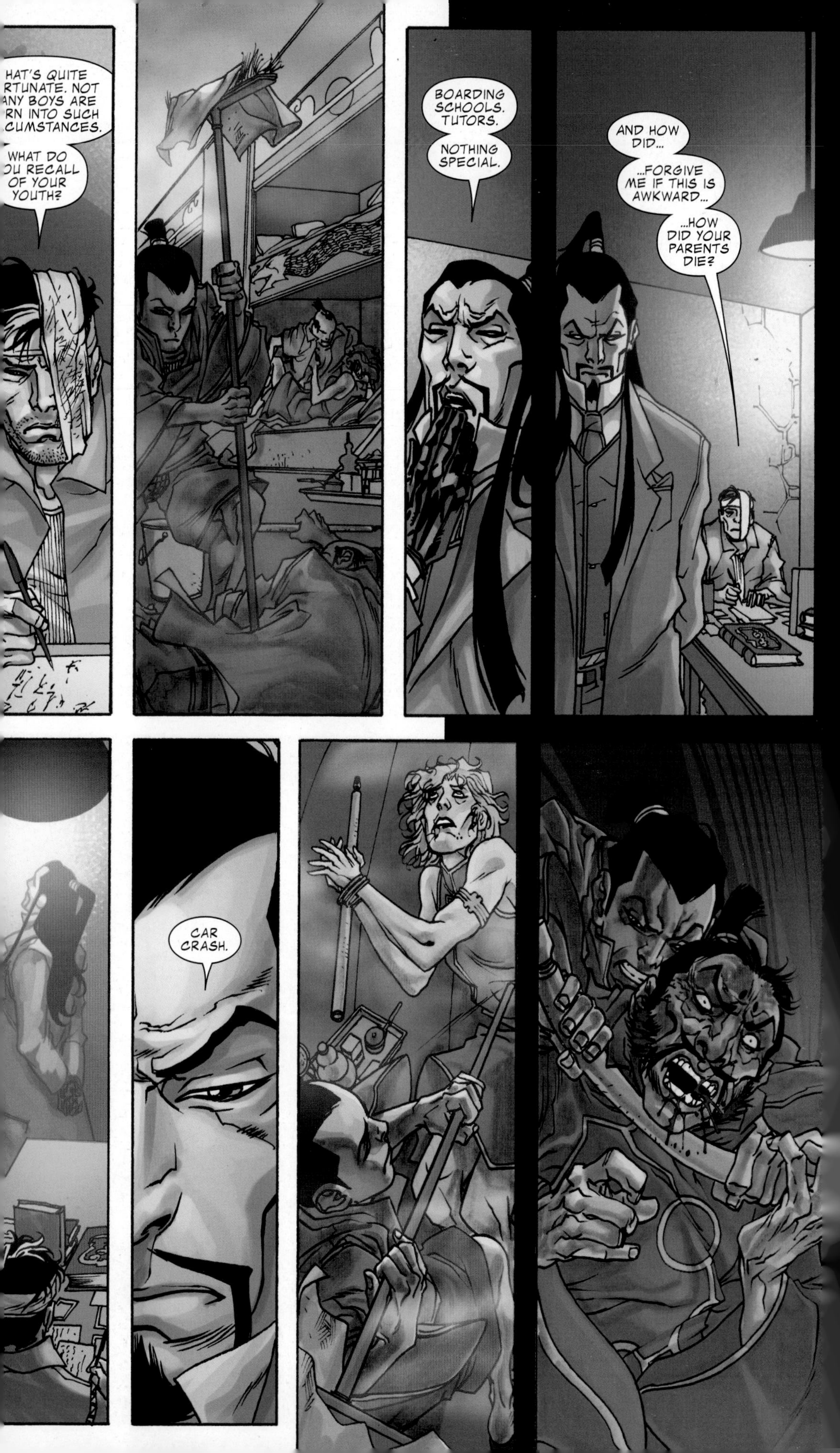
HAT'S QUITE
RTUNATE. NOT
ANY BOYS ARE
RN INTO SUCH
CUMSTANCES.
WHAT DO
OU RECALL
OF YOUR
YOUTH?
BOARDING
SCHOOLS.
TUTORS.
NOTHING
SPECIAL.
AND HOW
DID...
...FORGIVE
ME IF THIS IS
AWKWARD...
...HOW
DID YOUR
PARENTS
DIE?
CAR
CRASH.

"I WAS TAKEN IN BY MY MOTHER'S STERN SISTER AND RAISED IN THE FINEST BOARDING SCHOOLS EUROPE AND ASIA HAD TO OFFER.

"I EXCELLED IN MY STUDIES, OF COURSE, AND GRADUATED RATHER EARLY."

THEN WHAT HAPPENED?

"THE WAR OF LIBERATION.

COMMUNIST CHANGED EVERYTHING.

"THE REVOLUTION WELCOMED ME INTO ITS ARMS.

"I WAS A HERO OF THE REVOLUTION.

"I AM OF THE KHAN. I UNDERSTAND THE LONG VIEW.

"I CARRIED MAO'S MESSAGE FAR AND WIDE."

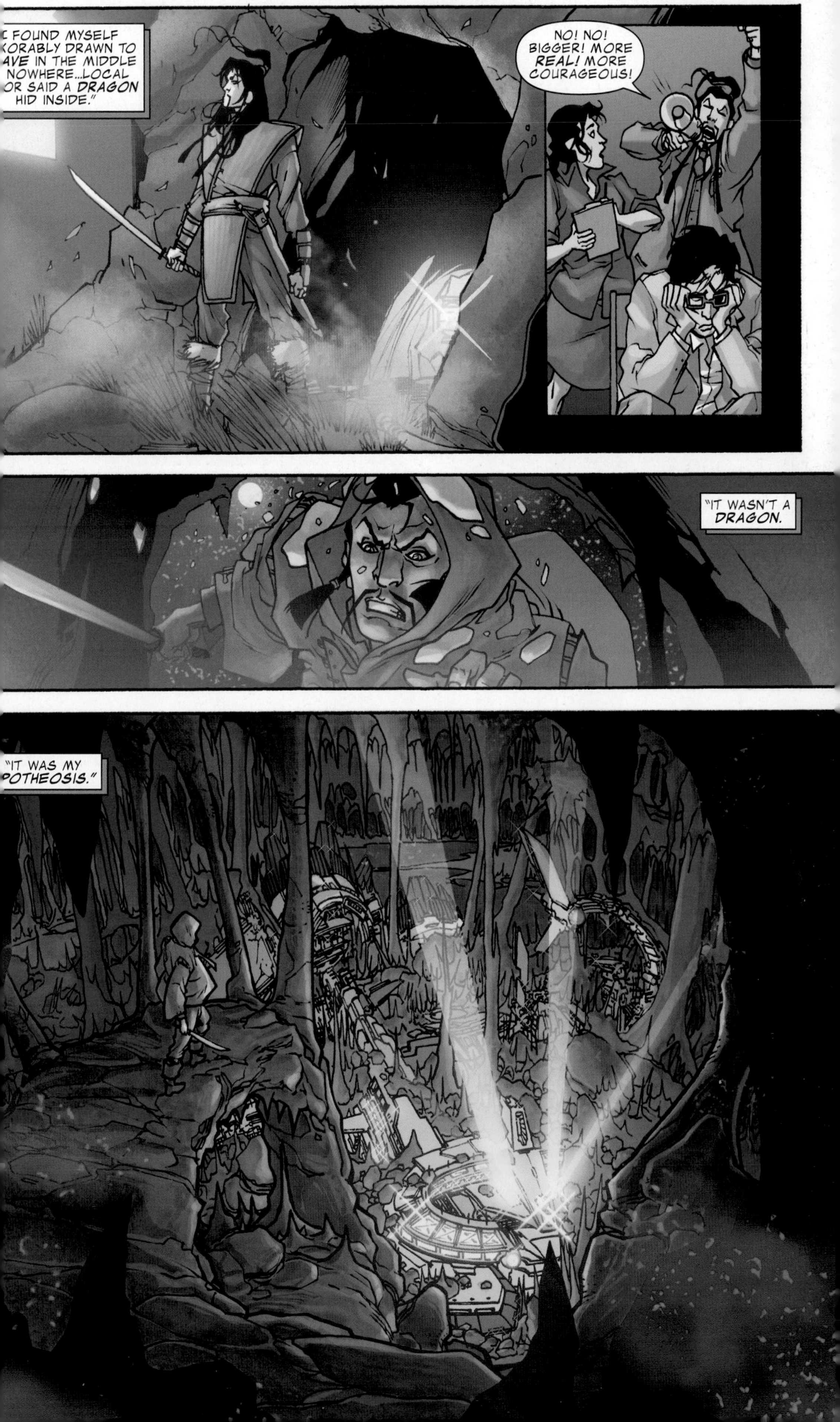

FOUND MYSELF XORABLY DRAWN TO AVE IN THE MIDDLE NOWHERE...LOCAL OR SAID A DRAGON HID INSIDE."
NO! NO! BIGGER! MORE REAL! MORE COURAGEOUS!
"IT WASN'T A DRAGON.
"IT WAS MY POTHEOSIS."

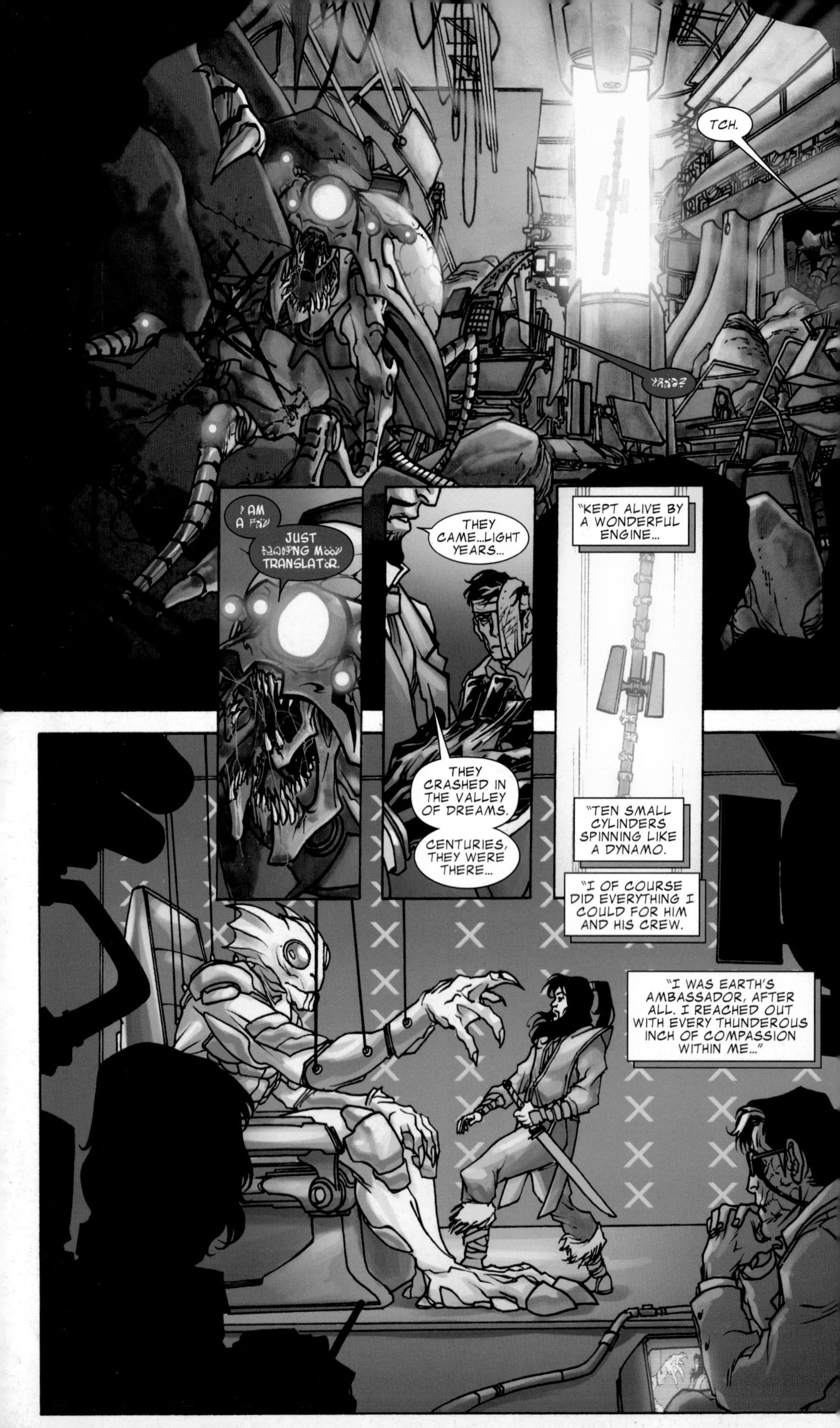
TCH.
I AM A
JUST
TRANSLATOR.
THEY CAME...LIGHT YEARS...
THEY CRASHED IN THE VALLEY OF DREAMS.
CENTURIES, THEY WERE THERE...
"KEPT ALIVE BY A WONDERFUL ENGINE...
"TEN SMALL CYLINDERS SPINNING LIKE A DYNAMO.
"I OF COURSE DID EVERYTHING I COULD FOR HIM AND HIS CREW.
"I WAS EARTH'S AMBASSADOR, AFTER ALL. I REACHED OUT WITH EVERY THUNDEROUS INCH OF COMPASSION WITHIN ME..."

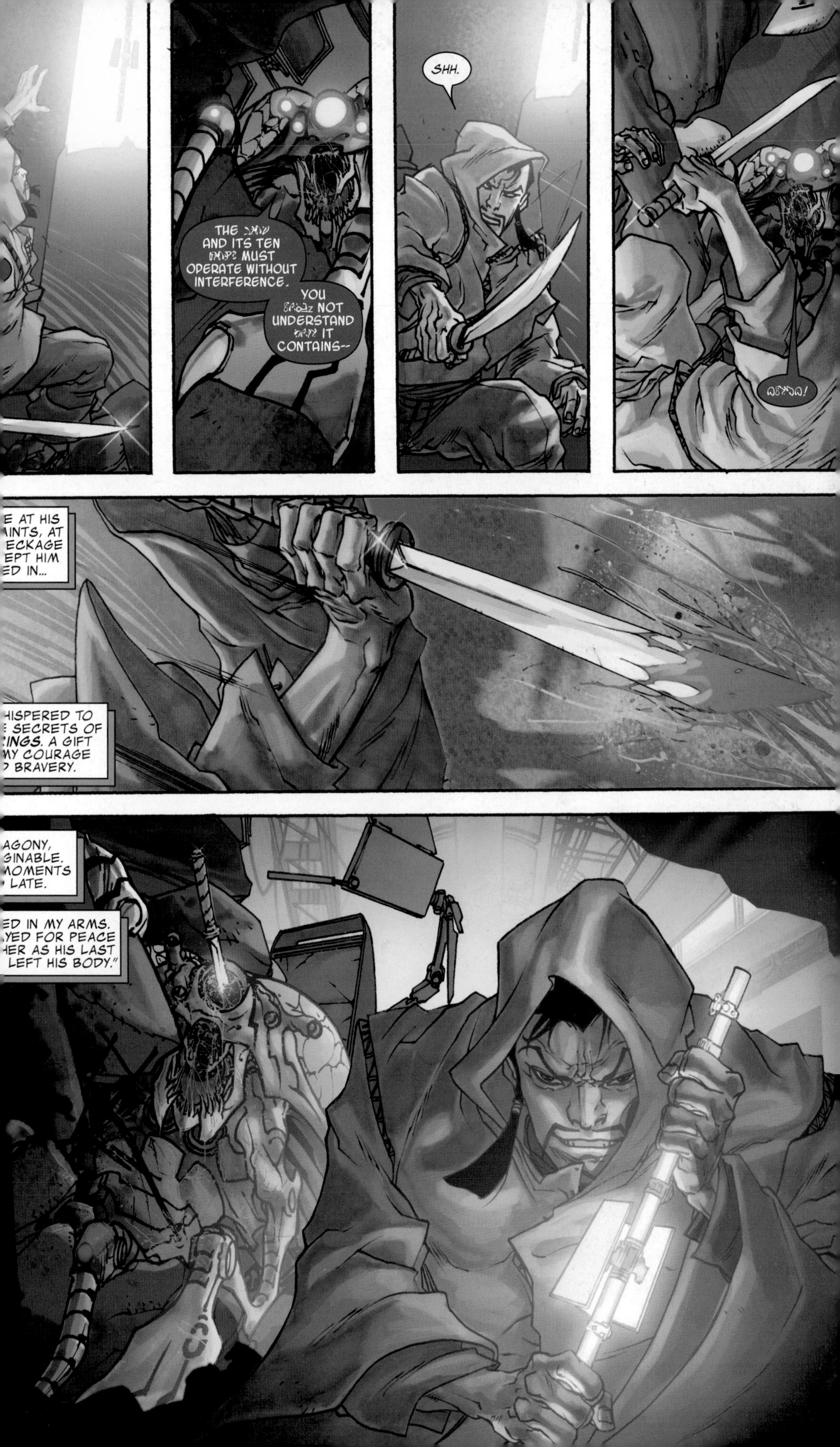
THE AND ITS TEN MUST OPERATE WITHOUT INTERFERENCE.
YOU NOT UNDERSTAND IT CONTAINS--
SHH.
E AT HIS AINTS, AT ECKAGE EPT HIM ED IN...
HISPERED TO E SECRETS OF RINGS. A GIFT MY COURAGE D BRAVERY.
AGONY, GINABLE. MOMENTS LATE.
ED IN MY ARMS. YED FOR PEACE HER AS HIS LAST LEFT HIS BODY."

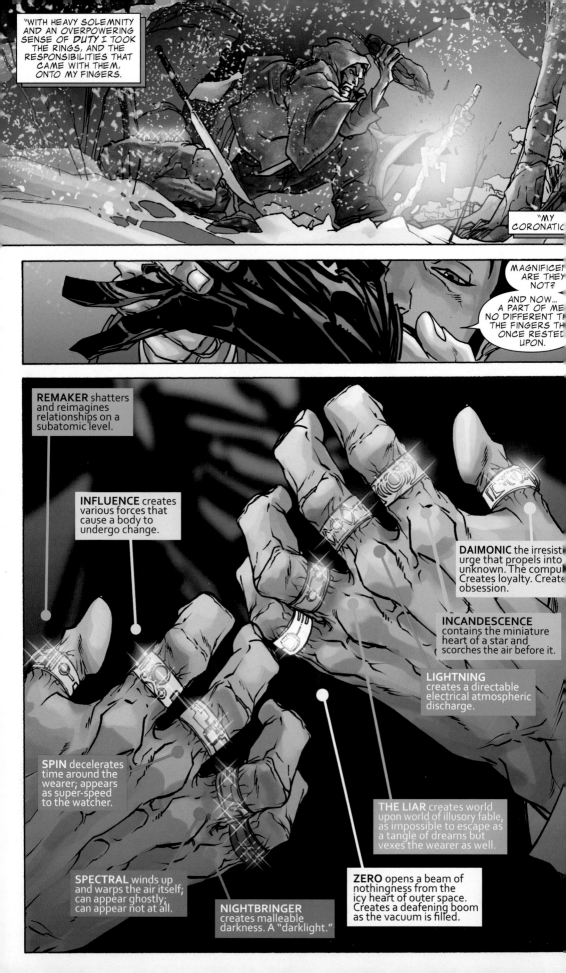

"WITH HEAVY SOLEMNITY AND AN OVERPOWERING SENSE OF *DUTY* I TOOK THE RINGS, AND THE RESPONSIBILITIES THAT CAME WITH THEM, ONTO MY FINGERS.

"MY CORONATIC

MAGNIFICEN ARE THEY NOT?

AND NOW... A PART OF ME NO DIFFERENT T THE FINGERS TH ONCE RESTED UPON.

REMAKER shatters and reimagines relationships on a subatomic level.

INFLUENCE creates various forces that cause a body to undergo change.

DAIMONIC the irresist urge that propels into unknown. The compu Creates loyalty. Create obsession.

INCANDESCENCE contains the miniature heart of a star and scorches the air before it.

LIGHTNING creates a directable electrical atmospheric discharge.

SPIN decelerates time around the wearer; appears as super-speed to the watcher.

THE LIAR creates world upon world of illusory fable, as impossible to escape as a tangle of dreams but vexes the wearer as well.

SPECTRAL winds up and warps the air itself; can appear ghostly; can appear not at all.

NIGHTBRINGER creates malleable darkness. A "darklight."

ZERO opens a beam of nothingness from the icy heart of outer space. Creates a deafening boom as the vacuum is filled.

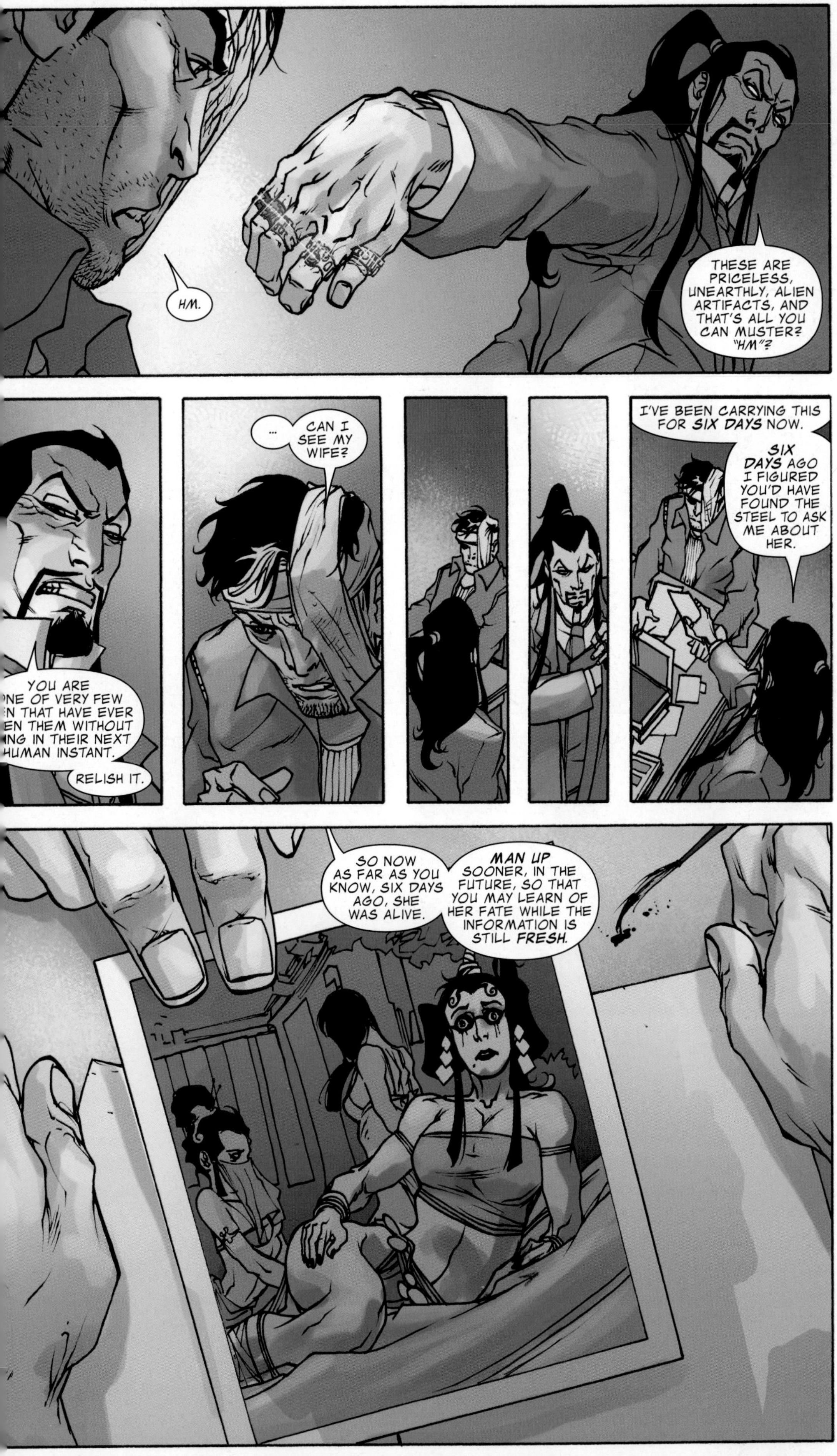

HM.
THESE ARE PRICELESS, UNEARTHLY, ALIEN ARTIFACTS, AND THAT'S ALL YOU CAN MUSTER? "HM"?
YOU ARE ONE OF VERY FEW MEN THAT HAVE EVER SEEN THEM WITHOUT DYING IN THEIR NEXT HUMAN INSTANT.
RELISH IT.
...
CAN I SEE MY WIFE?
I'VE BEEN CARRYING THIS FOR SIX DAYS NOW.
SIX DAYS AGO I FIGURED YOU'D HAVE FOUND THE STEEL TO ASK ME ABOUT HER.
SO NOW AS FAR AS YOU KNOW, SIX DAYS AGO, SHE WAS ALIVE.
MAN UP SOONER, IN THE FUTURE, SO THAT YOU MAY LEARN OF HER FATE WHILE THE INFORMATION IS STILL FRESH.

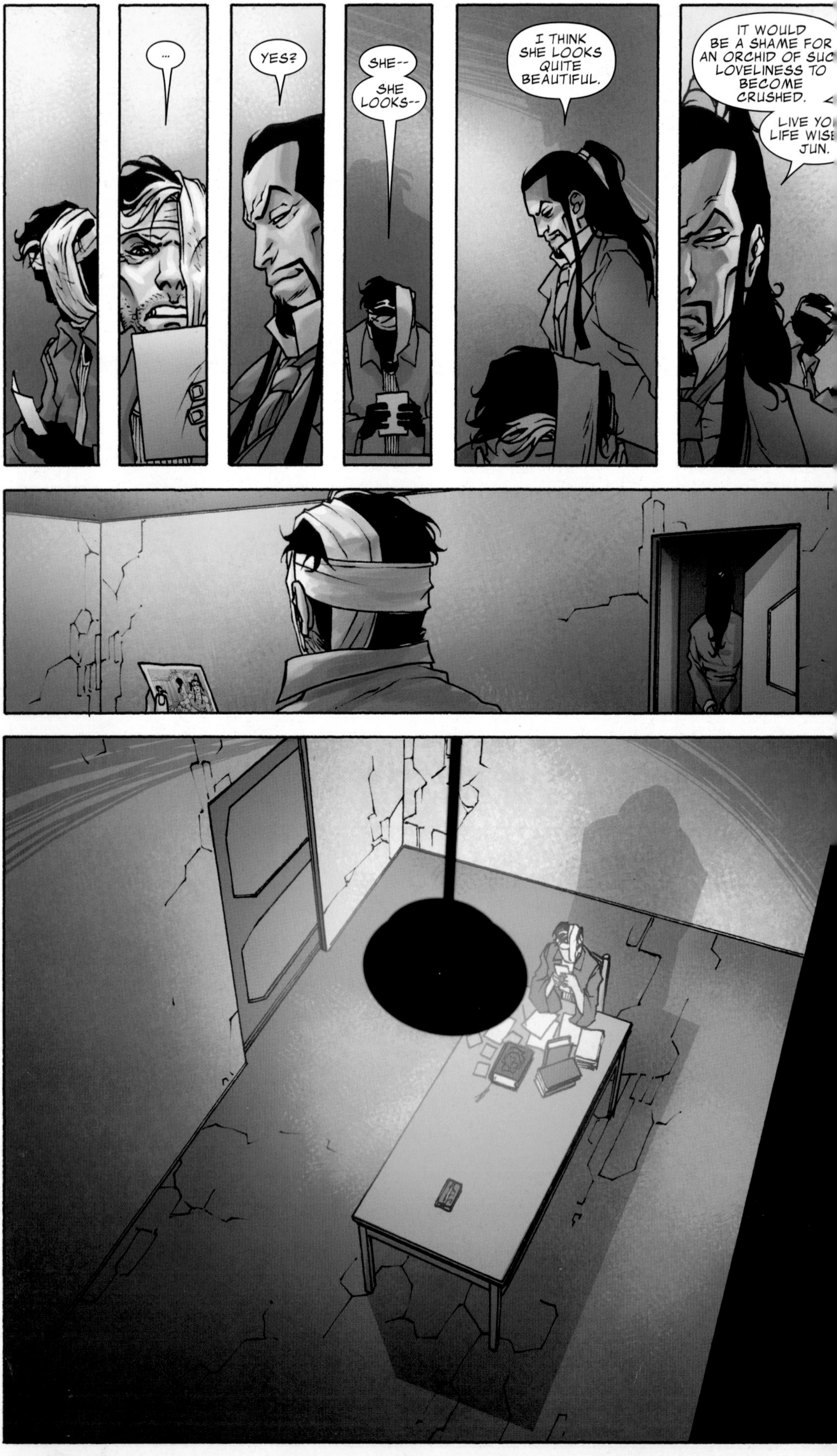
...
YES?
SHE--
SHE LOOKS--
I THINK SHE LOOKS QUITE BEAUTIFUL.
IT WOULD BE A SHAME FOR AN ORCHID OF SUC LOVELINESS TO BECOME CRUSHED.
LIVE YO LIFE WISE JUN.

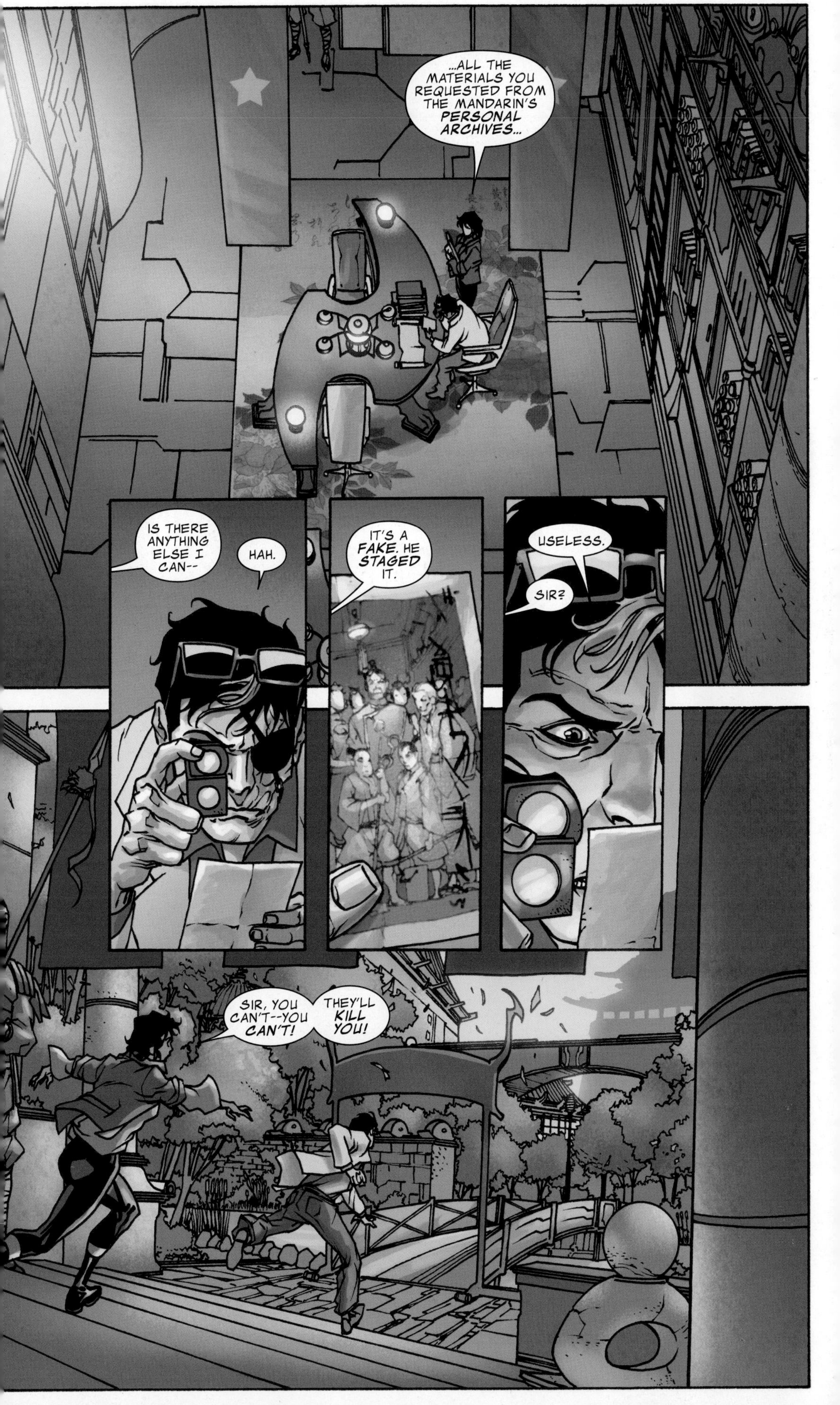
...ALL THE MATERIALS YOU REQUESTED FROM THE MANDARIN'S PERSONAL ARCHIVES...
IS THERE ANYTHING ELSE I CAN--
HAH.
IT'S A FAKE. HE STAGED IT.
USELESS.
SIR?
SIR, YOU CAN'T--YOU CAN'T!
THEY'LL KILL YOU!

GOD.

HALT!

I NE
TO S
HI/

AND
AM N
ASKI

GUARDS!
GUARDS!

HALT!
HALT!

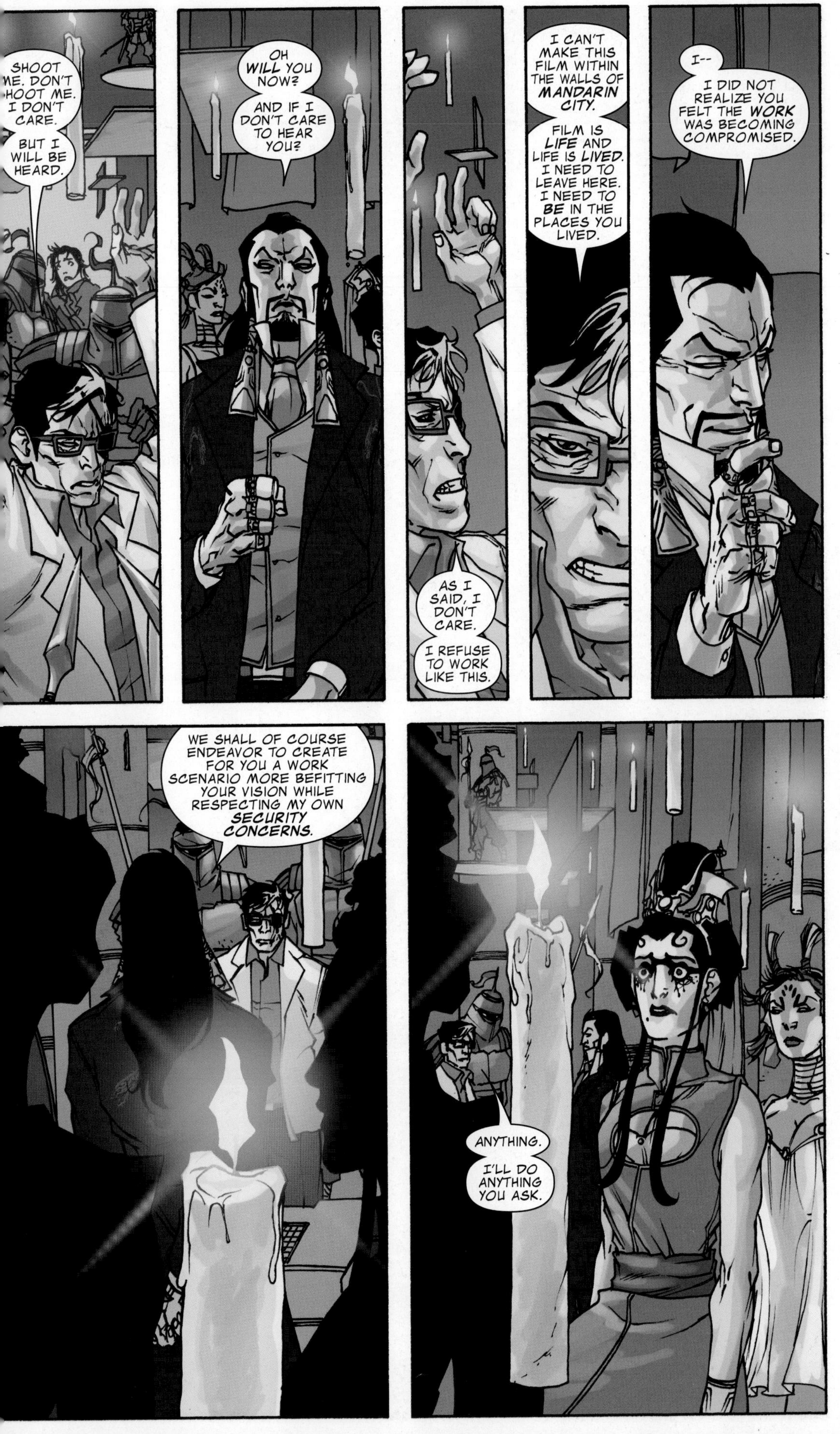

SHOOT ME. DON'T SHOOT ME. I DON'T CARE.
BUT I WILL BE HEARD.
OH WILL YOU NOW?
AND IF I DON'T CARE TO HEAR YOU?
AS I SAID, I DON'T CARE.
I REFUSE TO WORK LIKE THIS.
I CAN'T MAKE THIS FILM WITHIN THE WALLS OF MANDARIN CITY.
FILM IS LIFE AND LIFE IS LIVED. I NEED TO LEAVE HERE. I NEED TO BE IN THE PLACES YOU LIVED.
I--
I DID NOT REALIZE YOU FELT THE WORK WAS BECOMING COMPROMISED.
WE SHALL OF COURSE ENDEAVOR TO CREATE FOR YOU A WORK SCENARIO MORE BEFITTING YOUR VISION WHILE RESPECTING MY OWN SECURITY CONCERNS.
ANYTHING.
I'LL DO ANYTHING YOU ASK.

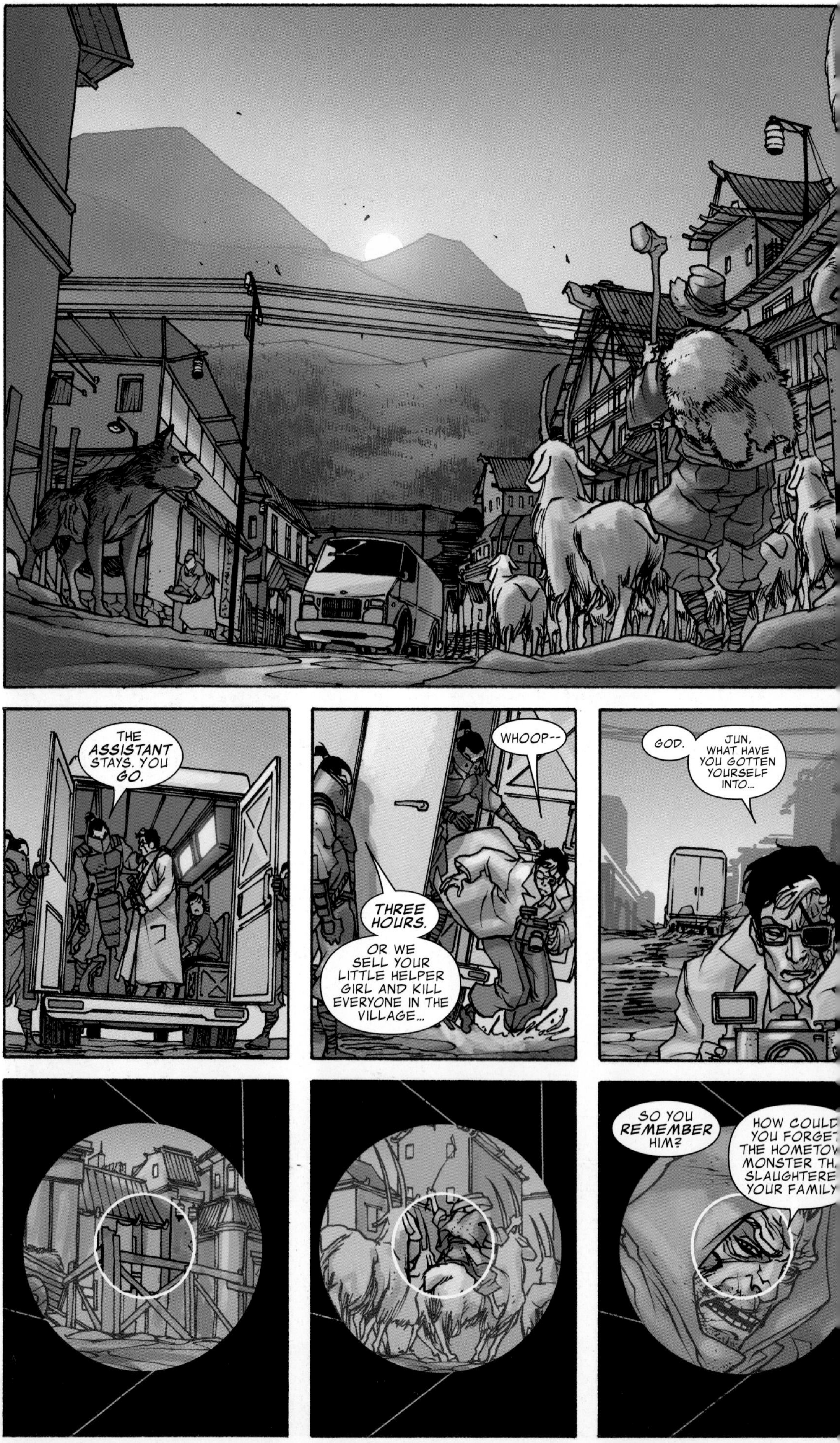
THE ASSISTANT STAYS. YOU GO.
WHOOP--
THREE HOURS.
OR WE SELL YOUR LITTLE HELPER GIRL AND KILL EVERYONE IN THE VILLAGE...
GOD.
JUN, WHAT HAVE YOU GOTTEN YOURSELF INTO...
SO YOU REMEMBER HIM?
HOW COULD YOU FORGET THE HOMETOW MONSTER TH SLAUGHTERE YOUR FAMILY

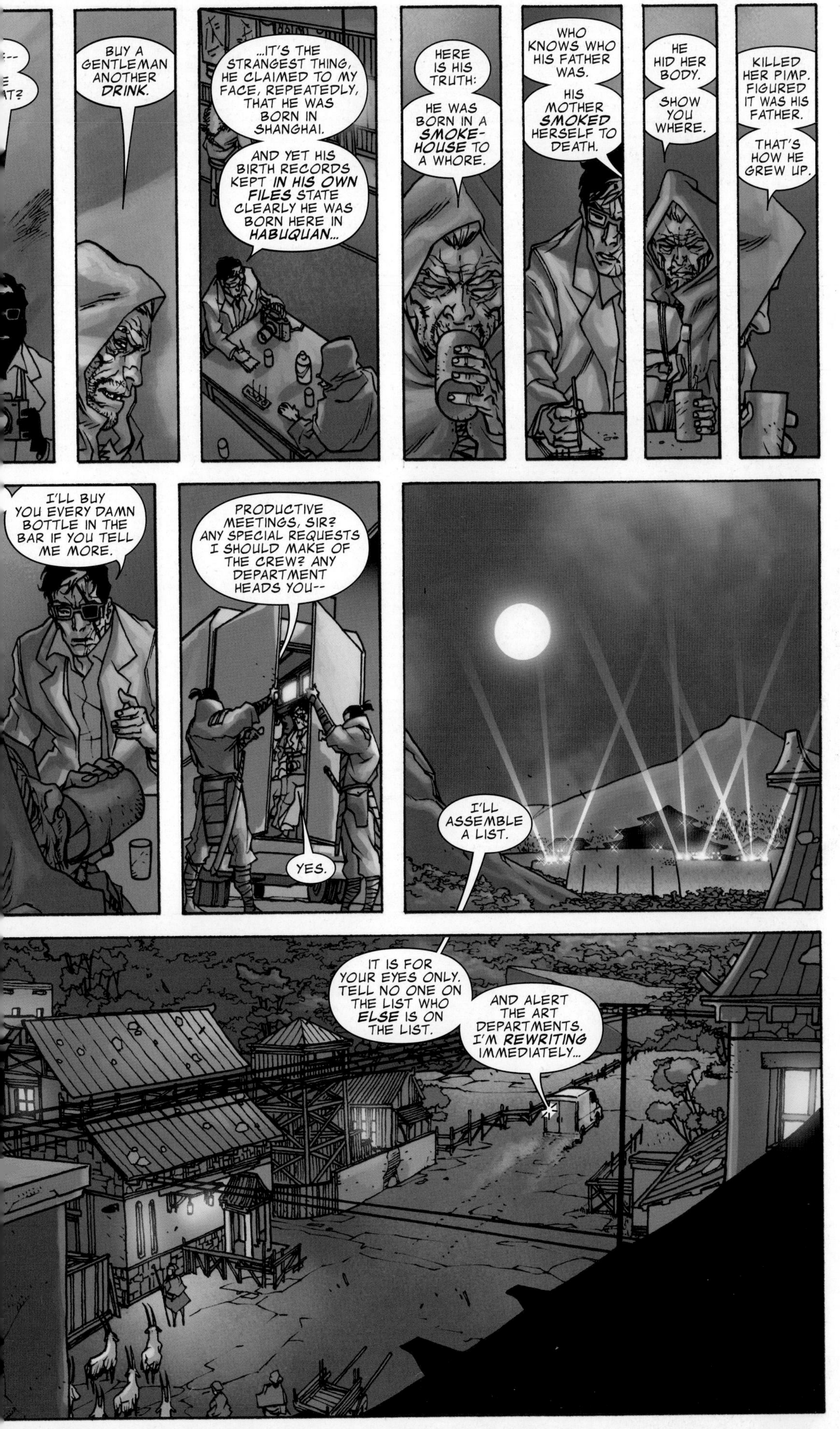
BUY A GENTLEMAN ANOTHER DRINK.
...IT'S THE STRANGEST THING, HE CLAIMED TO MY FACE, REPEATEDLY, THAT HE WAS BORN IN SHANGHAI.
AND YET HIS BIRTH RECORDS KEPT IN HIS OWN FILES STATE CLEARLY HE WAS BORN HERE IN HABUQUAN...
HERE IS HIS TRUTH:
HE WAS BORN IN A SMOKE-HOUSE TO A WHORE.
WHO KNOWS WHO HIS FATHER WAS.
HIS MOTHER SMOKED HERSELF TO DEATH.
HE HID HER BODY.
SHOW YOU WHERE.
KILLED HER PIMP. FIGURED IT WAS HIS FATHER.
THAT'S HOW HE GREW UP.
I'LL BUY YOU EVERY DAMN BOTTLE IN THE BAR IF YOU TELL ME MORE.
PRODUCTIVE MEETINGS, SIR? ANY SPECIAL REQUESTS I SHOULD MAKE OF THE CREW? ANY DEPARTMENT HEADS YOU--
YES.
I'LL ASSEMBLE A LIST.
IT IS FOR YOUR EYES ONLY. TELL NO ONE ON THE LIST WHO ELSE IS ON THE LIST.
AND ALERT THE ART DEPARTMENTS. I'M REWRITING IMMEDIATELY...

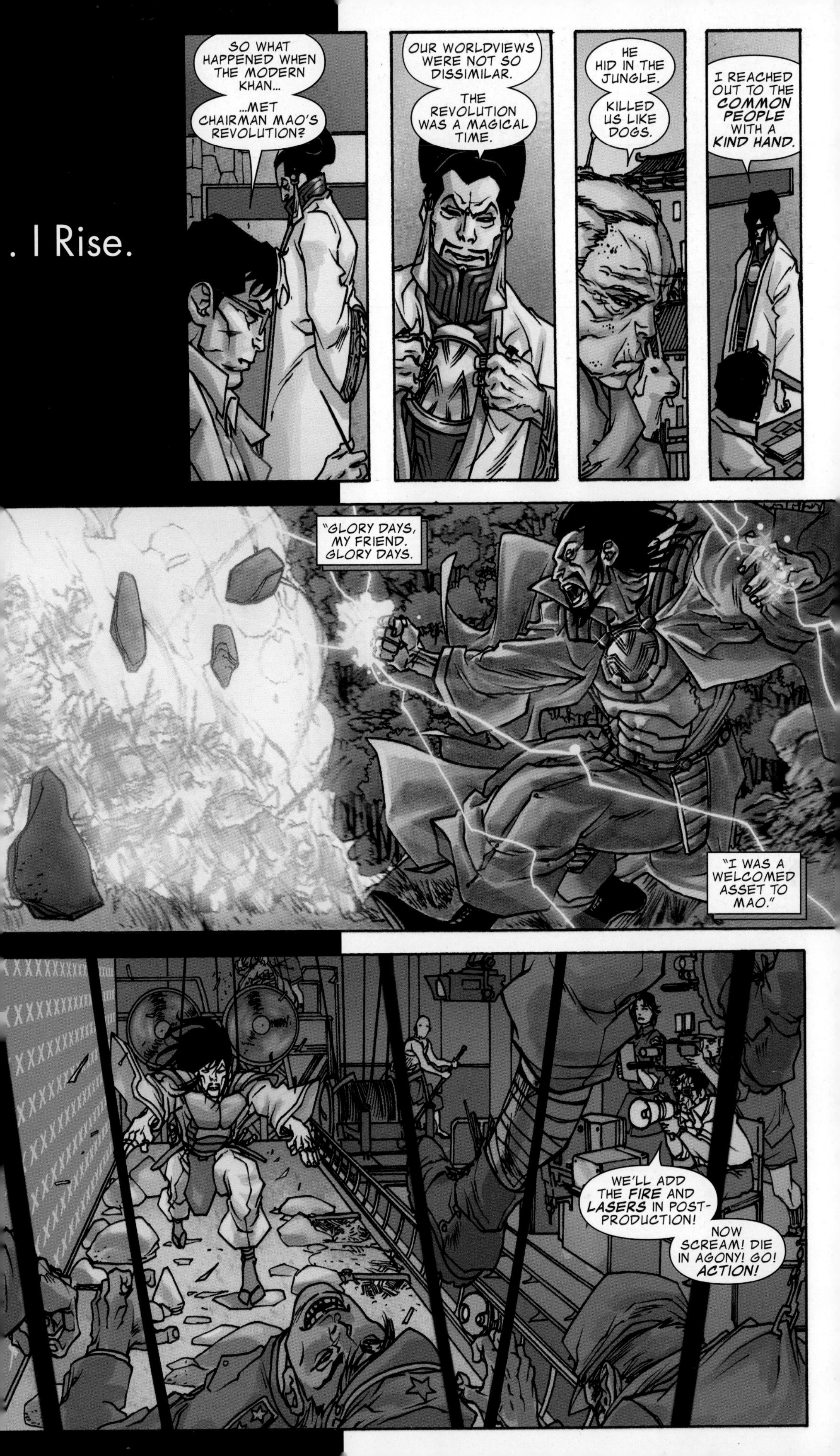
. I Rise.
SO WHAT HAPPENED WHEN THE MODERN KHAN...
...MET CHAIRMAN MAO'S REVOLUTION?
OUR WORLDVIEWS WERE NOT SO DISSIMILAR.
THE REVOLUTION WAS A MAGICAL TIME.
HE HID IN THE JUNGLE.
KILLED US LIKE DOGS.
I REACHED OUT TO THE COMMON PEOPLE WITH A KIND HAND.
"GLORY DAYS, MY FRIEND. GLORY DAYS.
"I WAS A WELCOMED ASSET TO MAO."
WE'LL ADD THE FIRE AND LASERS IN POST-PRODUCTION!
NOW SCREAM! DIE IN AGONY! GO! ACTION!

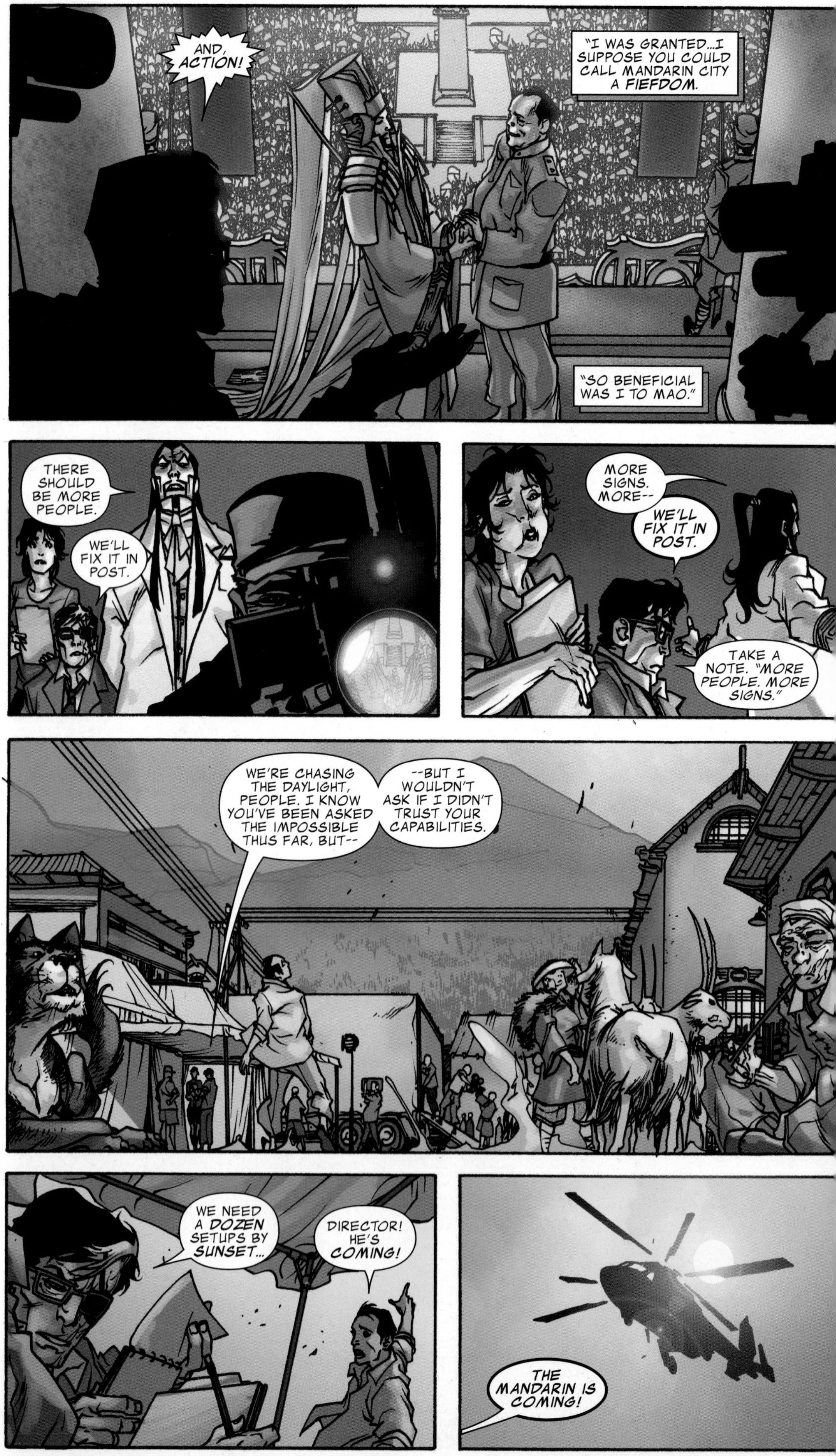
AND, ACTION!
"I WAS GRANTED...I SUPPOSE YOU COULD CALL MANDARIN CITY A FIEFDOM.
"SO BENEFICIAL WAS I TO MAO."
THERE SHOULD BE MORE PEOPLE.
WE'LL FIX IT IN POST.
MORE SIGNS. MORE--
WE'LL FIX IT IN POST.
TAKE A NOTE. "MORE PEOPLE. MORE SIGNS."
WE'RE CHASING THE DAYLIGHT, PEOPLE. I KNOW YOU'VE BEEN ASKED THE IMPOSSIBLE THUS FAR, BUT--
--BUT I WOULDN'T ASK IF I DIDN'T TRUST YOUR CAPABILITIES.
WE NEED A DOZEN SETUPS BY SUNSET...
DIRECTOR! HE'S COMING!
THE MANDARIN IS COMING!

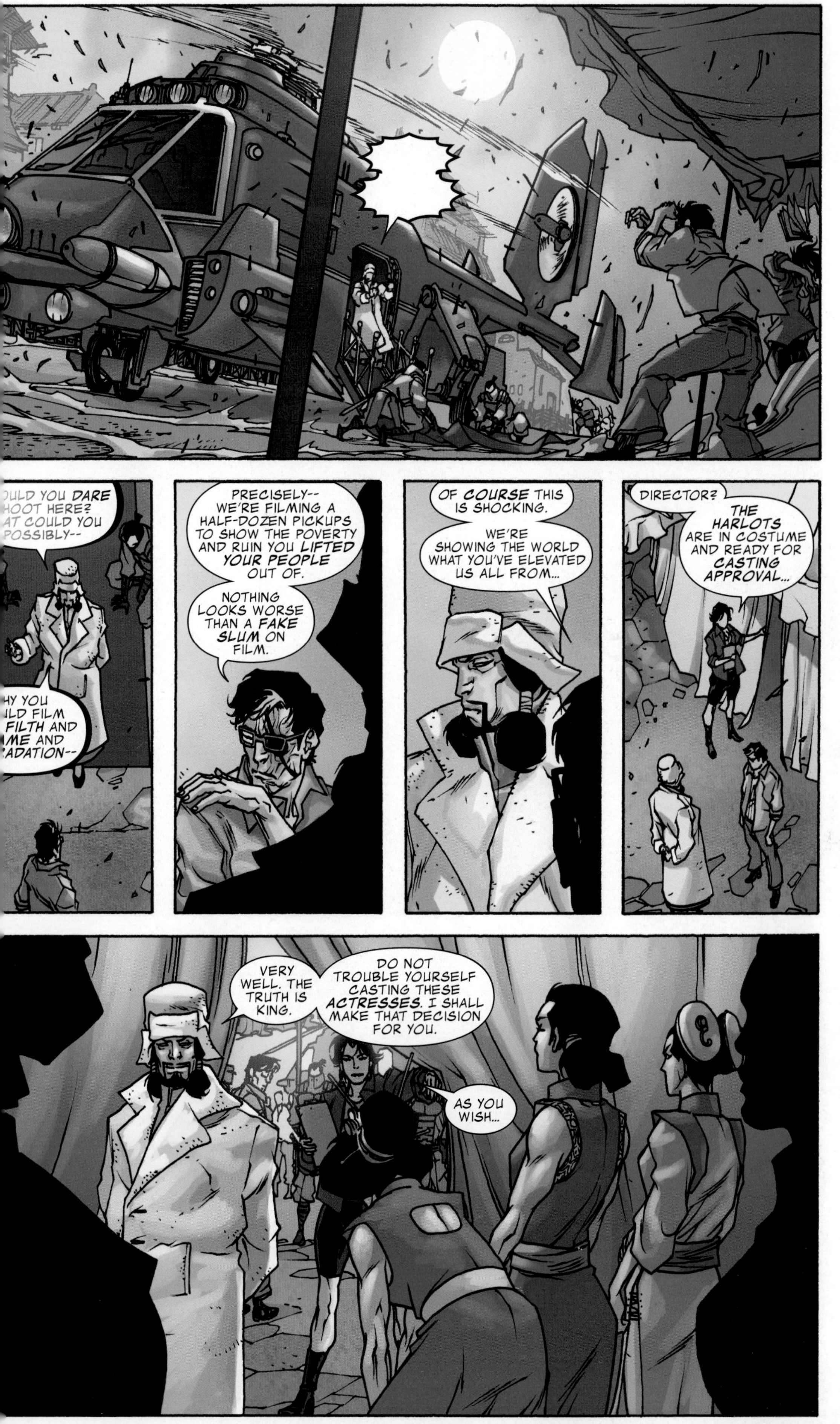
OULD YOU DARE HOOT HERE? AT COULD YOU POSSIBLY--
HY YOU ULD FILM FILTH AND ME AND CADATION--
PRECISELY-- WE'RE FILMING A HALF-DOZEN PICKUPS TO SHOW THE POVERTY AND RUIN YOU LIFTED YOUR PEOPLE OUT OF.
NOTHING LOOKS WORSE THAN A FAKE SLUM ON FILM.
OF COURSE THIS IS SHOCKING.
WE'RE SHOWING THE WORLD WHAT YOU'VE ELEVATED US ALL FROM...
DIRECTOR?
THE HARLOTS ARE IN COSTUME AND READY FOR CASTING APPROVAL...
VERY WELL. THE TRUTH IS KING.
DO NOT TROUBLE YOURSELF CASTING THESE ACTRESSES. I SHALL MAKE THAT DECISION FOR YOU.
AS YOU WISH...

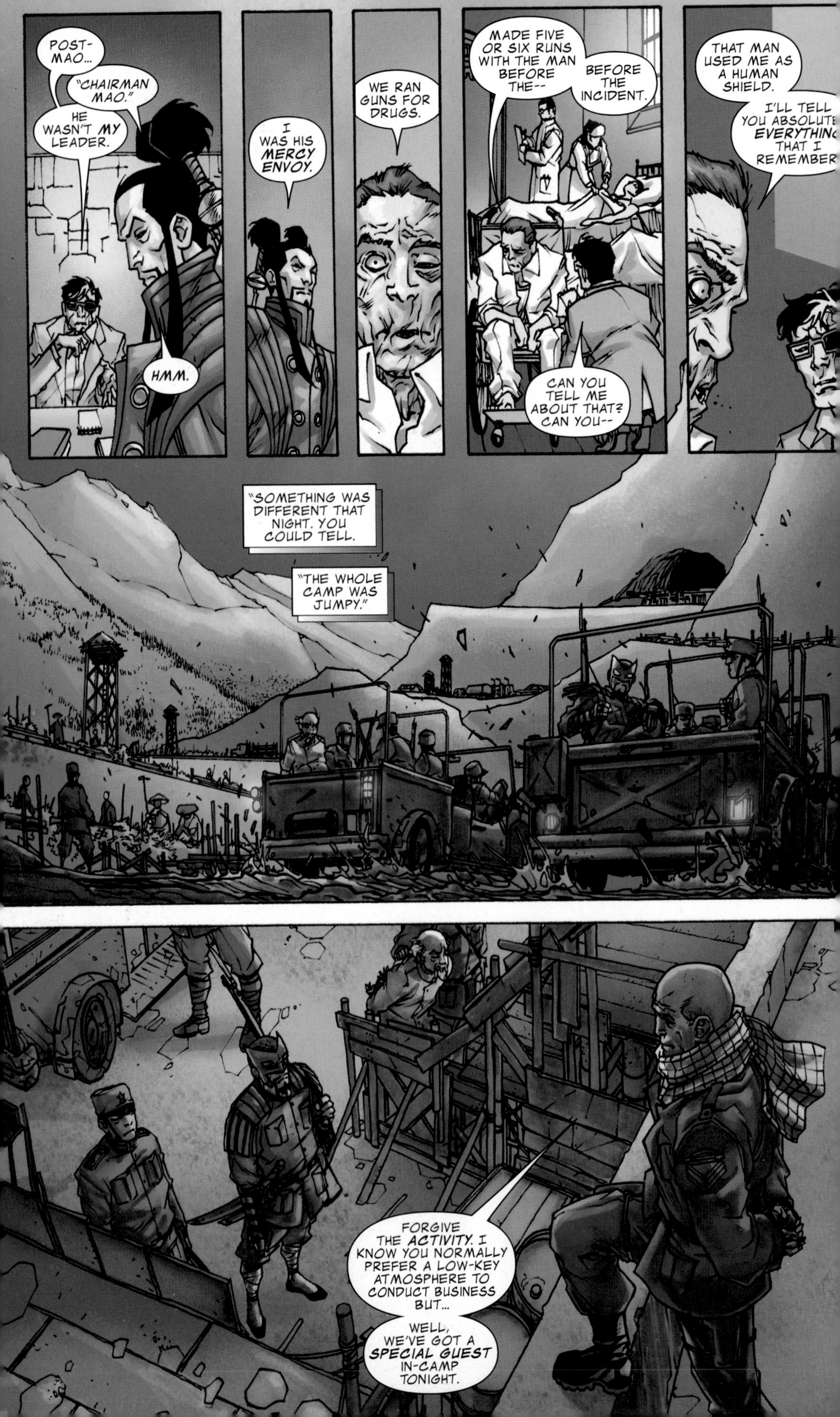
POST-MAO...
"CHAIRMAN MAO."
HE WASN'T MY LEADER.
HMM.
I WAS HIS MERCY ENVOY.
WE RAN GUNS FOR DRUGS.
MADE FIVE OR SIX RUNS WITH THE MAN BEFORE THE--
BEFORE THE INCIDENT.
CAN YOU TELL ME ABOUT THAT? CAN YOU--
THAT MAN USED ME AS A HUMAN SHIELD.
I'LL TELL YOU ABSOLUTE EVERYTHING THAT I REMEMBER
"SOMETHING WAS DIFFERENT THAT NIGHT. YOU COULD TELL.
"THE WHOLE CAMP WAS JUMPY."
FORGIVE THE ACTIVITY. I KNOW YOU NORMALLY PREFER A LOW-KEY ATMOSPHERE TO CONDUCT BUSINESS BUT...
WELL, WE'VE GOT A SPECIAL GUEST IN-CAMP TONIGHT.

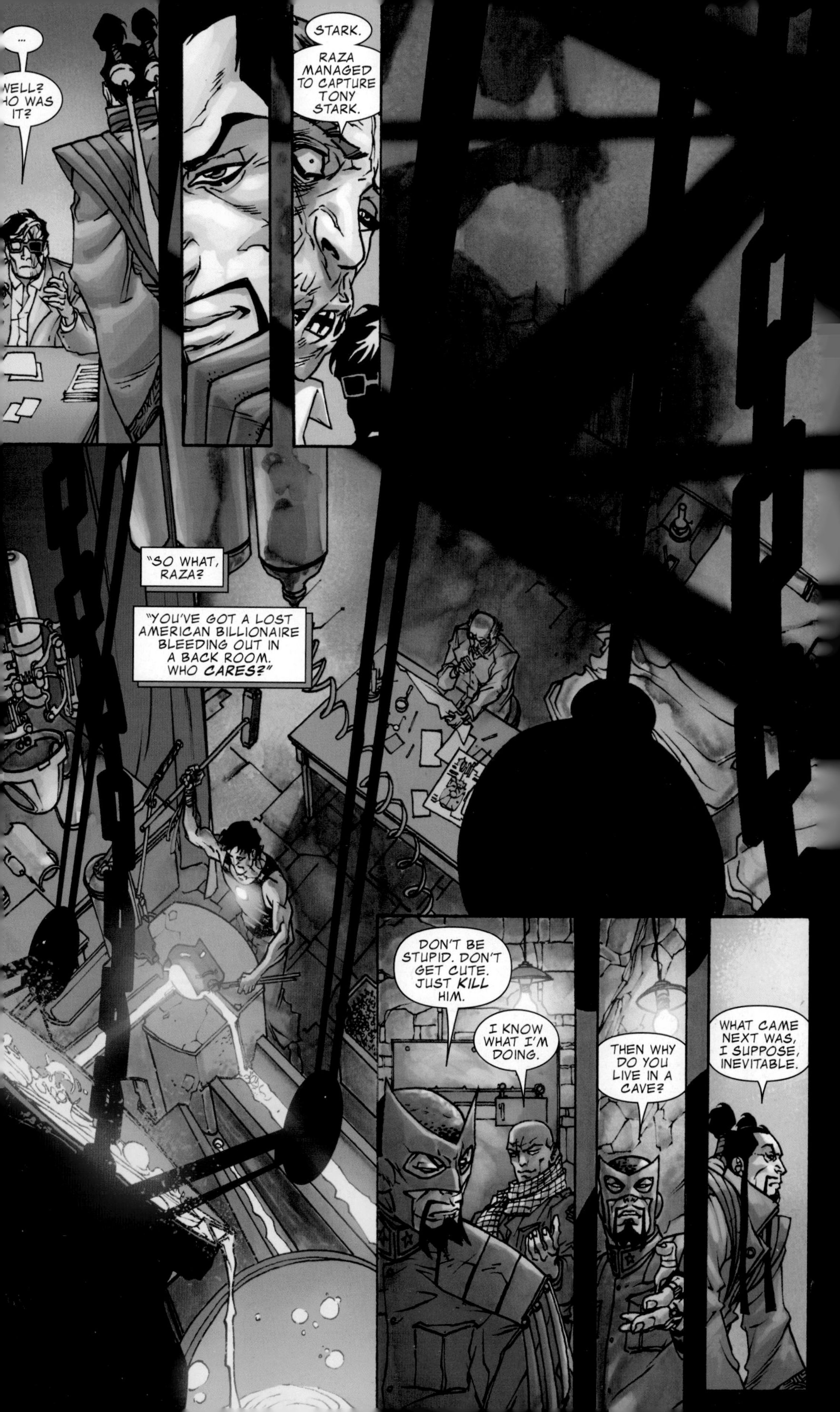

...
WELL? HO WAS IT?
STARK.
RAZA MANAGED TO CAPTURE TONY STARK.
"SO WHAT, RAZA?
"YOU'VE GOT A LOST AMERICAN BILLIONAIRE BLEEDING OUT IN A BACK ROOM. WHO CARES?"
DON'T BE STUPID. DON'T GET CUTE. JUST KILL HIM.
I KNOW WHAT I'M DOING.
THEN WHY DO YOU LIVE IN A CAVE?
WHAT CAME NEXT WAS, I SUPPOSE, INEVITABLE.

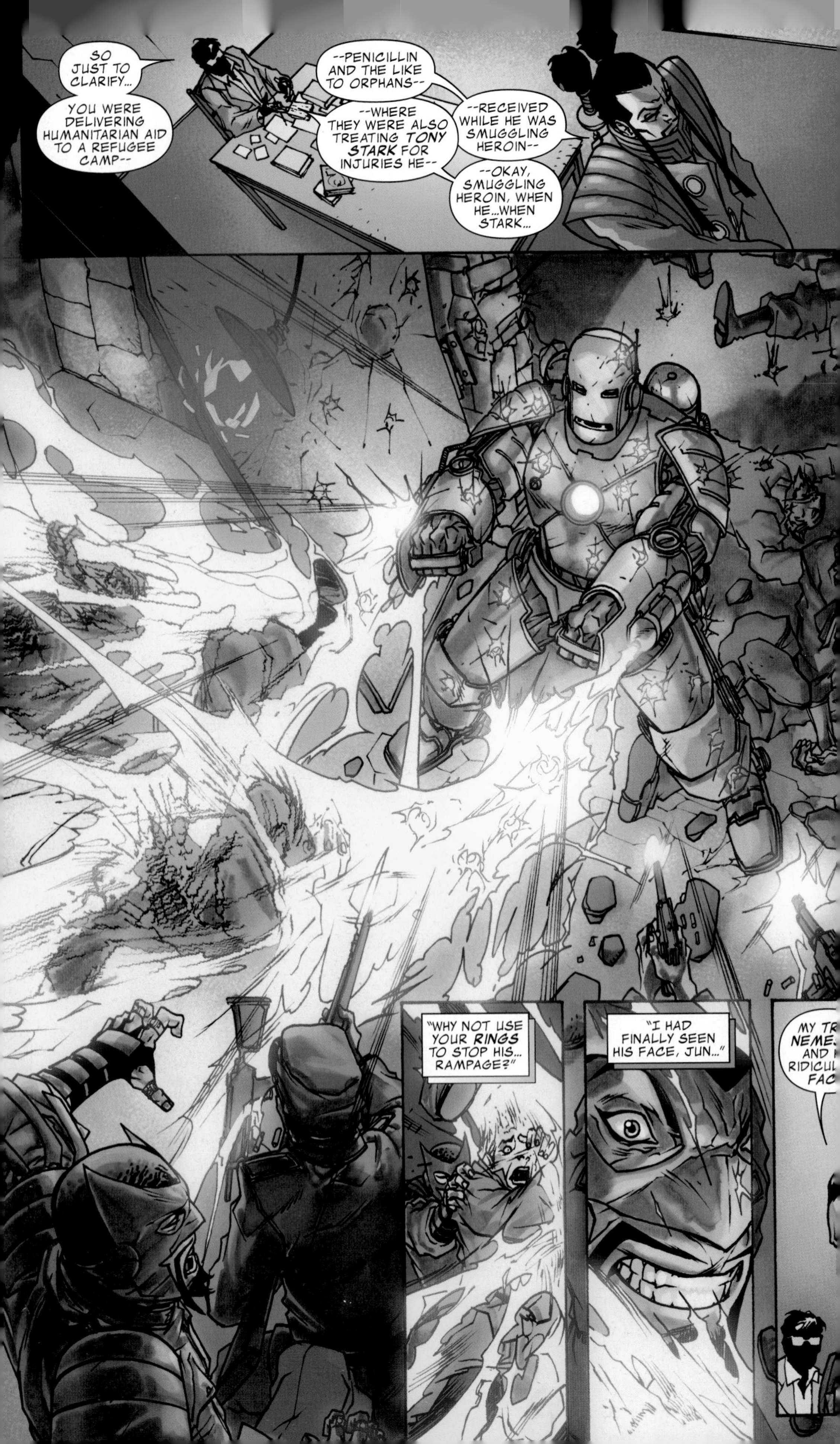
SO JUST TO CLARIFY...
YOU WERE DELIVERING HUMANITARIAN AID TO A REFUGEE CAMP--
--PENICILLIN AND THE LIKE TO ORPHANS--
--WHERE THEY WERE ALSO TREATING TONY STARK FOR INJURIES HE--
--RECEIVED WHILE HE WAS SMUGGLING HEROIN--
--OKAY, SMUGGLING HEROIN, WHEN HE...WHEN STARK...
"WHY NOT USE YOUR RINGS TO STOP HIS... RAMPAGE?"
"I HAD FINALLY SEEN HIS FACE, JUN..."

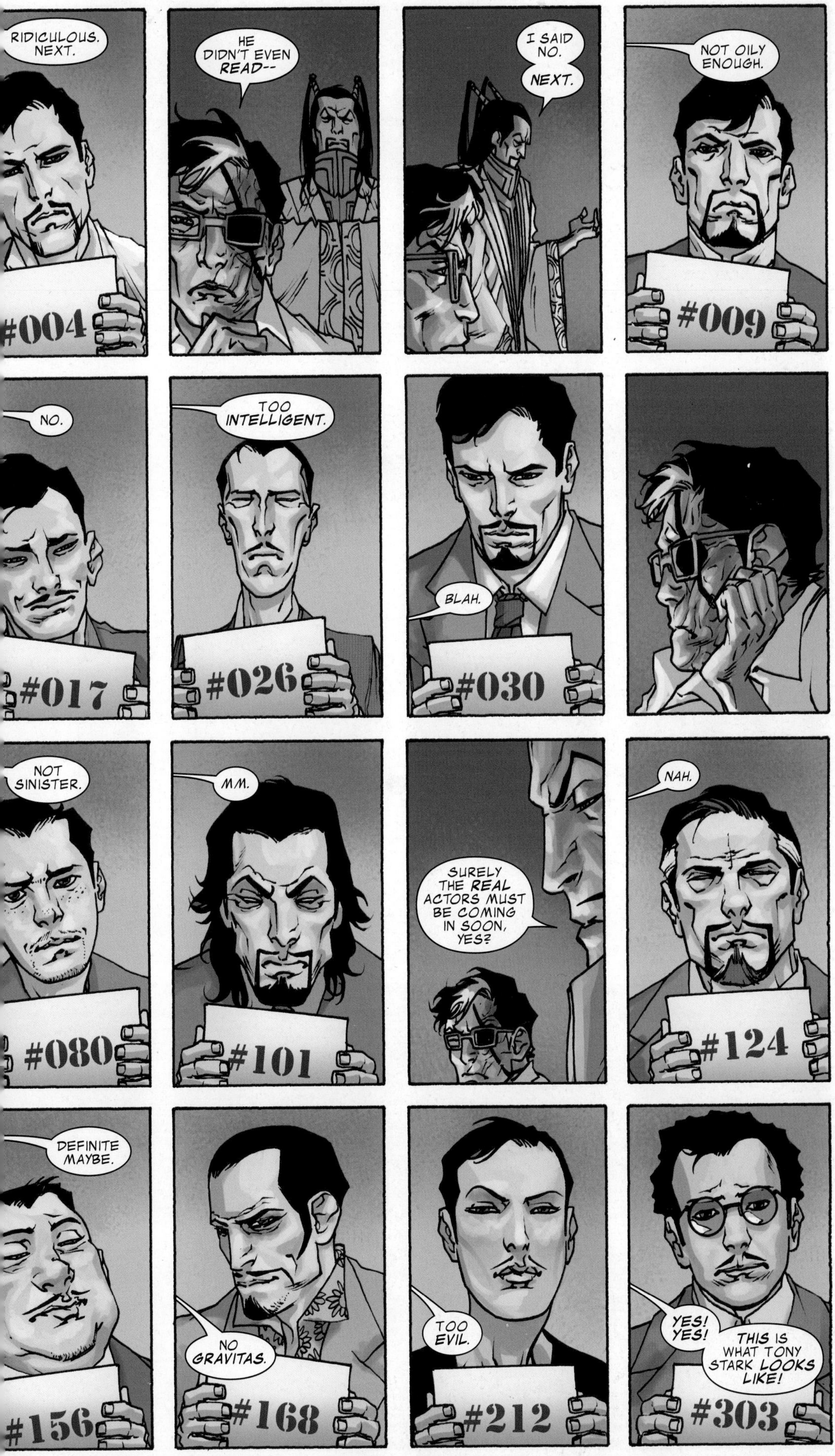
RIDICULOUS. NEXT.
#004
HE DIDN'T EVEN READ--
I SAID NO.
NEXT.
NOT OILY ENOUGH.
#009
NO.
#017
TOO INTELLIGENT.
#026
BLAH.
#030
NOT SINISTER.
#080
MM.
#101
SURELY THE REAL ACTORS MUST BE COMING IN SOON, YES?
NAH.
#124
DEFINITE MAYBE.
#156
NO GRAVITAS.
#168
TOO EVIL.
#212
YES! YES!
THIS IS WHAT TONY STARK LOOKS LIKE!
#303

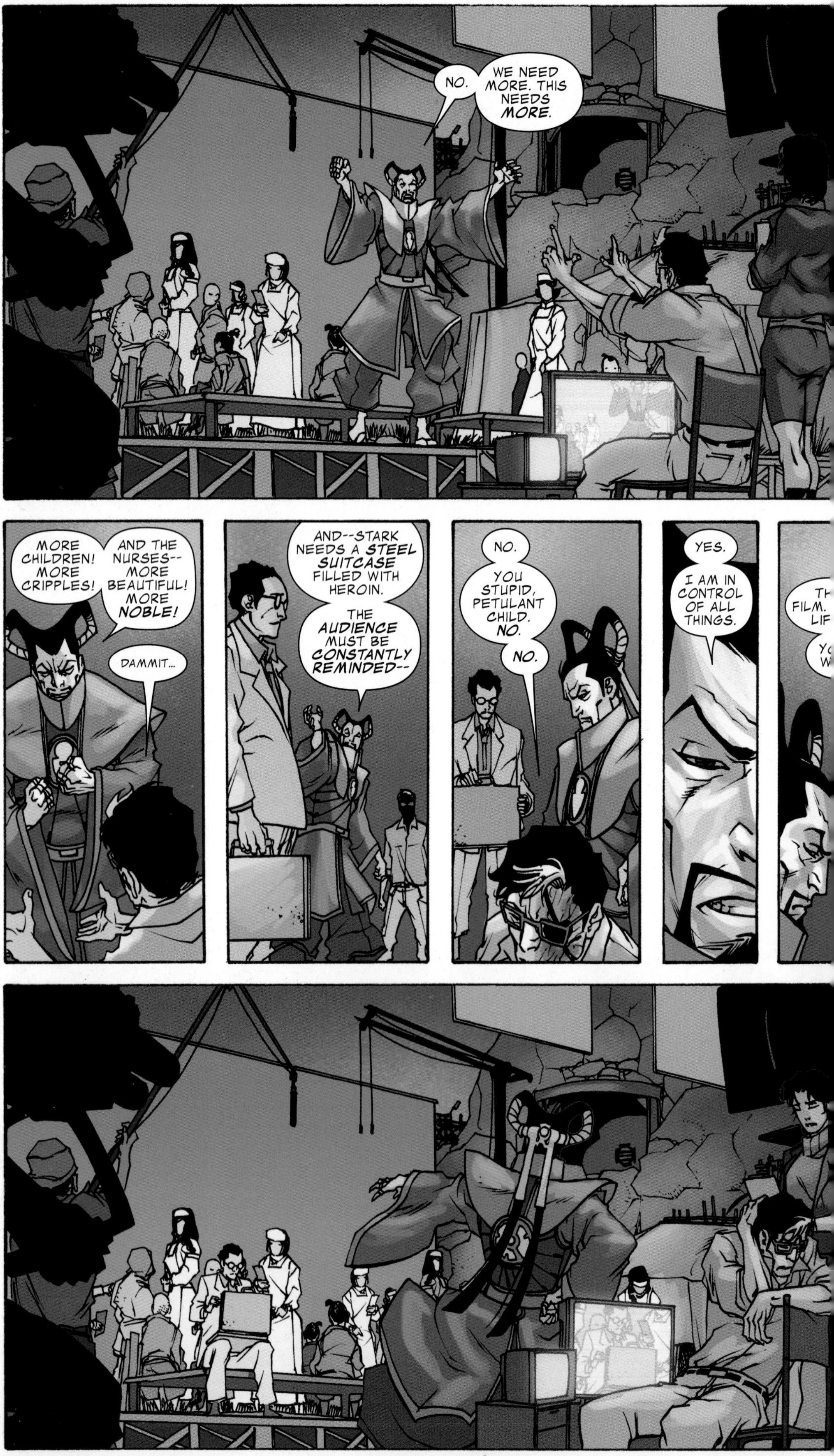
NO.
WE NEED MORE. THIS NEEDS MORE.
MORE CHILDREN! MORE CRIPPLES!
AND THE NURSES-- MORE BEAUTIFUL! MORE NOBLE!
DAMMIT...
AND--STARK NEEDS A STEEL SUITCASE FILLED WITH HEROIN.
THE AUDIENCE MUST BE CONSTANTLY REMINDED--
NO.
YOU STUPID, PETULANT CHILD. NO.
NO.
YES.
I AM IN CONTROL OF ALL THINGS.

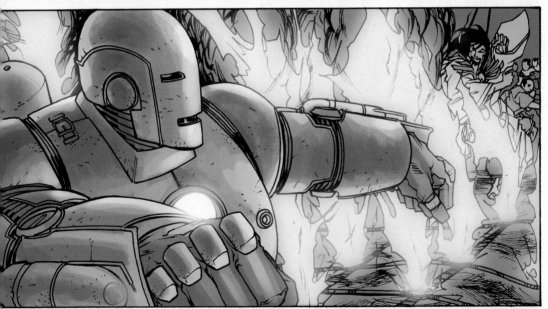

YES. YES, IT WAS JUST LIKE THIS...

CUT!

CUT!

COWARD! YOU LOOKED COWARDLY!

PLAYING THE BEAT, I FELT--

SILENCE!

PLAY IT FEARLESS.

OR YOU WILL DIE.

HANG ON-- HANG ON--

YOU--YOU CAN'T JUST THREATEN THE PERFORMANCE YOU WANT OUT OF AN ACTOR--

MY FILM

I'LL DIRE IT HOW LIKE

OH GOD--

--O GOD GOD

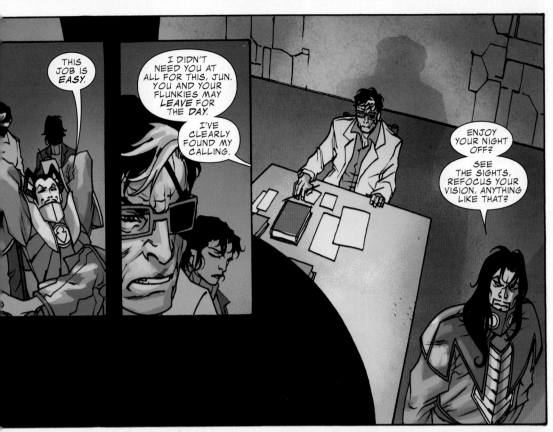

THIS JOB IS *EASY.*

I DIDN'T NEED YOU AT ALL FOR THIS, JUN. YOU AND YOUR FLUNKIES MAY *LEAVE* FOR THE *DAY.*

I'VE CLEARLY FOUND MY CALLING.

ENJOY YOUR NIGHT OFF?

SEE THE SIGHTS, REFOCUS YOUR VISION, ANYTHING LIKE THAT?

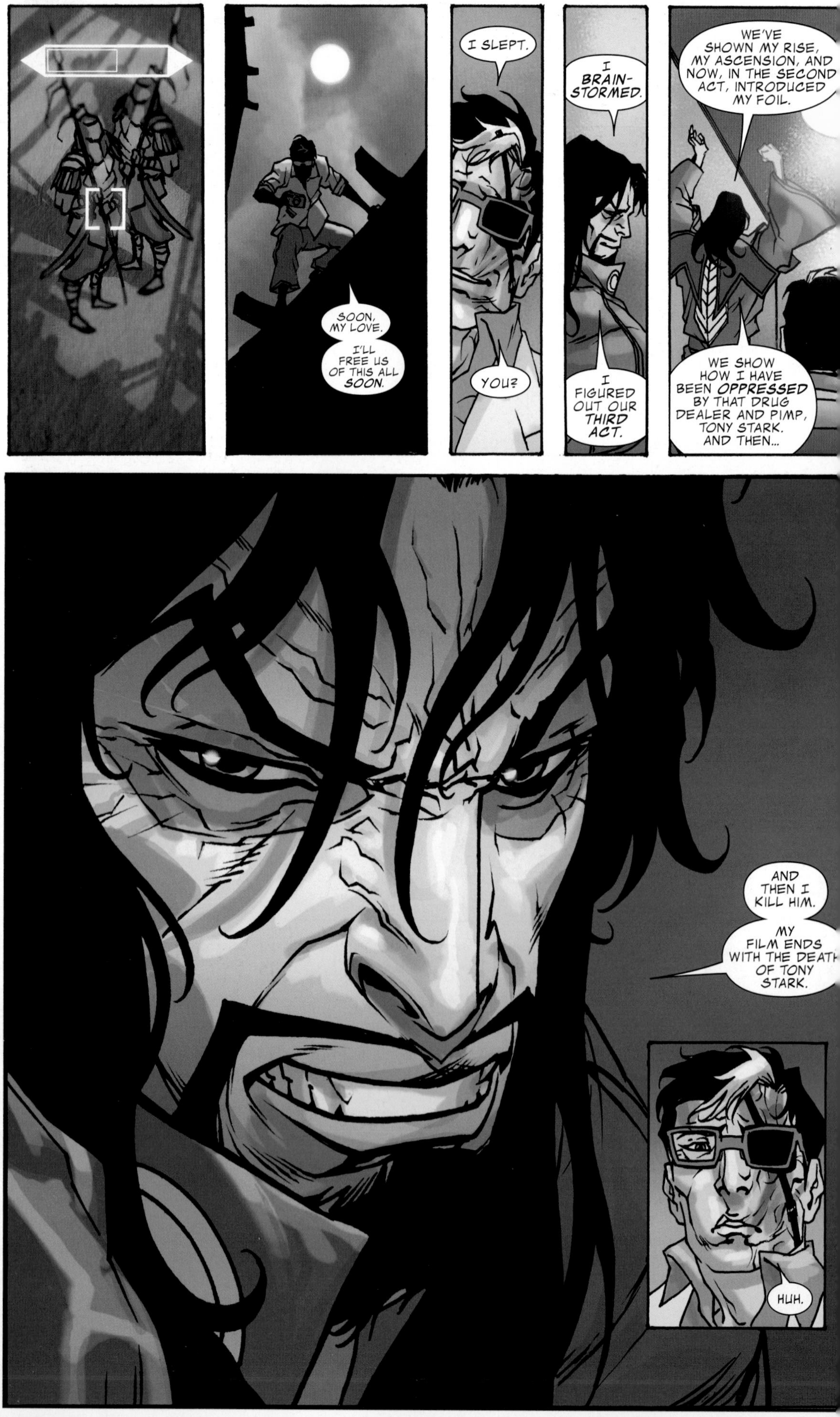
SOON, MY LOVE.
I'LL FREE US OF THIS ALL SOON.
I SLEPT.
YOU?
I BRAIN-STORMED.
I FIGURED OUT OUR THIRD ACT.
WE'VE SHOWN MY RISE, MY ASCENSION, AND NOW, IN THE SECOND ACT, INTRODUCED MY FOIL.
WE SHOW HOW I HAVE BEEN OPPRESSED BY THAT DRUG DEALER AND PIMP, TONY STARK. AND THEN...
AND THEN I KILL HIM.
MY FILM ENDS WITH THE DEATH OF TONY STARK.
HUH.

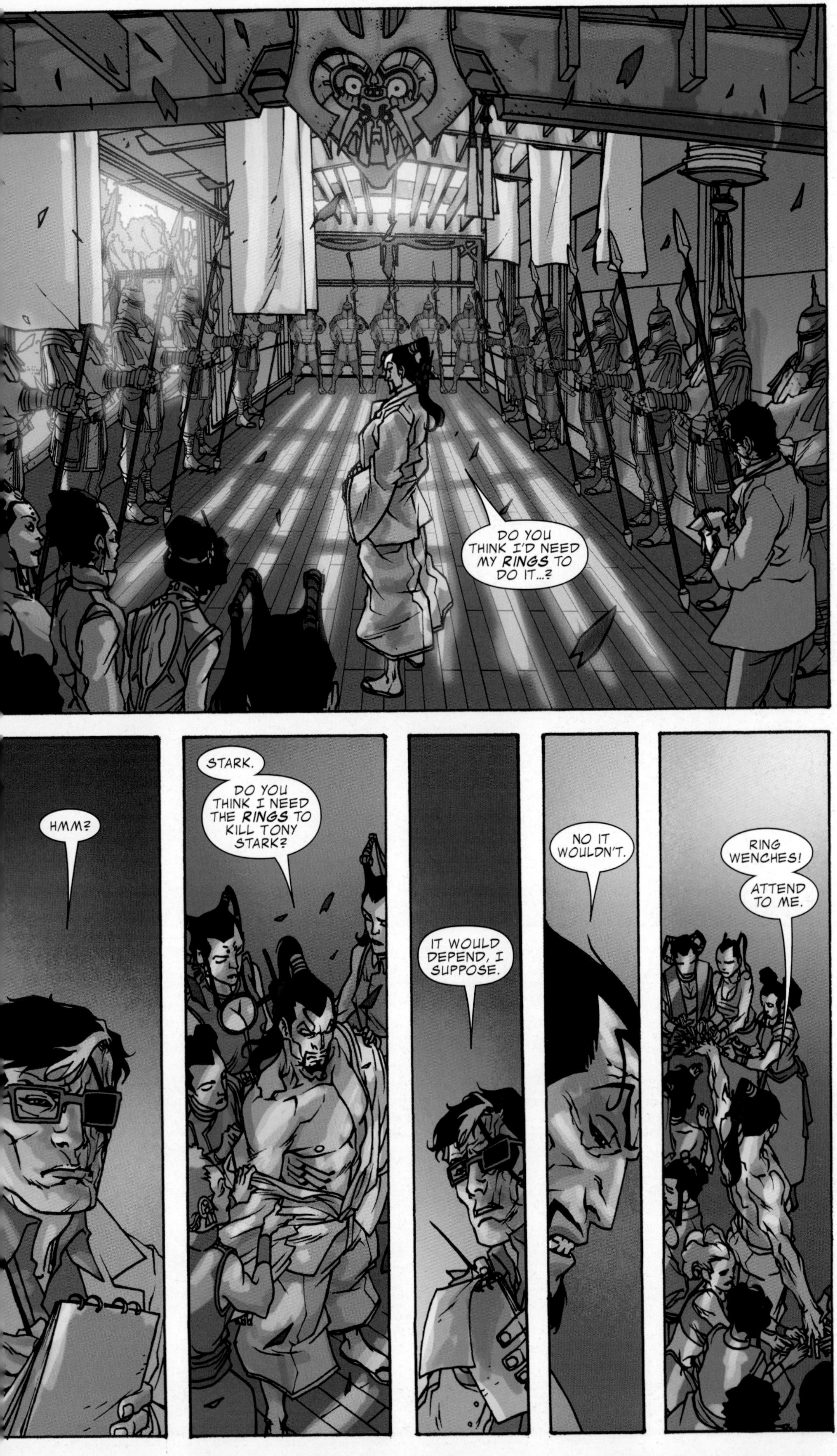

DO YOU THINK I'D NEED MY RINGS TO DO IT...?
HMM?
STARK.
DO YOU THINK I NEED THE RINGS TO KILL TONY STARK?
IT WOULD DEPEND, I SUPPOSE.
NO IT WOULDN'T.
RING WENCHES!
ATTEND TO ME.

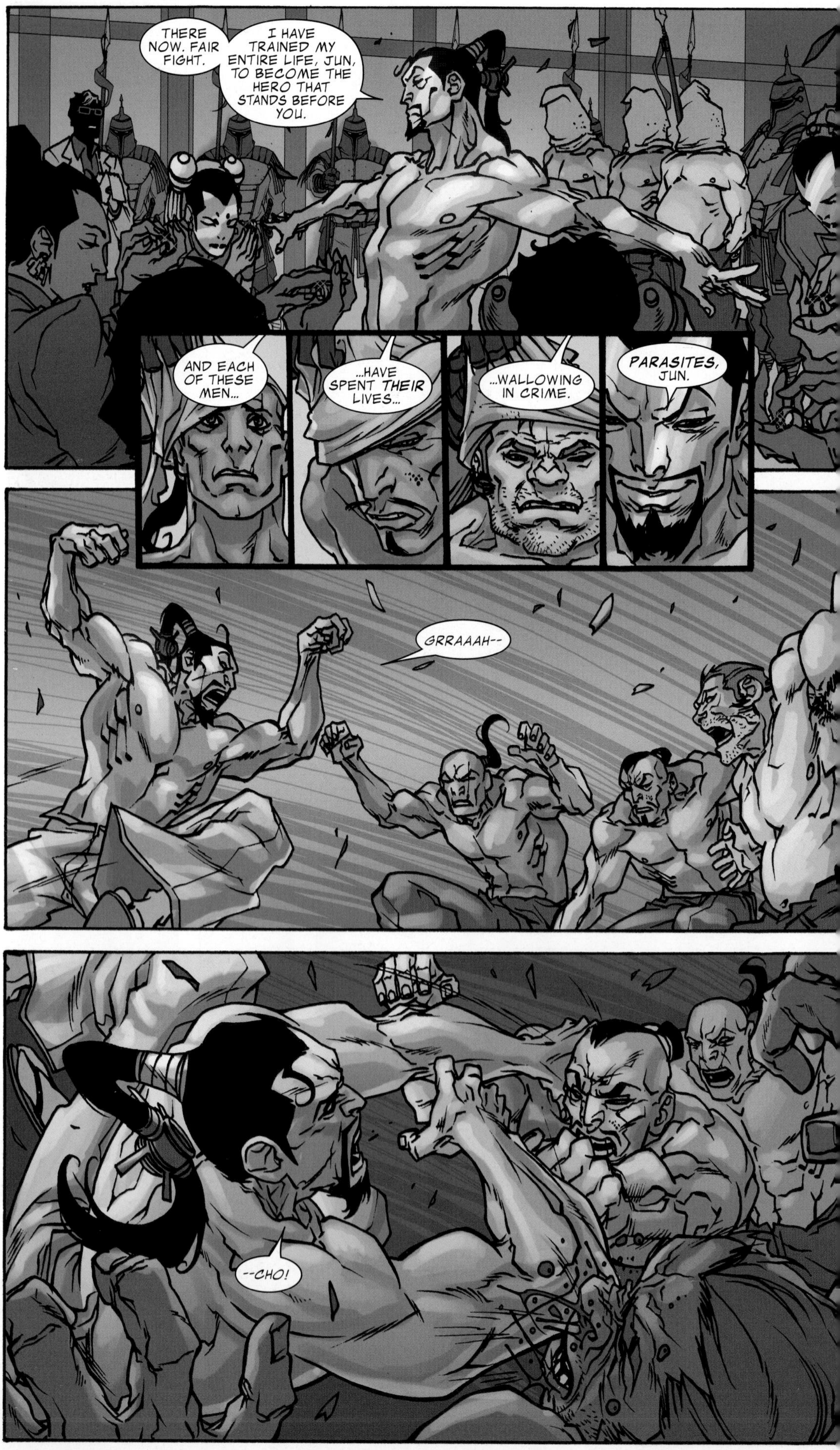
THERE NOW. FAIR FIGHT.
I HAVE TRAINED MY ENTIRE LIFE, JUN, TO BECOME THE HERO THAT STANDS BEFORE YOU.
AND EACH OF THESE MEN...
...HAVE SPENT THEIR LIVES...
...WALLOWING IN CRIME.
PARASITES, JUN.
GRRAAAH--
--CHO!

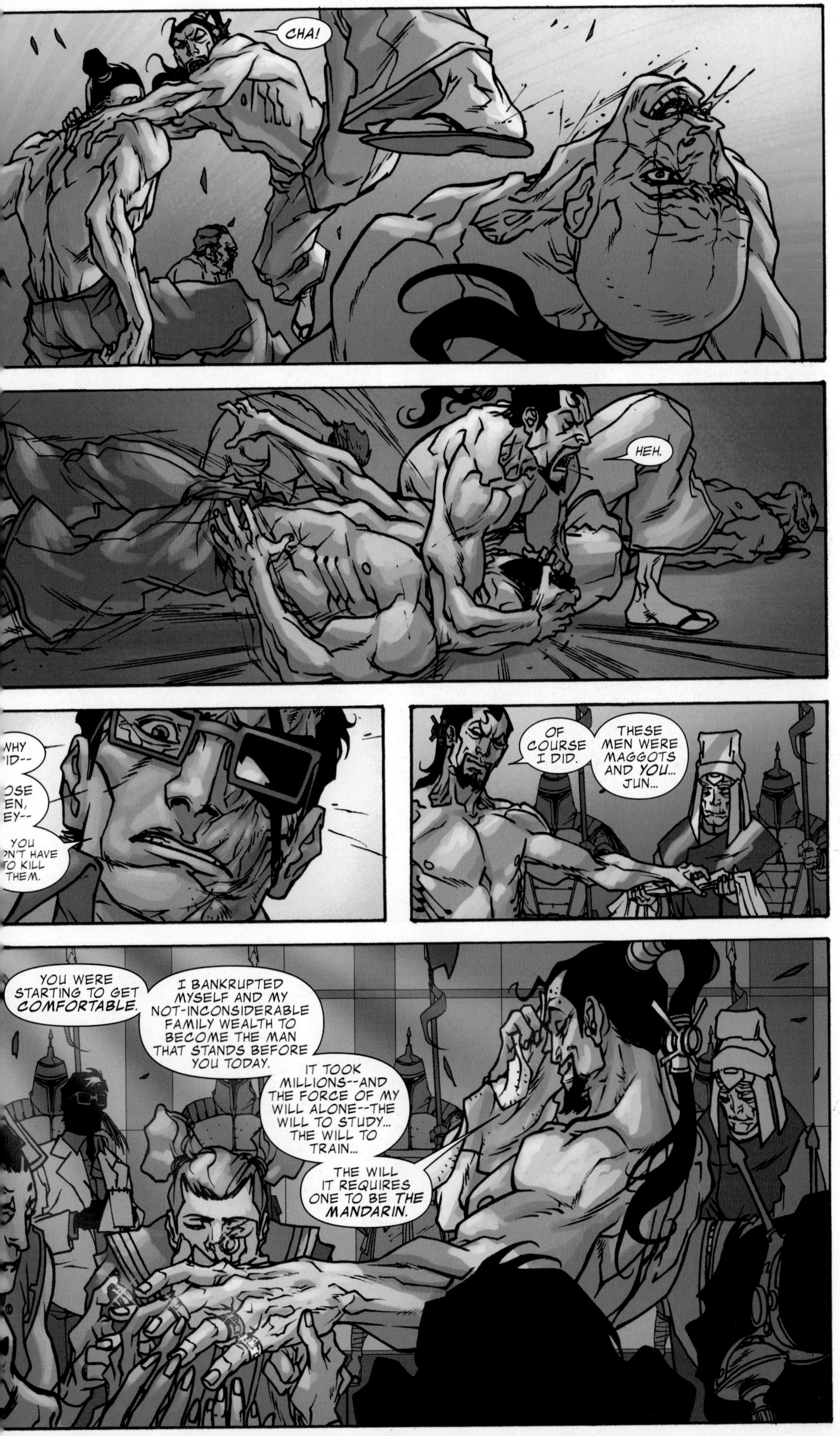
CHA!
HEH.
WHY ID--
OSE EN, EY--
YOU N'T HAVE O KILL THEM.
OF COURSE I DID.
THESE MEN WERE MAGGOTS AND YOU... JUN...
YOU WERE STARTING TO GET COMFORTABLE.
I BANKRUPTED MYSELF AND MY NOT-INCONSIDERABLE FAMILY WEALTH TO BECOME THE MAN THAT STANDS BEFORE YOU TODAY.
IT TOOK MILLIONS--AND THE FORCE OF MY WILL ALONE--THE WILL TO STUDY... THE WILL TO TRAIN...
THE WILL IT REQUIRES ONE TO BE THE MANDARIN.

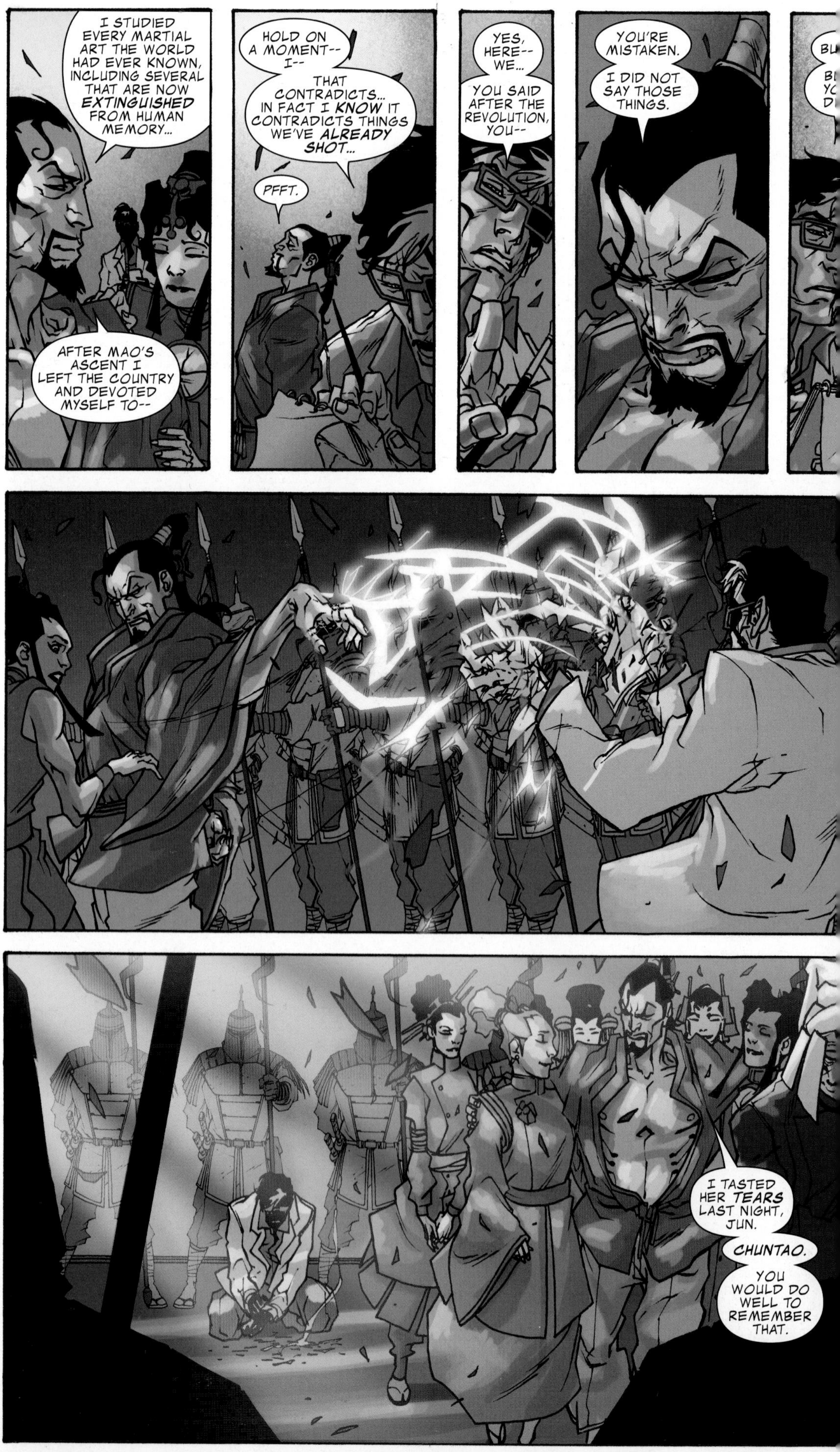
I STUDIED EVERY MARTIAL ART THE WORLD HAD EVER KNOWN, INCLUDING SEVERAL THAT ARE NOW EXTINGUISHED FROM HUMAN MEMORY...
AFTER MAO'S ASCENT I LEFT THE COUNTRY AND DEVOTED MYSELF TO--
HOLD ON A MOMENT-- I--
THAT CONTRADICTS... IN FACT I KNOW IT CONTRADICTS THINGS WE'VE ALREADY SHOT...
PFFT.
YES, HERE-- WE...
YOU SAID AFTER THE REVOLUTION, YOU--
YOU'RE MISTAKEN.
I DID NOT SAY THOSE THINGS.
I TASTED HER TEARS LAST NIGHT, JUN.
CHUNTAO.
YOU WOULD DO WELL TO REMEMBER THAT.

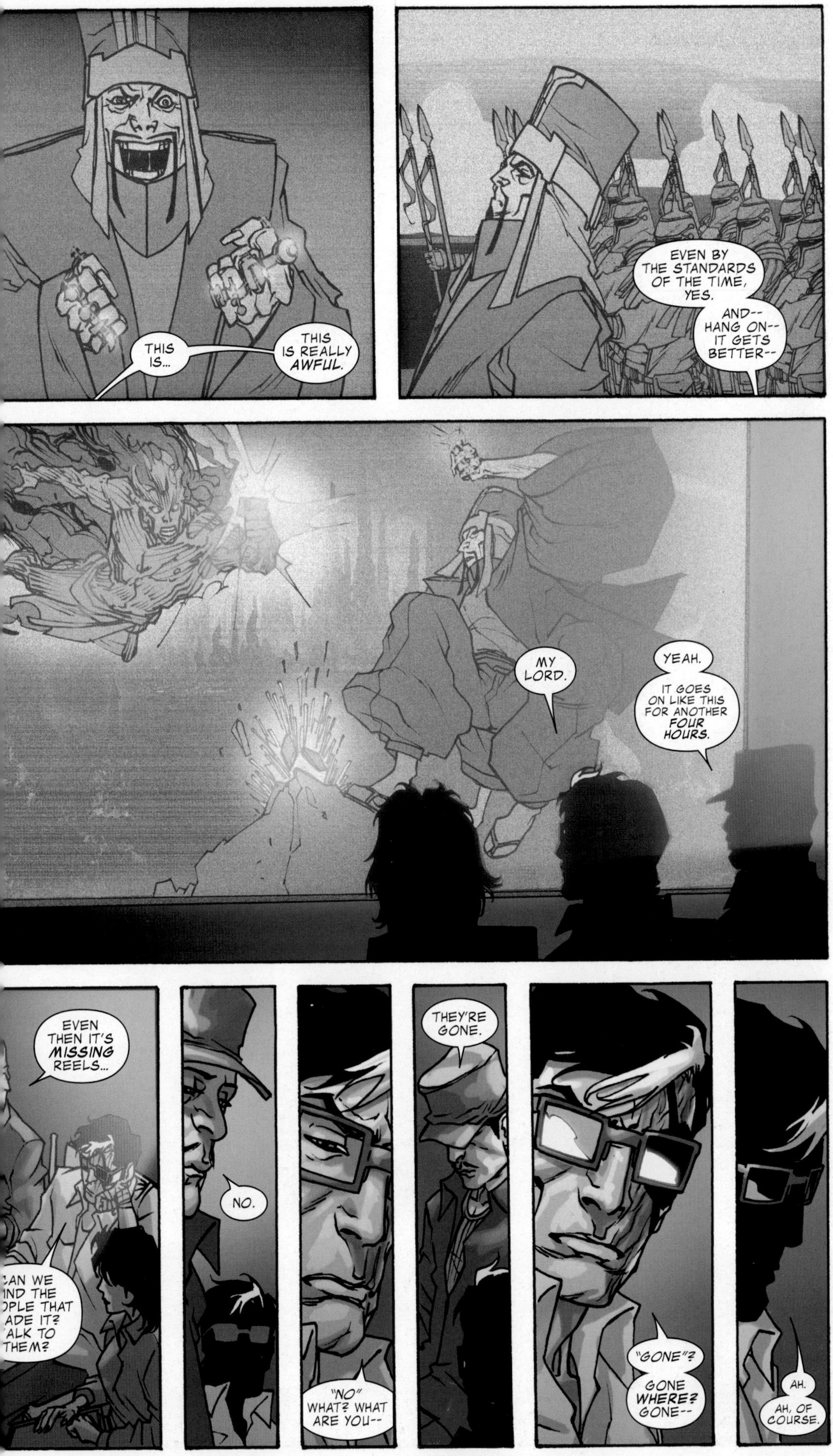
THIS IS...
THIS IS REALLY AWFUL.
EVEN BY THE STANDARDS OF THE TIME, YES.
AND-- HANG ON-- IT GETS BETTER--
MY LORD.
YEAH.
IT GOES ON LIKE THIS FOR ANOTHER FOUR HOURS.
EVEN THEN IT'S MISSING REELS...
CAN WE IND THE OPLE THAT ADE IT? TALK TO THEM?
NO.
"NO" WHAT? WHAT ARE YOU--
THEY'RE GONE.
"GONE"?
GONE WHERE? GONE--
AH.
AH, OF COURSE.

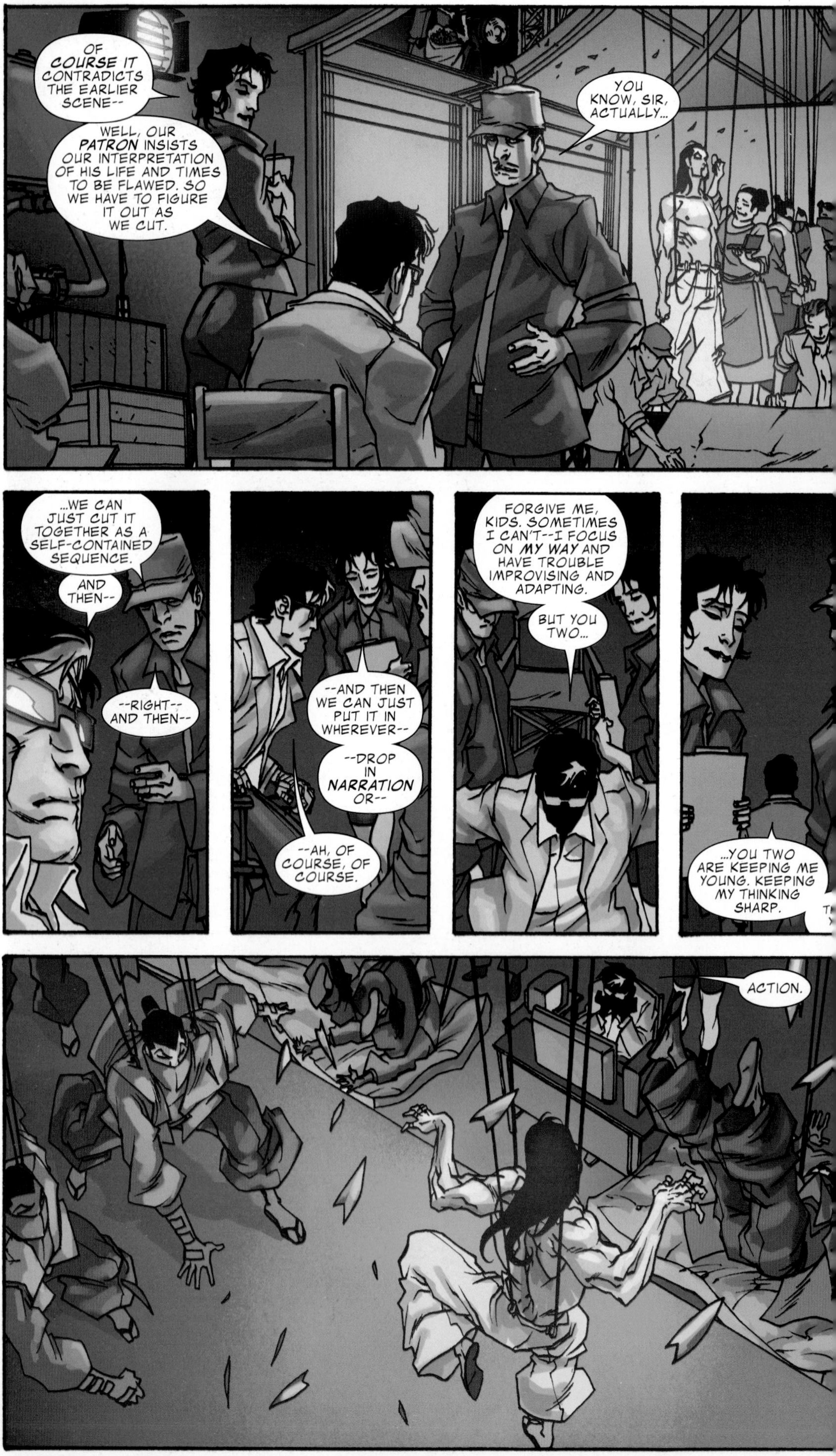
OF COURSE IT CONTRADICTS THE EARLIER SCENE--
WELL, OUR PATRON INSISTS OUR INTERPRETATION OF HIS LIFE AND TIMES TO BE FLAWED. SO WE HAVE TO FIGURE IT OUT AS WE CUT.
YOU KNOW, SIR, ACTUALLY...
...WE CAN JUST CUT IT TOGETHER AS A SELF-CONTAINED SEQUENCE.
AND THEN--
--RIGHT-- AND THEN--
--AND THEN WE CAN JUST PUT IT IN WHEREVER--
--DROP IN NARRATION OR--
--AH, OF COURSE, OF COURSE.
FORGIVE ME, KIDS. SOMETIMES I CAN'T--I FOCUS ON MY WAY AND HAVE TROUBLE IMPROVISING AND ADAPTING.
BUT YOU TWO...
...YOU TWO ARE KEEPING ME YOUNG. KEEPING MY THINKING SHARP.
ACTION.

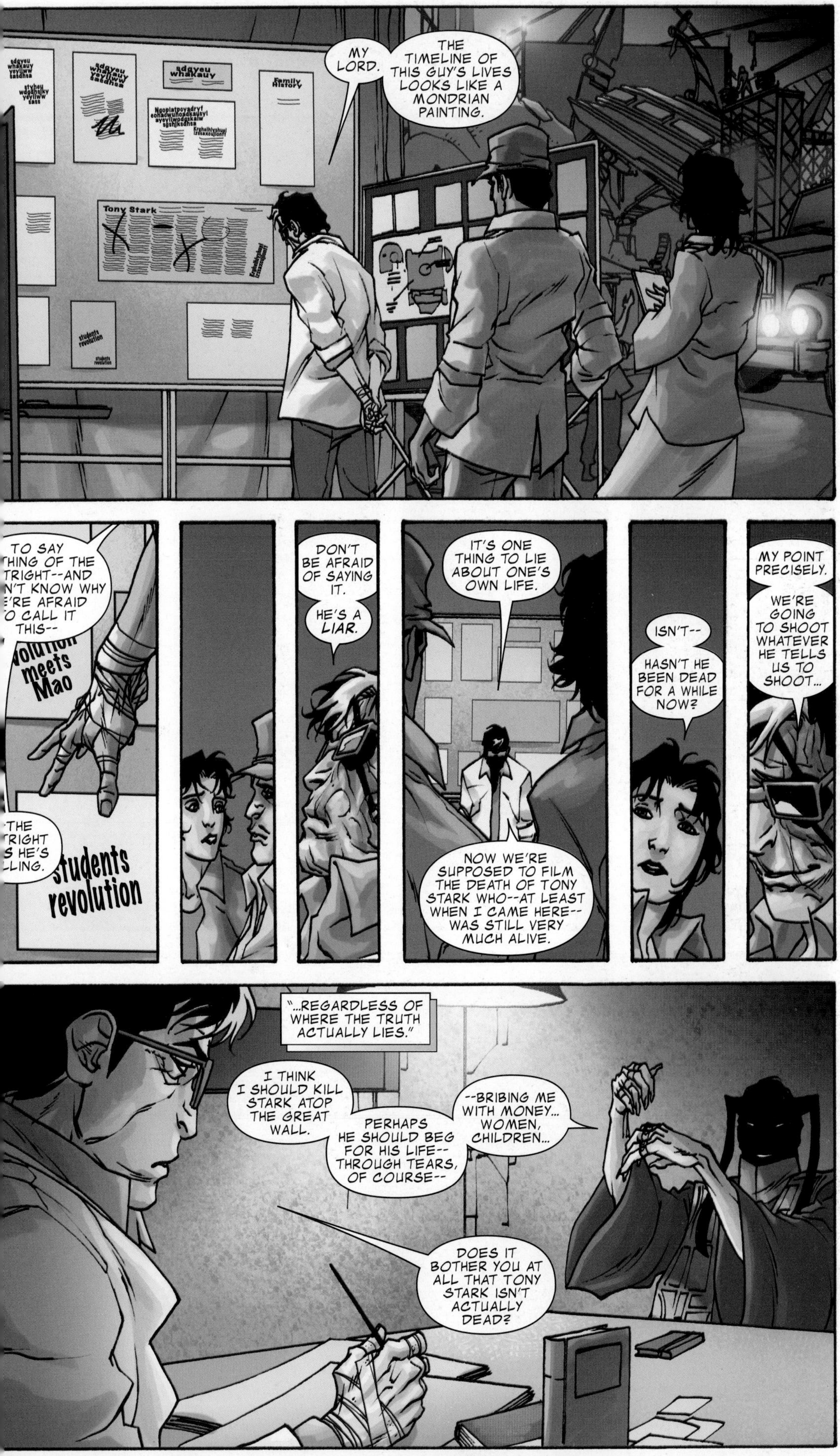

Tony Stark
Family history
students revolution
MY LORD.
THE TIMELINE OF THIS GUY'S LIVES LOOKS LIKE A MONDRIAN PAINTING.
TO SAY THING OF THE TRIGHT--AND N'T KNOW WHY E'RE AFRAID O CALL IT THIS--
volution meets Mao
-THE TRIGHT S HE'S LING.
students revolution
DON'T BE AFRAID OF SAYING IT.
HE'S A *LIAR*.
IT'S ONE THING TO LIE ABOUT ONE'S OWN LIFE.
NOW WE'RE SUPPOSED TO FILM THE DEATH OF TONY STARK WHO--AT LEAST WHEN I CAME HERE--WAS STILL VERY MUCH ALIVE.
ISN'T--
HASN'T HE BEEN DEAD FOR A WHILE NOW?
MY POINT PRECISELY.
WE'RE GOING TO SHOOT WHATEVER HE TELLS US TO SHOOT...
"...REGARDLESS OF WHERE THE TRUTH ACTUALLY LIES."
I THINK I SHOULD KILL STARK ATOP THE GREAT WALL.
PERHAPS HE SHOULD BEG FOR HIS LIFE--THROUGH TEARS, OF COURSE--
--BRIBING ME WITH MONEY... WOMEN, CHILDREN...
DOES IT BOTHER YOU AT ALL THAT TONY STARK ISN'T ACTUALLY DEAD?

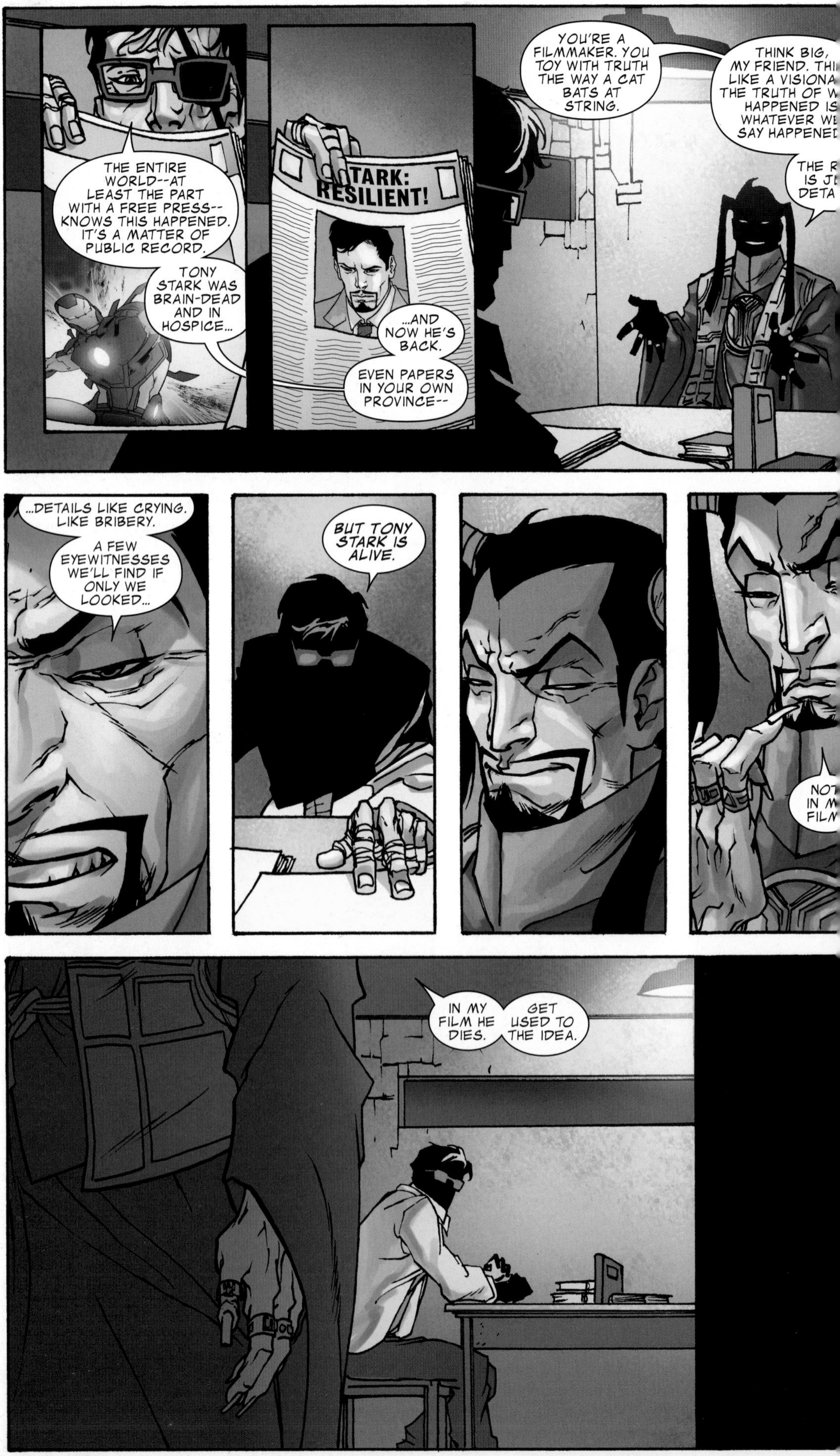
THE ENTIRE WORLD--AT LEAST THE PART WITH A FREE PRESS--KNOWS THIS HAPPENED. IT'S A MATTER OF PUBLIC RECORD.
TONY STARK WAS BRAIN-DEAD AND IN HOSPICE...
TARK: RESILIENT!
...AND NOW HE'S BACK.
EVEN PAPERS IN YOUR OWN PROVINCE--
YOU'RE A FILMMAKER. YOU TOY WITH TRUTH THE WAY A CAT BATS AT STRING.
THINK BIG, MY FRIEND. THI LIKE A VISIONA THE TRUTH OF W HAPPENED IS WHATEVER WE SAY HAPPENED
THE R IS J DETA
...DETAILS LIKE CRYING. LIKE BRIBERY.
A FEW EYEWITNESSES WE'LL FIND IF ONLY WE LOOKED...
BUT TONY STARK IS ALIVE.
NOT IN M FILM
IN MY FILM HE DIES.
GET USED TO THE IDEA.

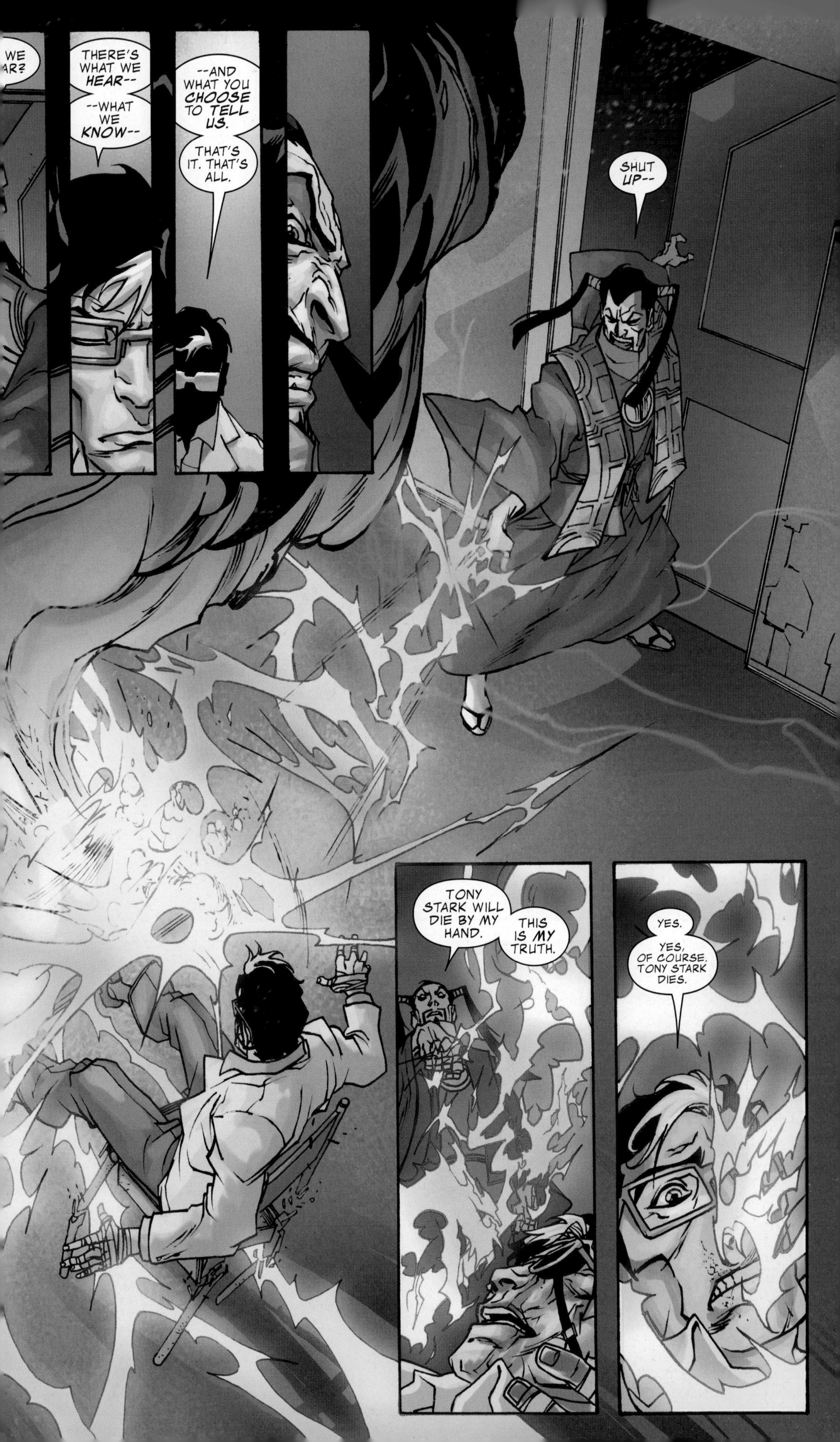
WE
AR?
THERE'S WHAT WE HEAR--
--WHAT WE KNOW--
--AND WHAT YOU CHOOSE TO TELL US.
THAT'S IT. THAT'S ALL.
SHUT UP--
TONY STARK WILL DIE BY MY HAND.
THIS IS MY TRUTH.
YES.
YES, OF COURSE. TONY STARK DIES.

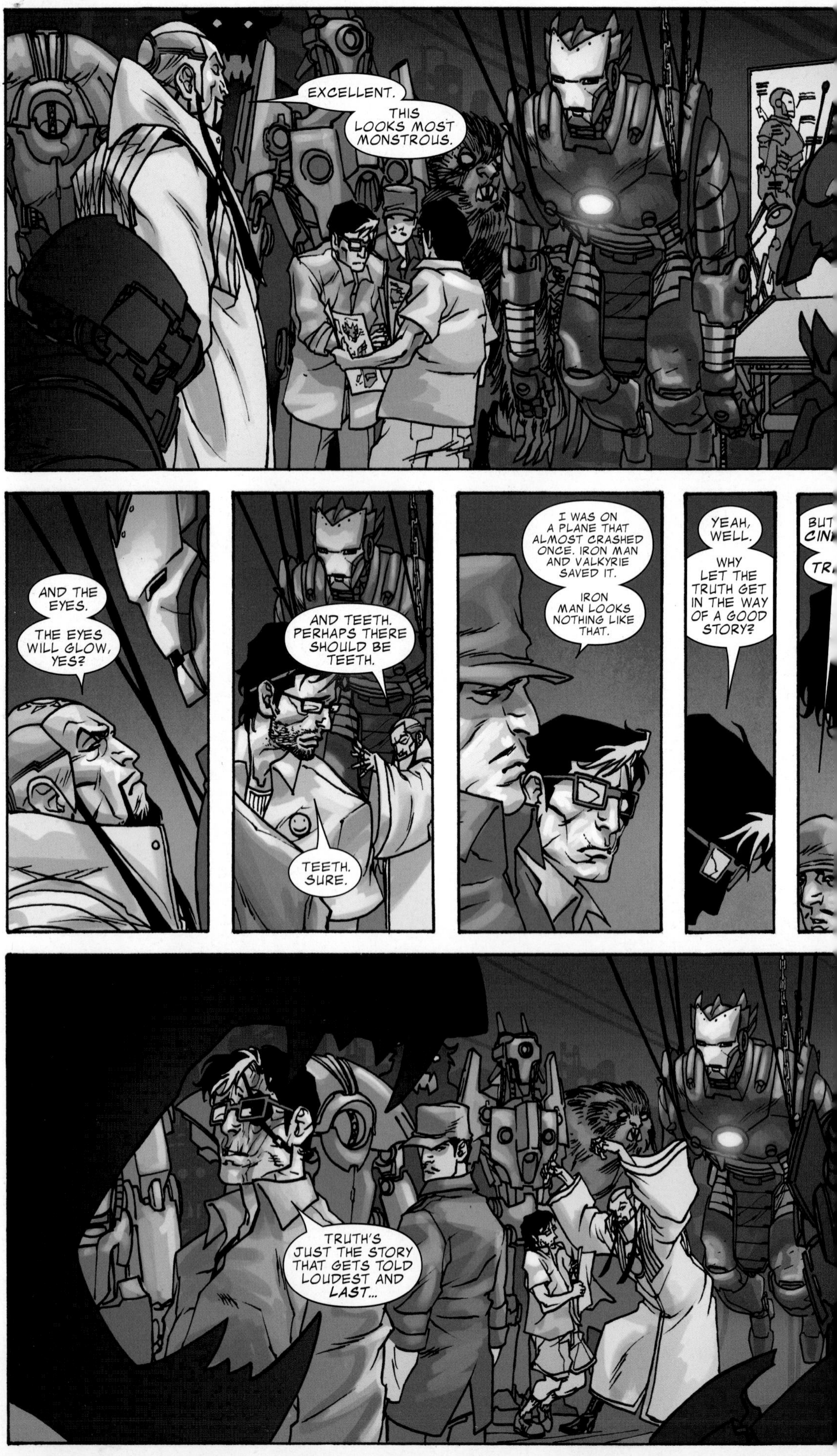
EXCELLENT.
THIS LOOKS MOST MONSTROUS.
AND THE EYES.
THE EYES WILL GLOW, YES?
AND TEETH. PERHAPS THERE SHOULD BE TEETH.
TEETH. SURE.
I WAS ON A PLANE THAT ALMOST CRASHED ONCE. IRON MAN AND VALKYRIE SAVED IT.
IRON MAN LOOKS NOTHING LIKE THAT.
YEAH, WELL.
WHY LET THE TRUTH GET IN THE WAY OF A GOOD STORY?
BUT
TRUTH'S JUST THE STORY THAT GETS TOLD LOUDEST AND *LAST*...

SO WE *END* WITH THE DOLLY *IN* TO THE SUIT AND JUST--

--YEAH--

--REALLY DO IT, YOU KNOW?

'S THE N OF THE E SO WE ALLY...

...WE SHOULD...

SIR.

ARE YOU--

I'M FINE.

JUST CALL IT.

CALL "ACTION," START FILMING, AND DON'T STOP UNTIL THIS THING IS DESTROYED.

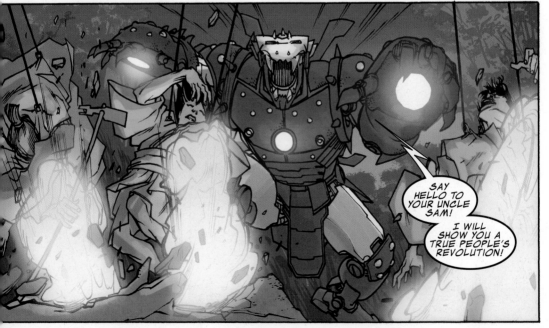

SAY HELLO TO YOUR UNCLE SAM!

I WILL SHOW YOU A *TRUE* PEOPLE'S REVOLUTION!

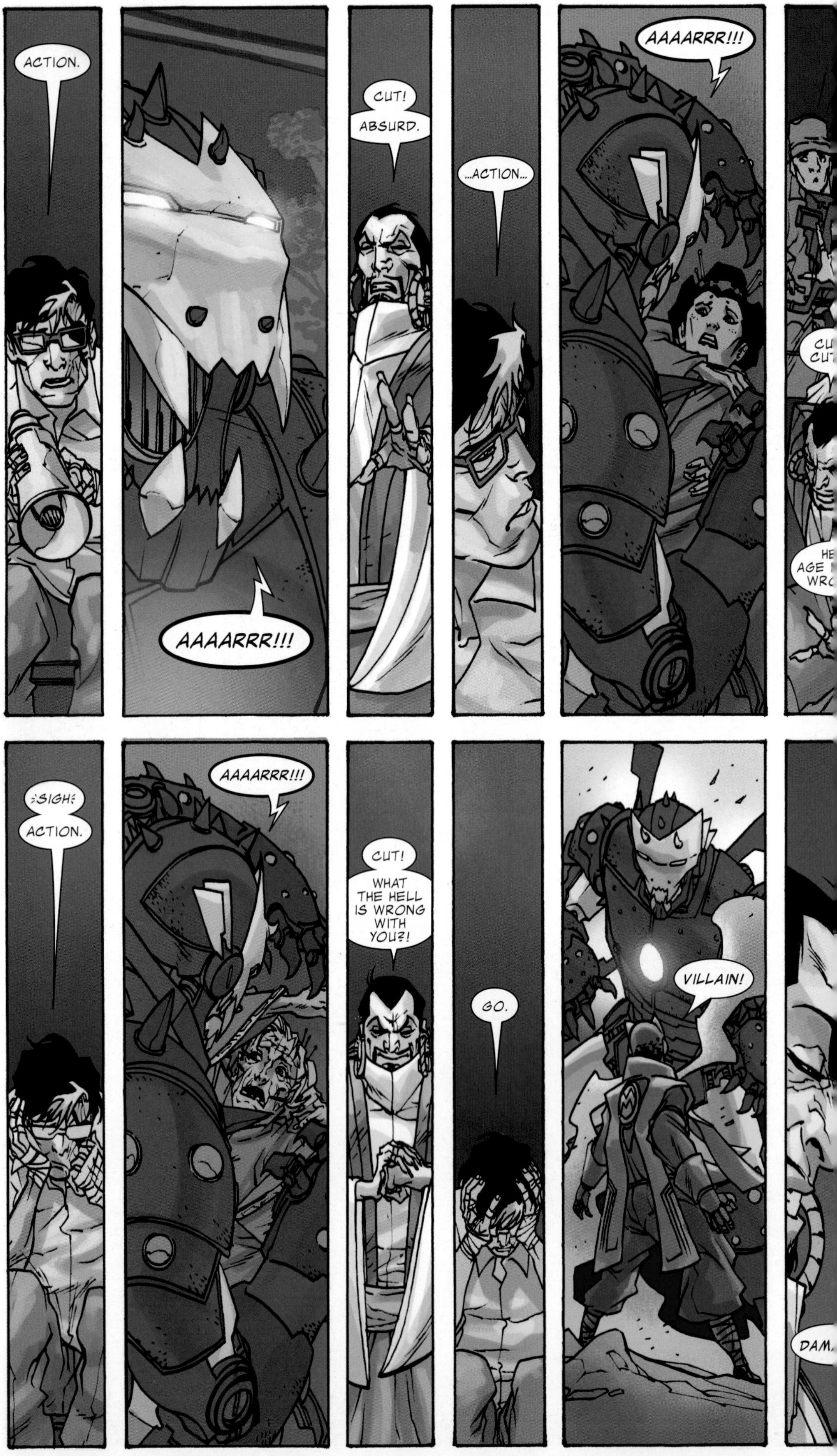
ACTION.
AAAARRR!!!
CUT!
ABSURD.
...ACTION...
AAAARRR!!!
:SIGH:
ACTION.
AAAARRR!!!
CUT!
WHAT THE HELL IS WRONG WITH YOU?!
GO.
VILLAIN!

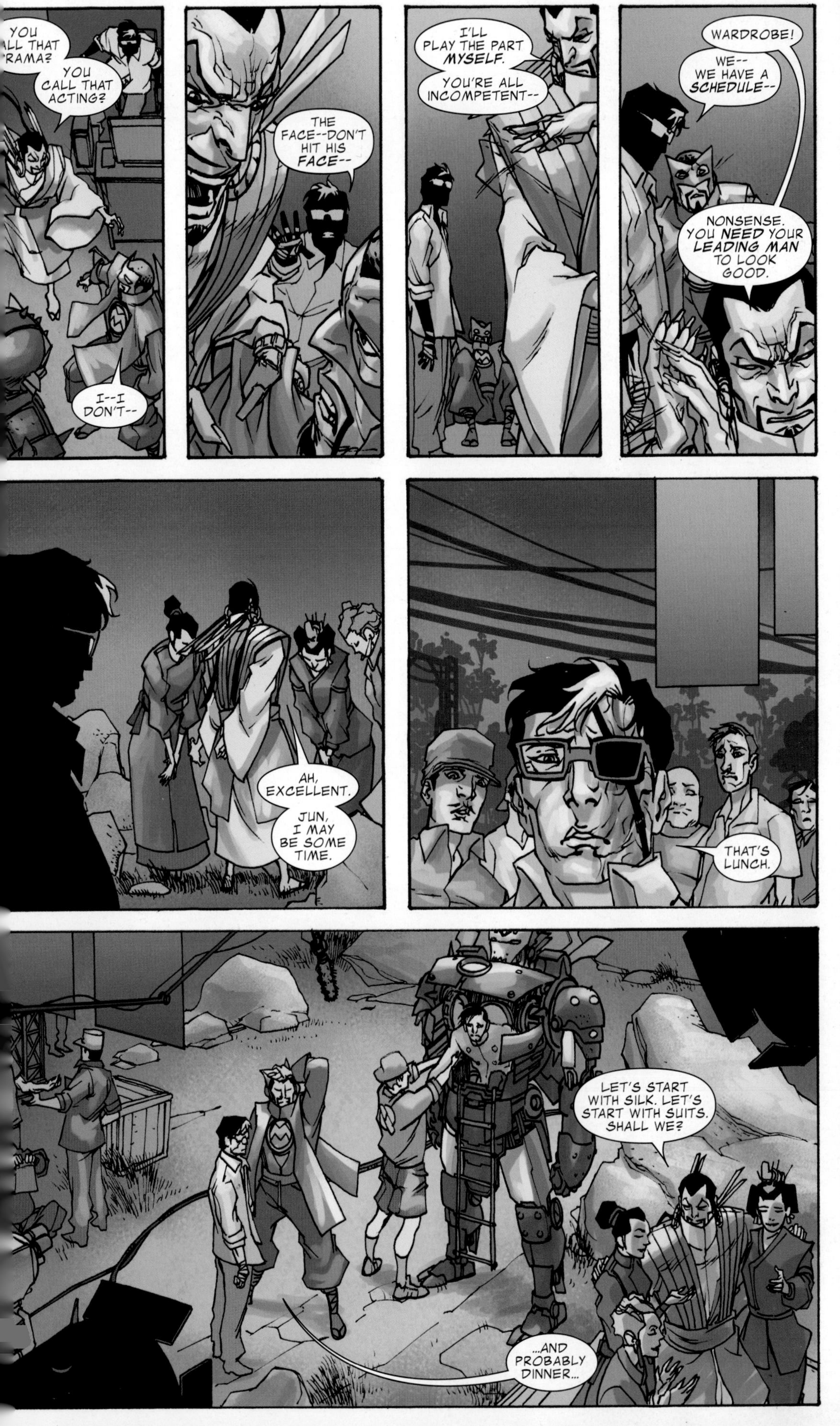
YOU ...ALL THAT ...RAMA?
YOU CALL THAT ACTING?
I--I DON'T--
THE FACE--DON'T HIT HIS FACE--
I'LL PLAY THE PART MYSELF.
YOU'RE ALL INCOMPETENT--
WARDROBE!
WE--
WE HAVE A SCHEDULE--
NONSENSE. YOU NEED YOUR LEADING MAN TO LOOK GOOD.
AH, EXCELLENT.
JUN, I MAY BE SOME TIME.
THAT'S LUNCH.
LET'S START WITH SILK. LET'S START WITH SUITS. SHALL WE?
...AND PROBABLY DINNER...

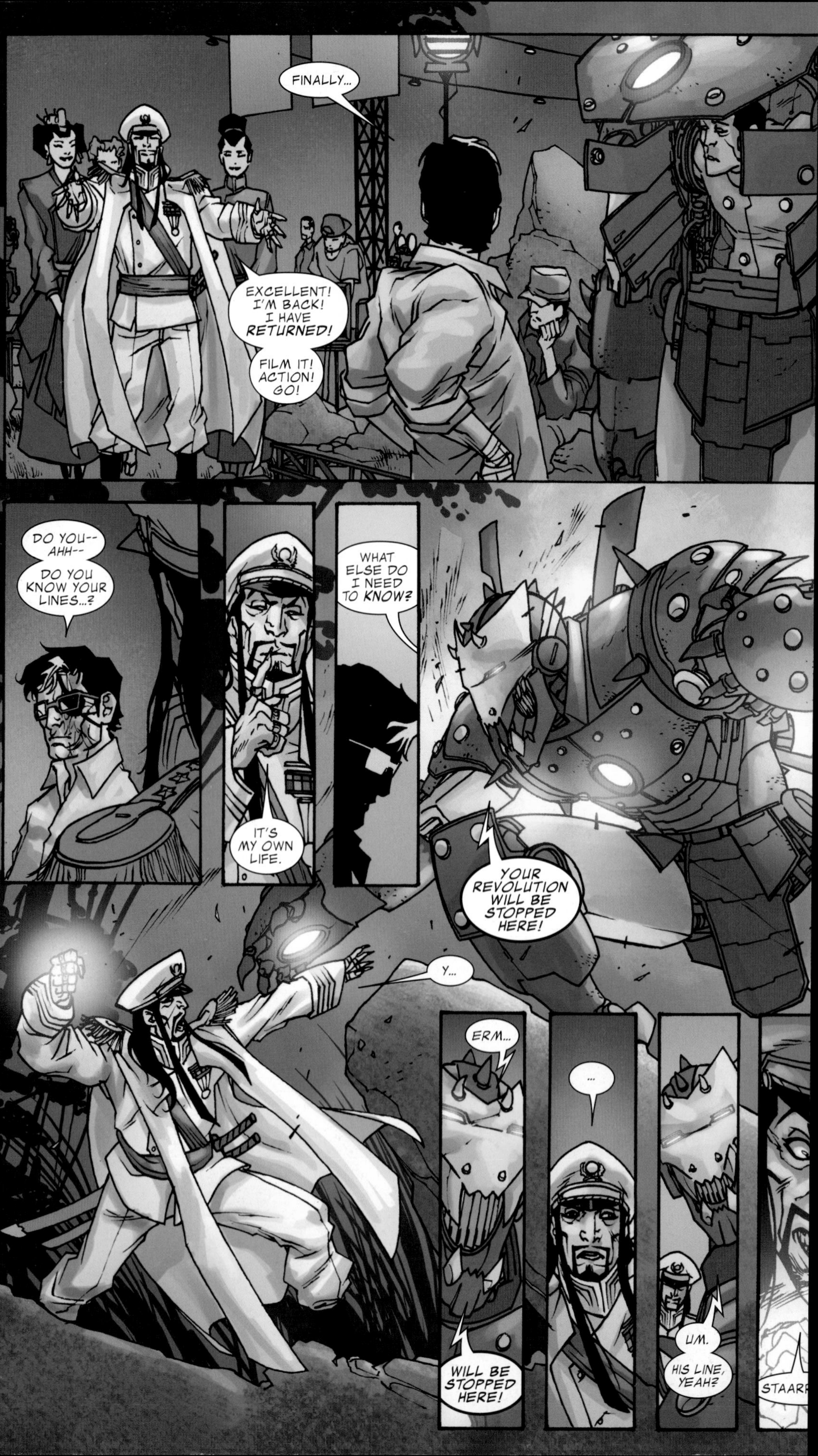

FINALLY...
EXCELLENT! I'M BACK! I HAVE RETURNED!
FILM IT! ACTION! GO!
DO YOU-- AHH--
DO YOU KNOW YOUR LINES...?
IT'S MY OWN LIFE.
WHAT ELSE DO I NEED TO KNOW?
YOUR REVOLUTION WILL BE STOPPED HERE!
Y...
ERM...
...
WILL BE STOPPED HERE!
UM.
HIS LINE, YEAH?
STAARR

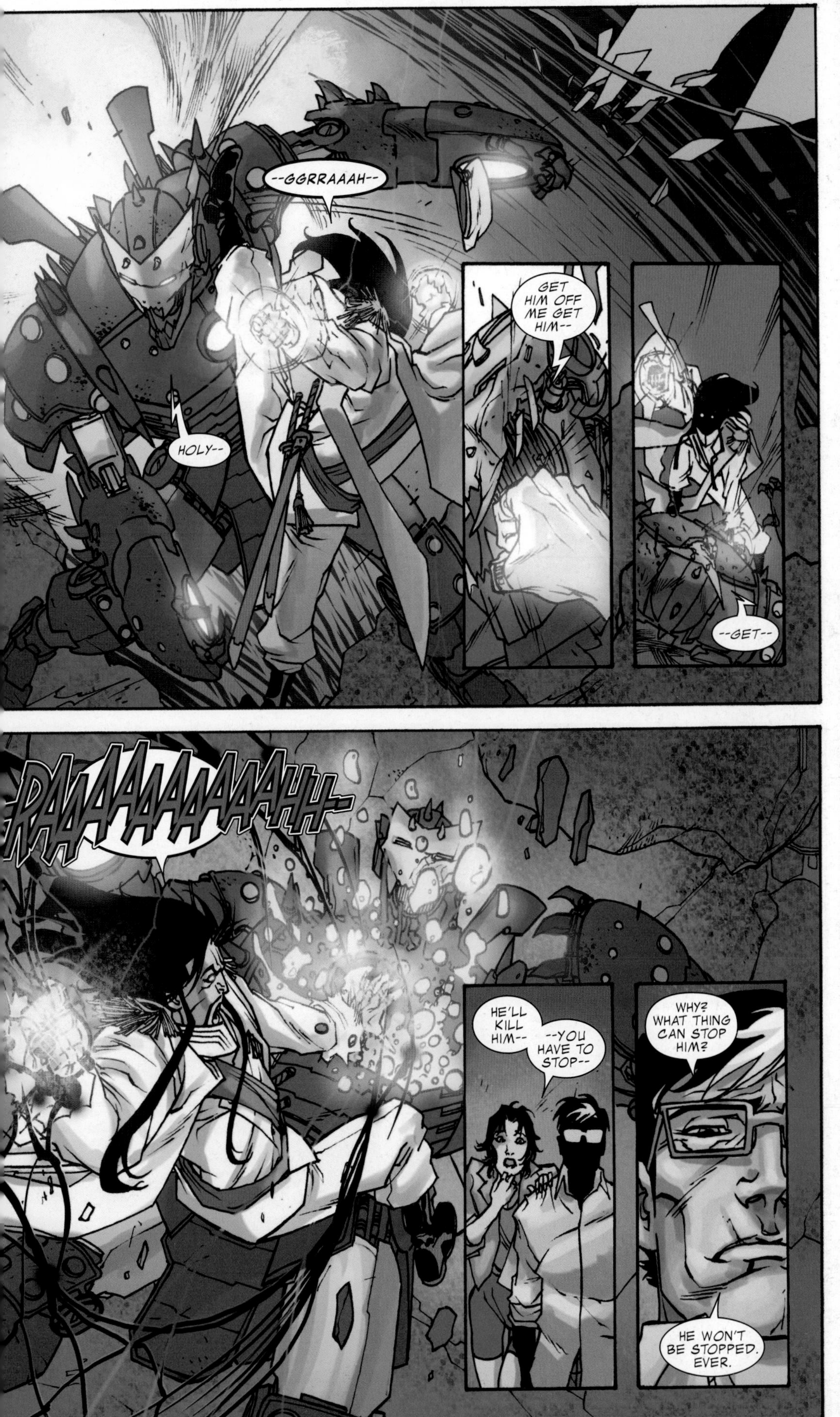
--GGRRAAAH--
HOLY--
GET HIM OFF ME GET HIM--
--GET--
RAAAAAAAAAAHH--
HE'LL KILL HIM--
--YOU HAVE TO STOP--
WHY? WHAT THING CAN STOP HIM?
HE WON'T BE STOPPED. EVER.

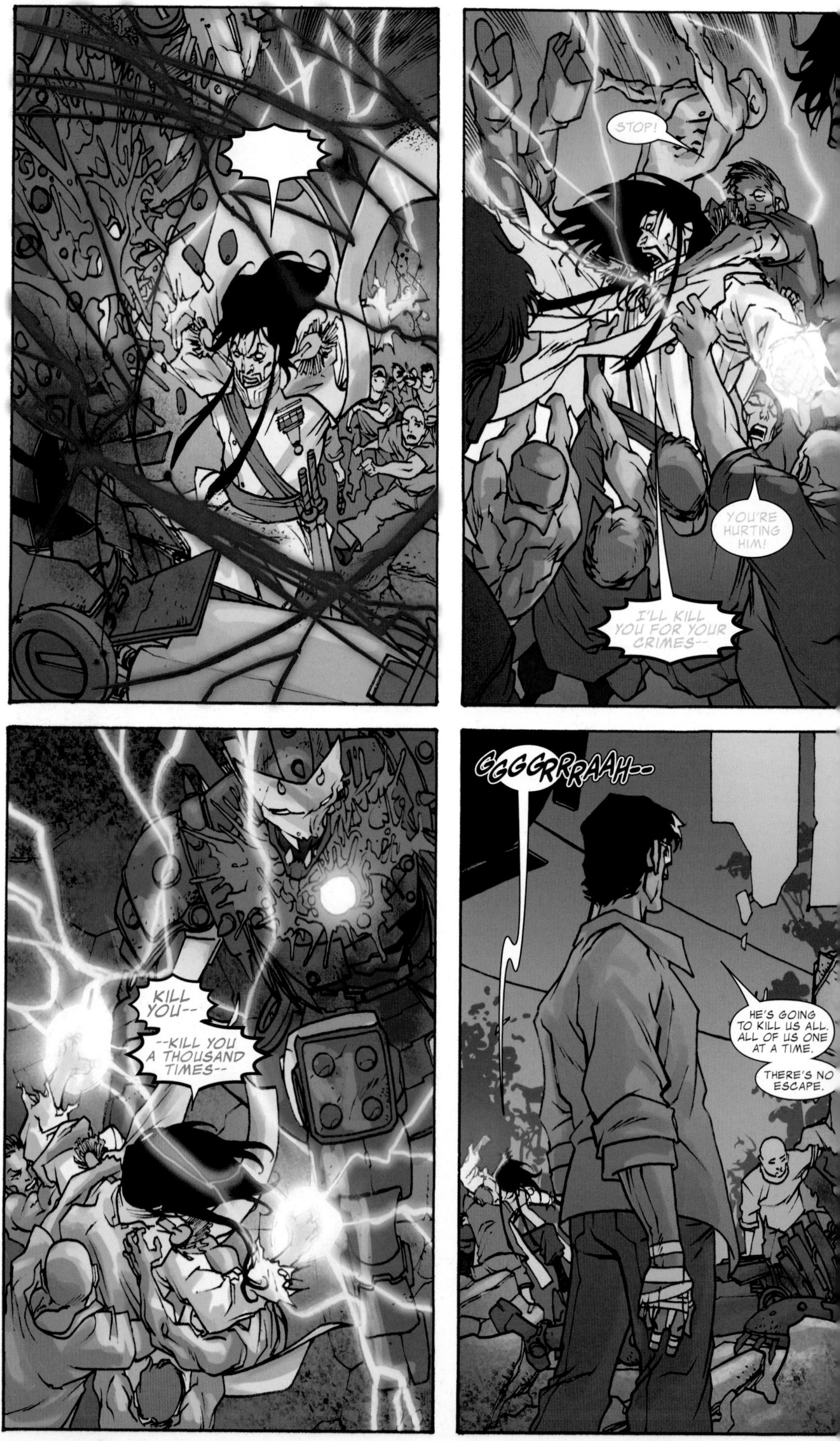
STOP!
YOU'RE HURTING HIM!
I'LL KILL YOU FOR YOUR CRIMES--
KILL YOU--
--KILL YOU A THOUSAND TIMES--
GGGGRRRAAH--
HE'S GOING TO KILL US ALL. ALL OF US ONE AT A TIME.
THERE'S NO ESCAPE.

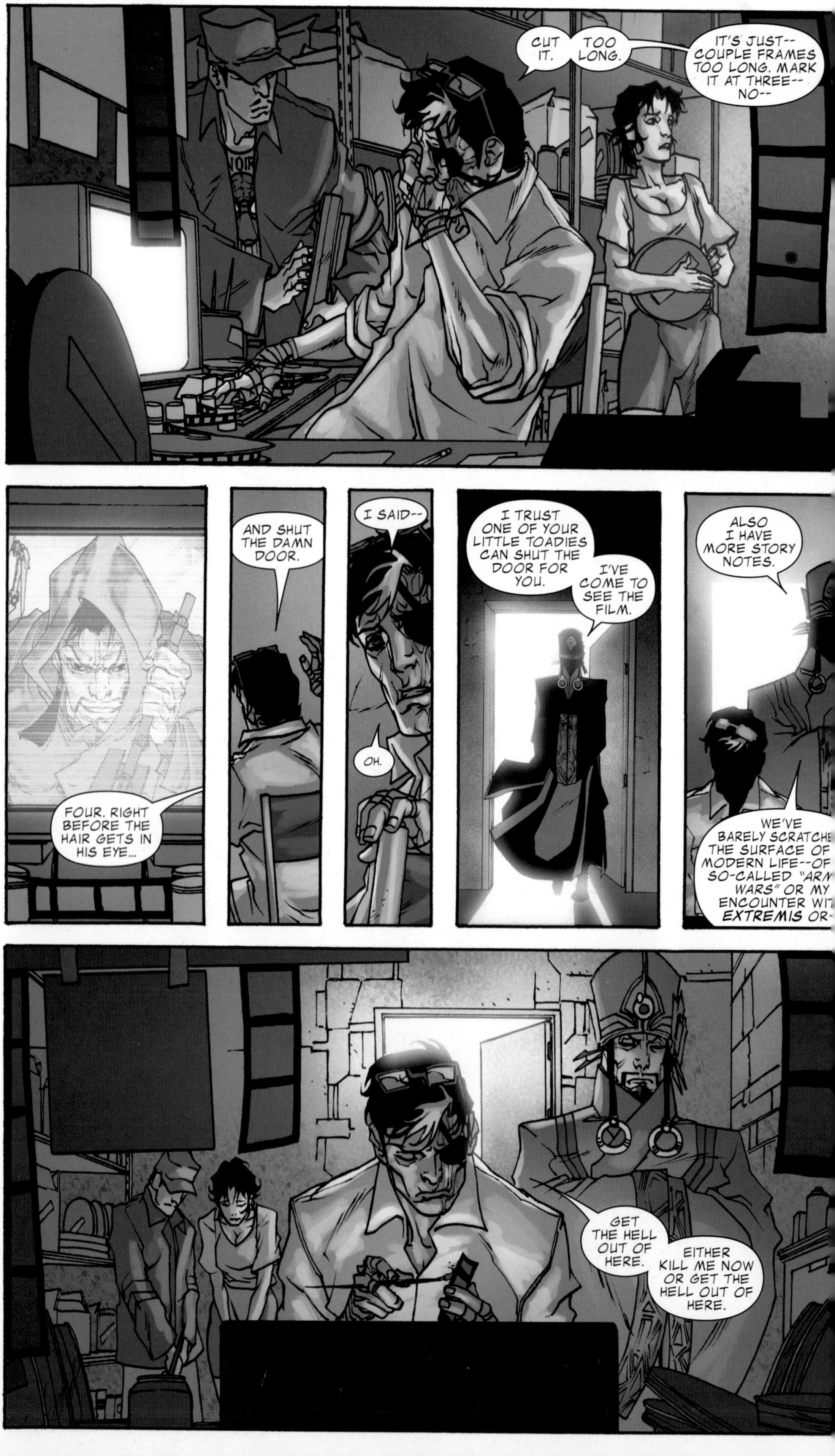
CUT IT.
TOO LONG.
IT'S JUST-- COUPLE FRAMES TOO LONG. MARK IT AT THREE-- NO--
FOUR. RIGHT BEFORE THE HAIR GETS IN HIS EYE...
AND SHUT THE DAMN DOOR.
I SAID--
OH.
I TRUST ONE OF YOUR LITTLE TOADIES CAN SHUT THE DOOR FOR YOU.
I'VE COME TO SEE THE FILM.
ALSO I HAVE MORE STORY NOTES.
WE'VE BARELY SCRATCHE THE SURFACE OF MODERN LIFE--OF SO-CALLED "ARM WARS" OR MY ENCOUNTER WIT EXTREMIS OR-
GET THE HELL OUT OF HERE.
EITHER KILL ME NOW OR GET THE HELL OUT OF HERE.

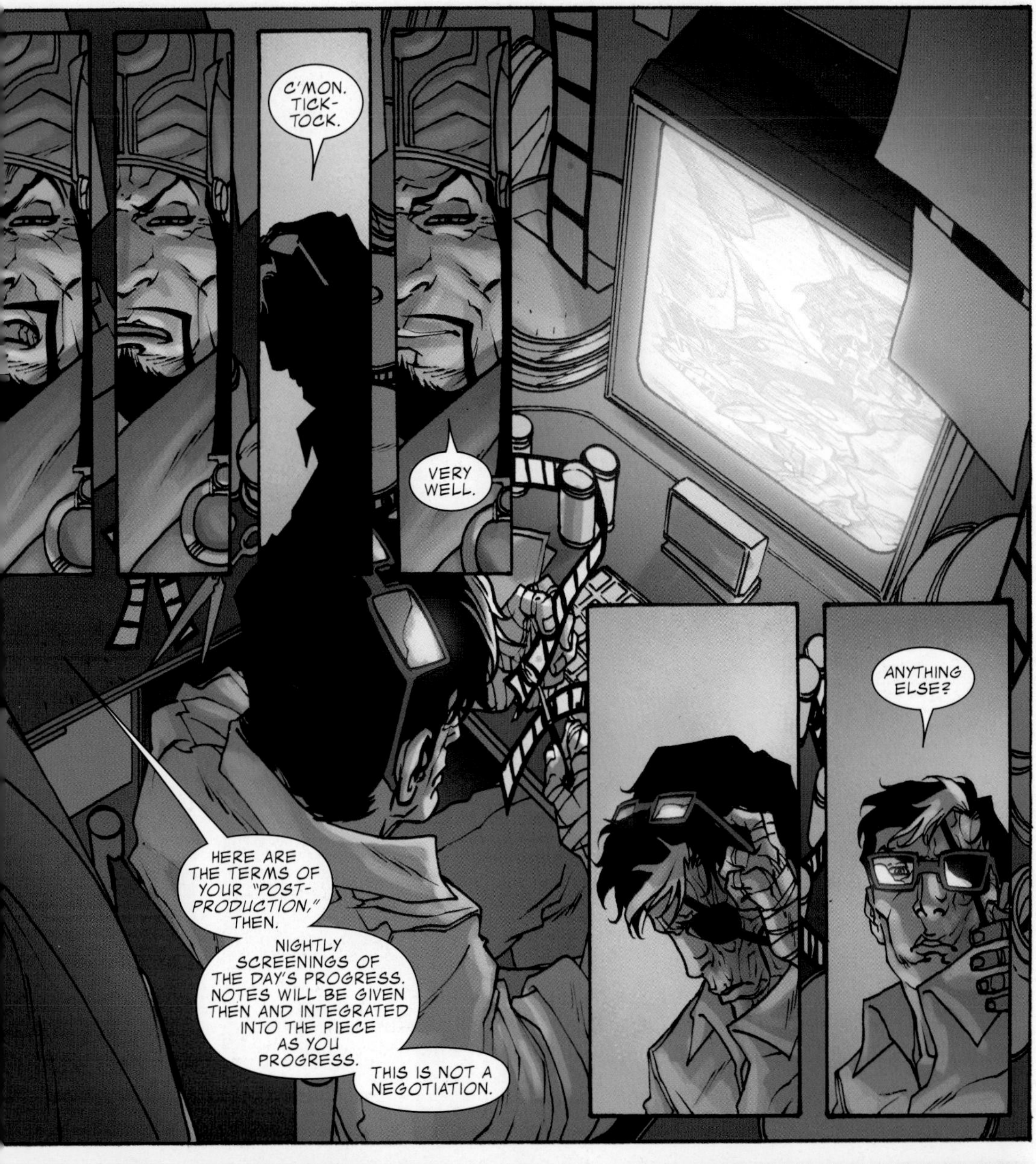
C'MON. TICK-TOCK.
VERY WELL.
HERE ARE THE TERMS OF YOUR "POST-PRODUCTION," THEN.
NIGHTLY SCREENINGS OF THE DAY'S PROGRESS. NOTES WILL BE GIVEN THEN AND INTEGRATED INTO THE PIECE AS YOU PROGRESS.
THIS IS NOT A NEGOTIATION.
ANYTHING ELSE?
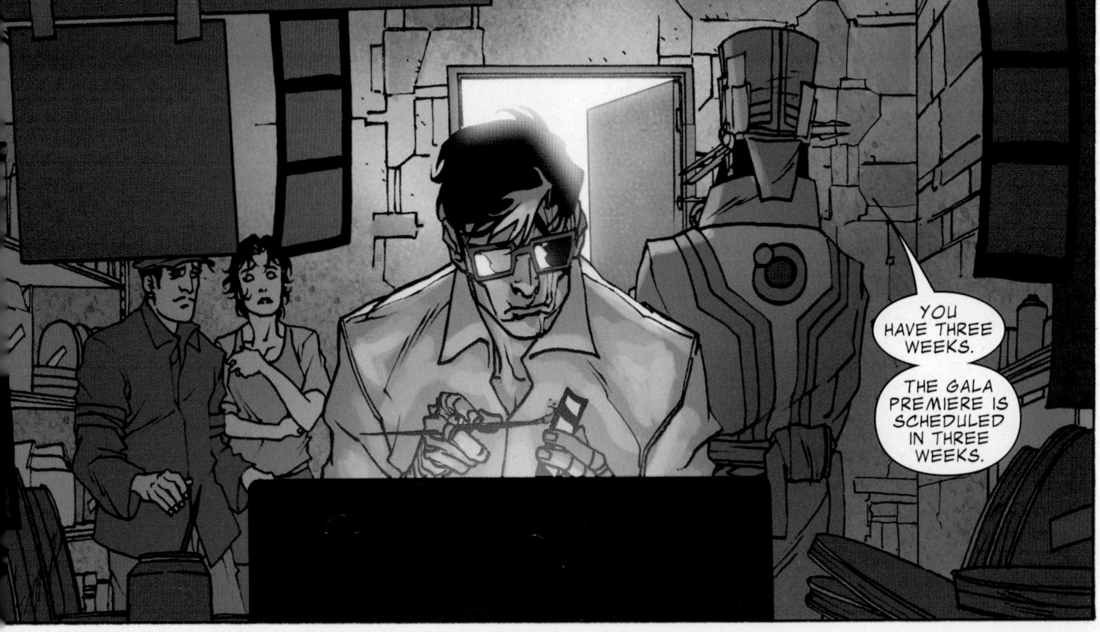
YOU HAVE THREE WEEKS.
THE GALA PREMIERE IS SCHEDULED IN THREE WEEKS.

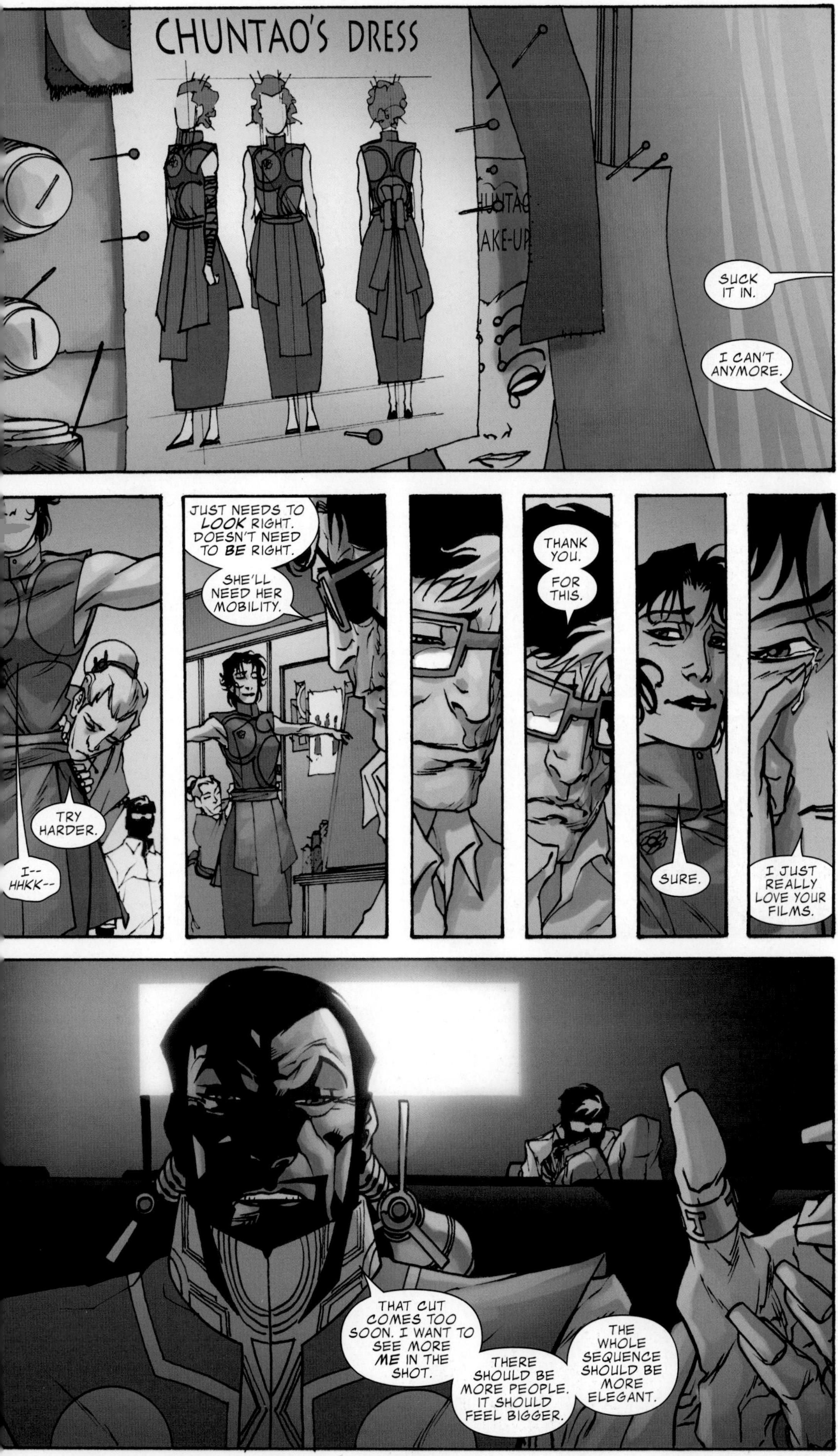

CHUNTAO'S DRESS
SUCK IT IN.
I CAN'T ANYMORE.
TRY HARDER.
I-- HHKK--
JUST NEEDS TO LOOK RIGHT. DOESN'T NEED TO BE RIGHT.
SHE'LL NEED HER MOBILITY.
THANK YOU.
FOR THIS.
SURE.
I JUST REALLY LOVE YOUR FILMS.
THAT CUT COMES TOO SOON. I WANT TO SEE MORE ME IN THE SHOT.
THERE SHOULD BE MORE PEOPLE. IT SHOULD FEEL BIGGER.
THE WHOLE SEQUENCE SHOULD BE MORE ELEGANT.

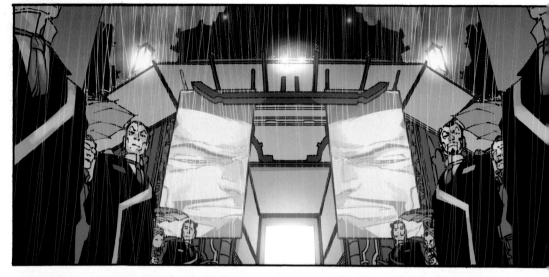

I HAVE ARRIVED.

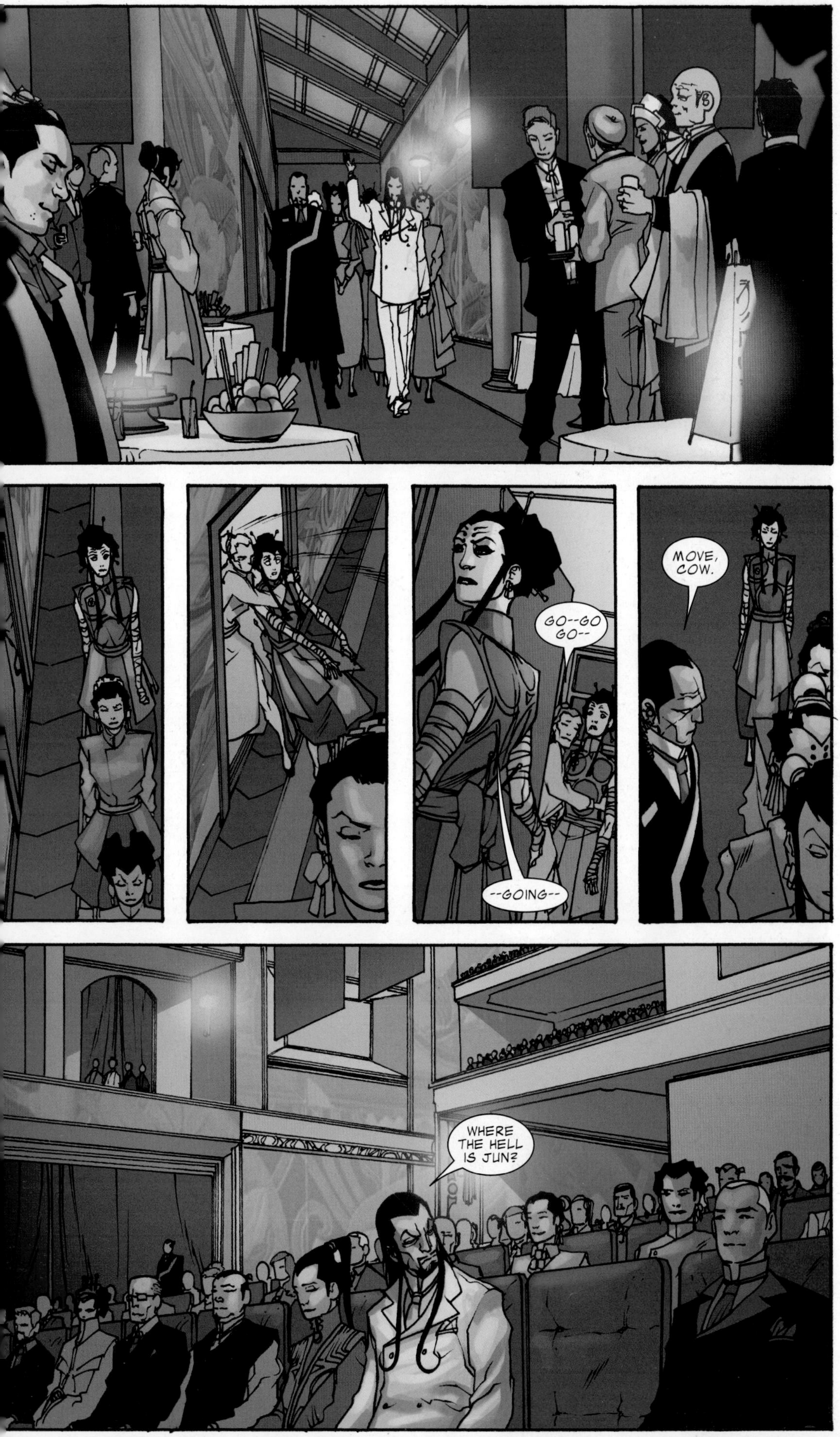
GO--GO GO--
--GOING--
MOVE, COW.
WHERE THE HELL IS JUN?

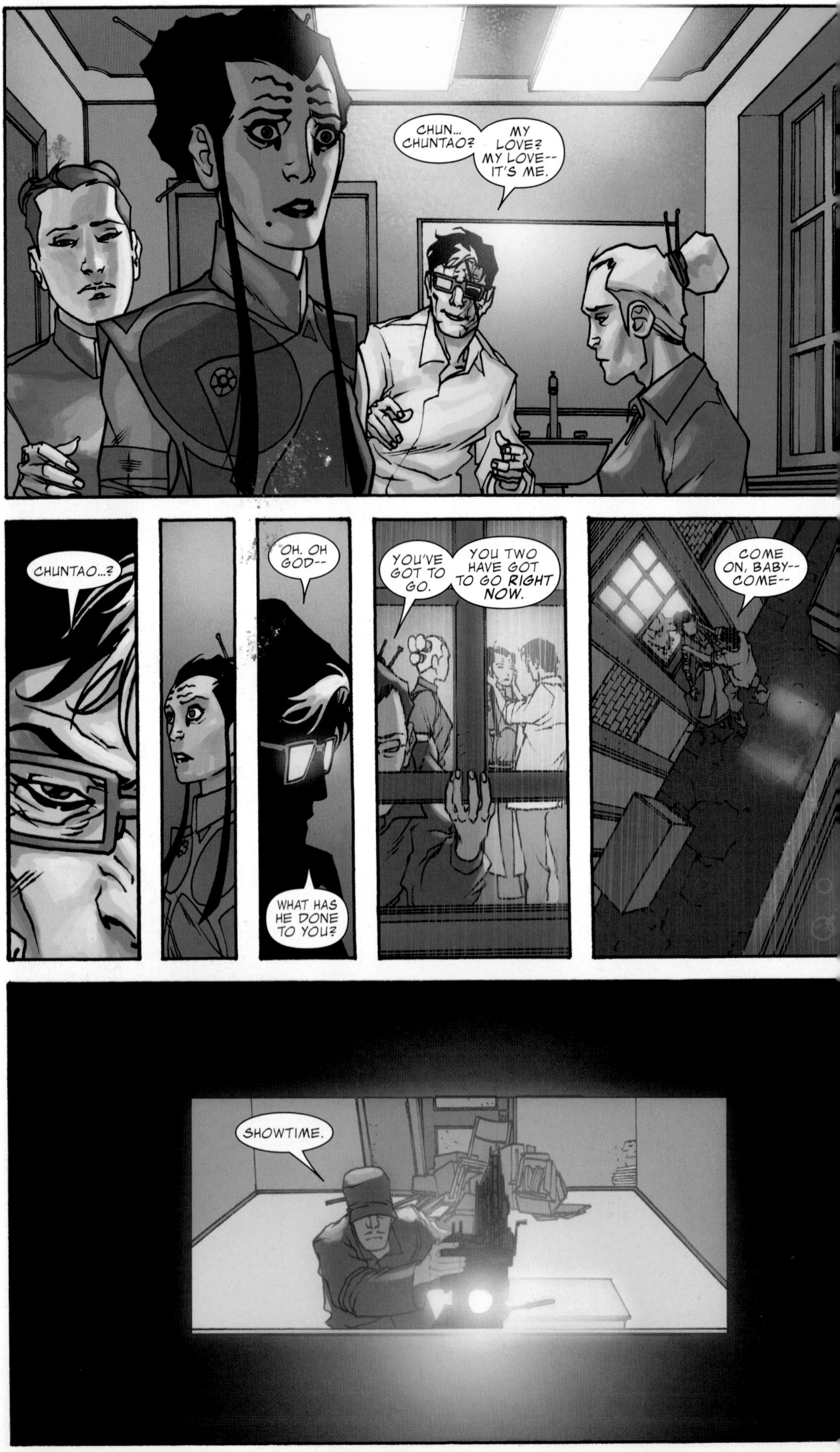

CHUN... CHUNTAO?
MY LOVE? MY LOVE-- IT'S ME.
CHUNTAO...?
OH. OH GOD--
WHAT HAS HE DONE TO YOU?
YOU'VE GOT TO GO.
YOU TWO HAVE GOT TO GO **RIGHT NOW.**
COME ON, BABY-- COME--
SHOWTIME.

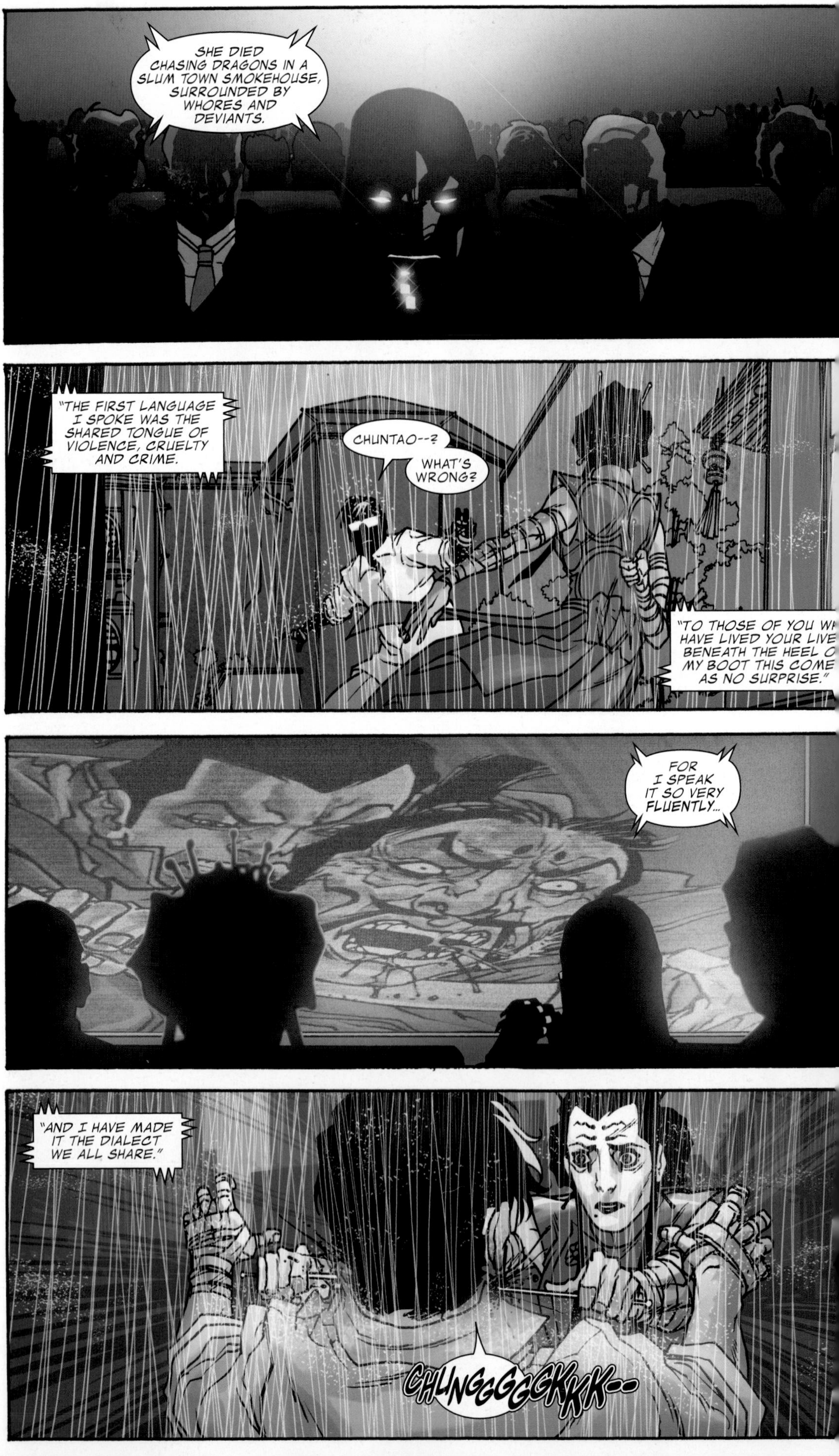

SHE DIED CHASING DRAGONS IN A SLUM TOWN SMOKEHOUSE, SURROUNDED BY WHORES AND DEVIANTS.
"THE FIRST LANGUAGE I SPOKE WAS THE SHARED TONGUE OF VIOLENCE, CRUELTY AND CRIME.
CHUNTAO--?
WHAT'S WRONG?
"TO THOSE OF YOU WH HAVE LIVED YOUR LIVE BENEATH THE HEEL O MY BOOT THIS COME AS NO SURPRISE."
FOR I SPEAK IT SO VERY FLUENTLY...
"AND I HAVE MADE IT THE DIALECT WE ALL SHARE."
CHUNGGGGGKKKK--

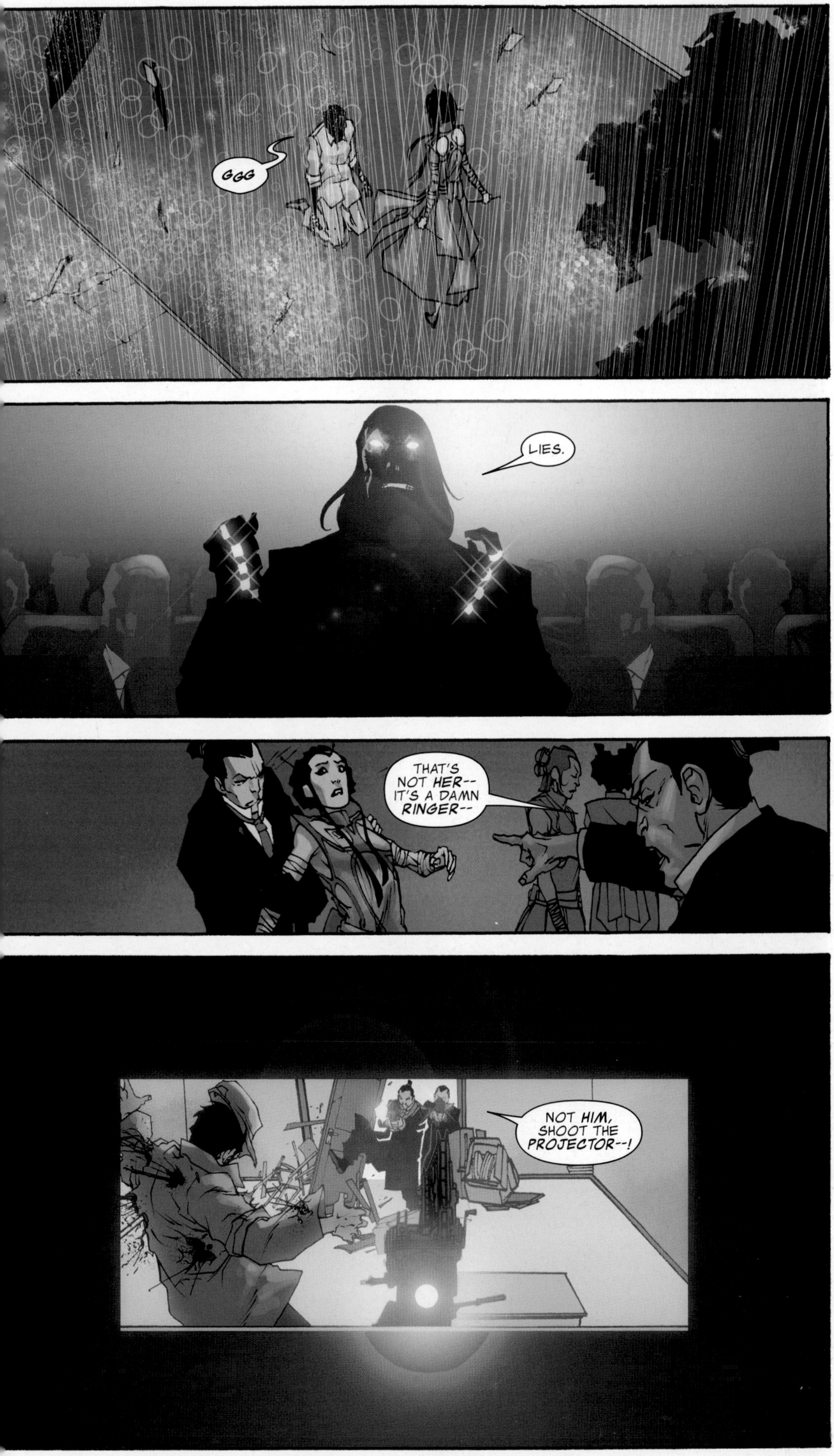
GGG
LIES.
THAT'S NOT HER-- IT'S A DAMN RINGER--
NOT HIM, SHOOT THE PROJECTOR--!

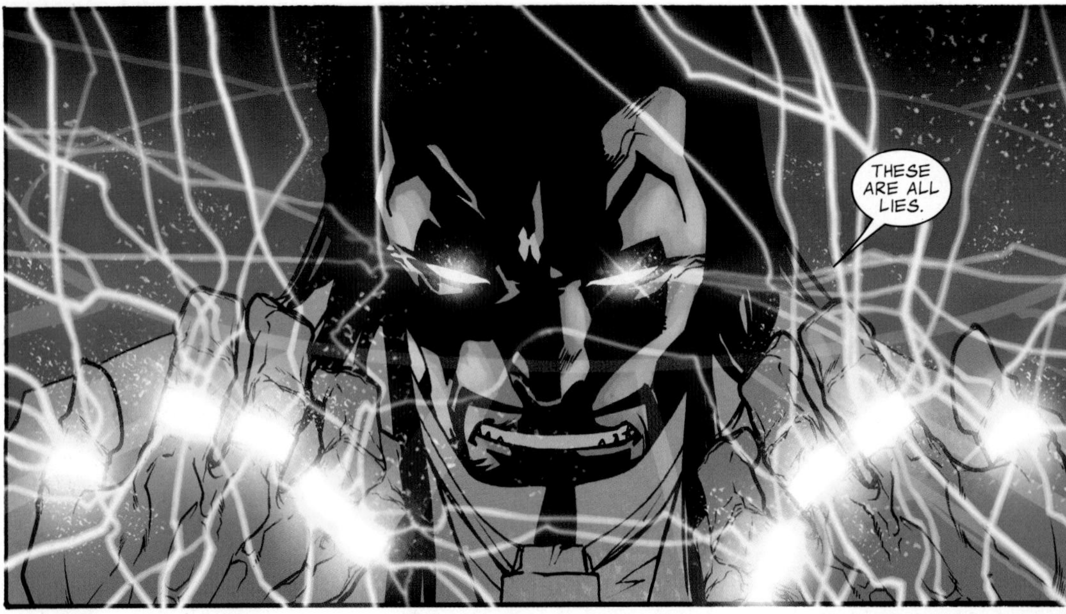
THESE ARE ALL LIES.
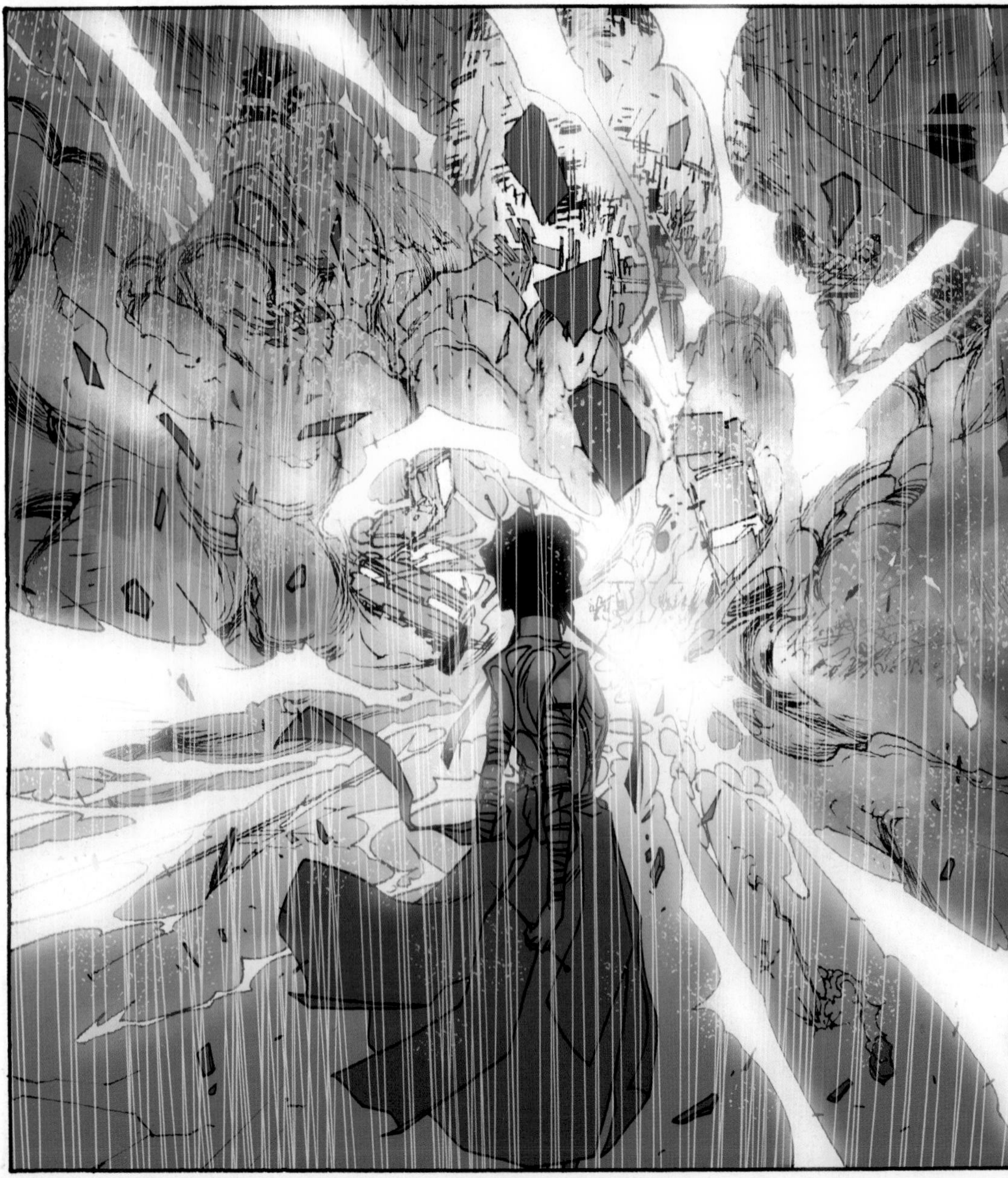

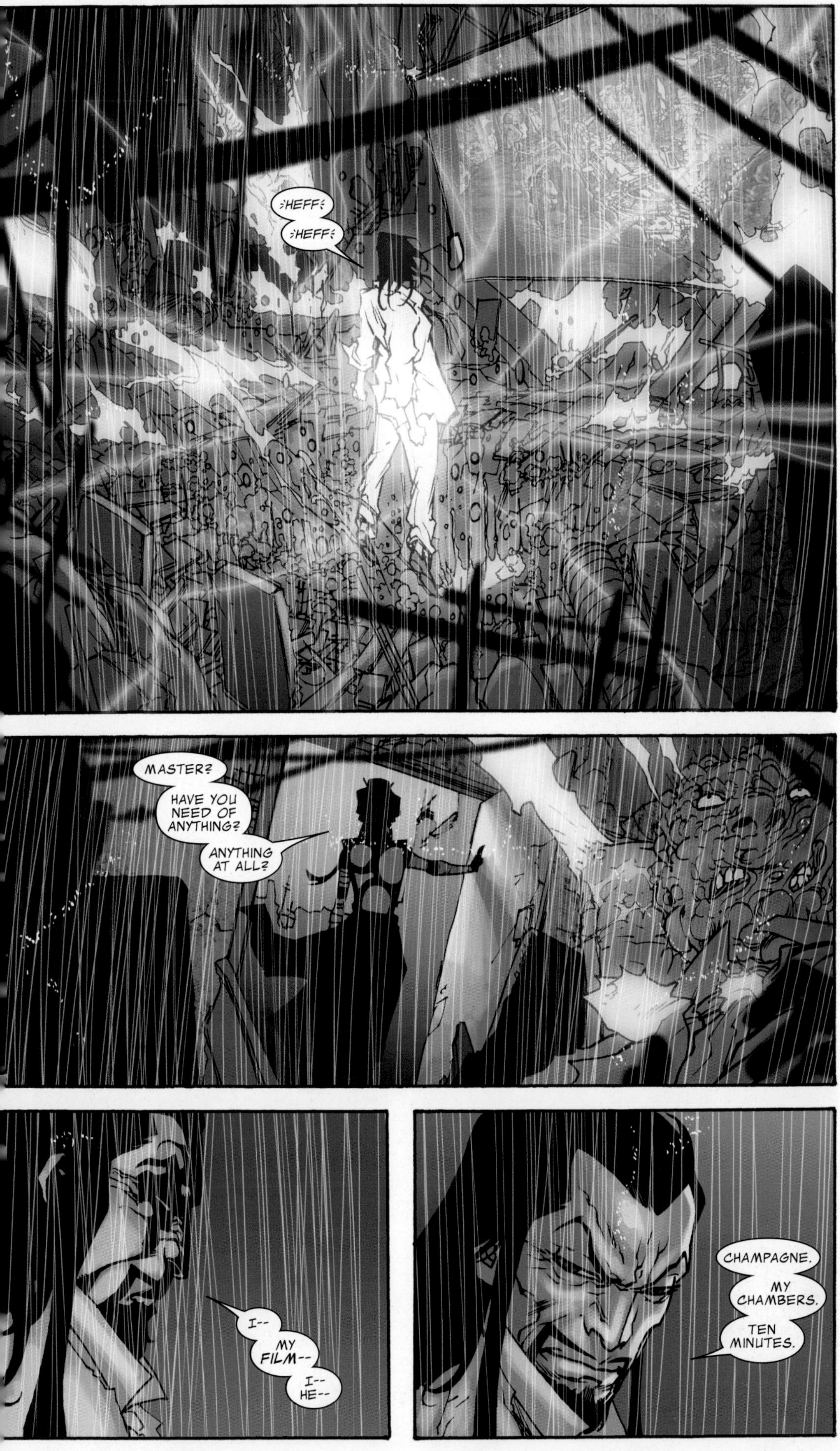

HEFF
HEFF
MASTER?
HAVE YOU NEED OF ANYTHING?
ANYTHING AT ALL?
I--
MY FILM--
I-- HE--
CHAMPAGNE.
MY CHAMBERS.
TEN MINUTES.

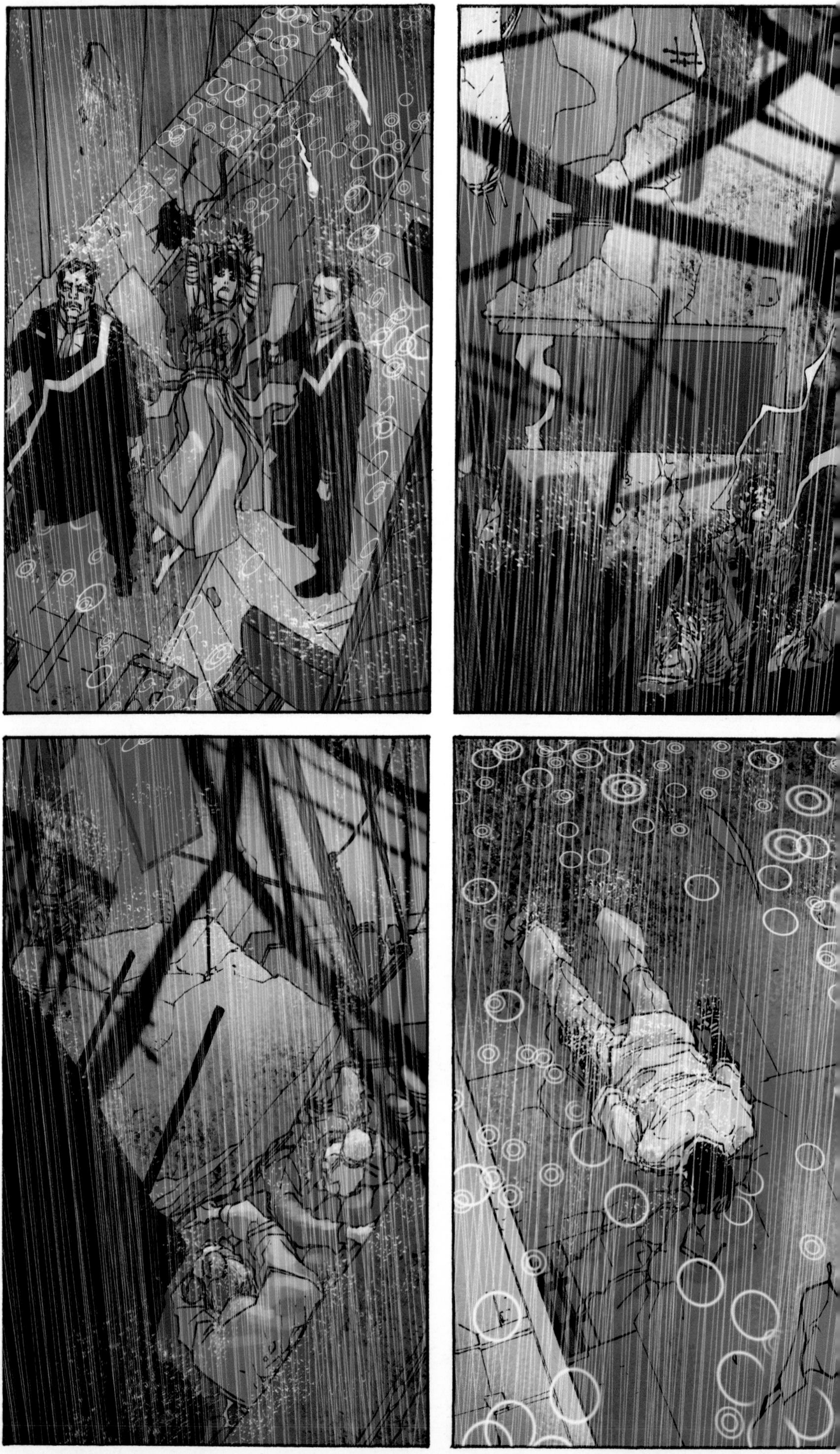

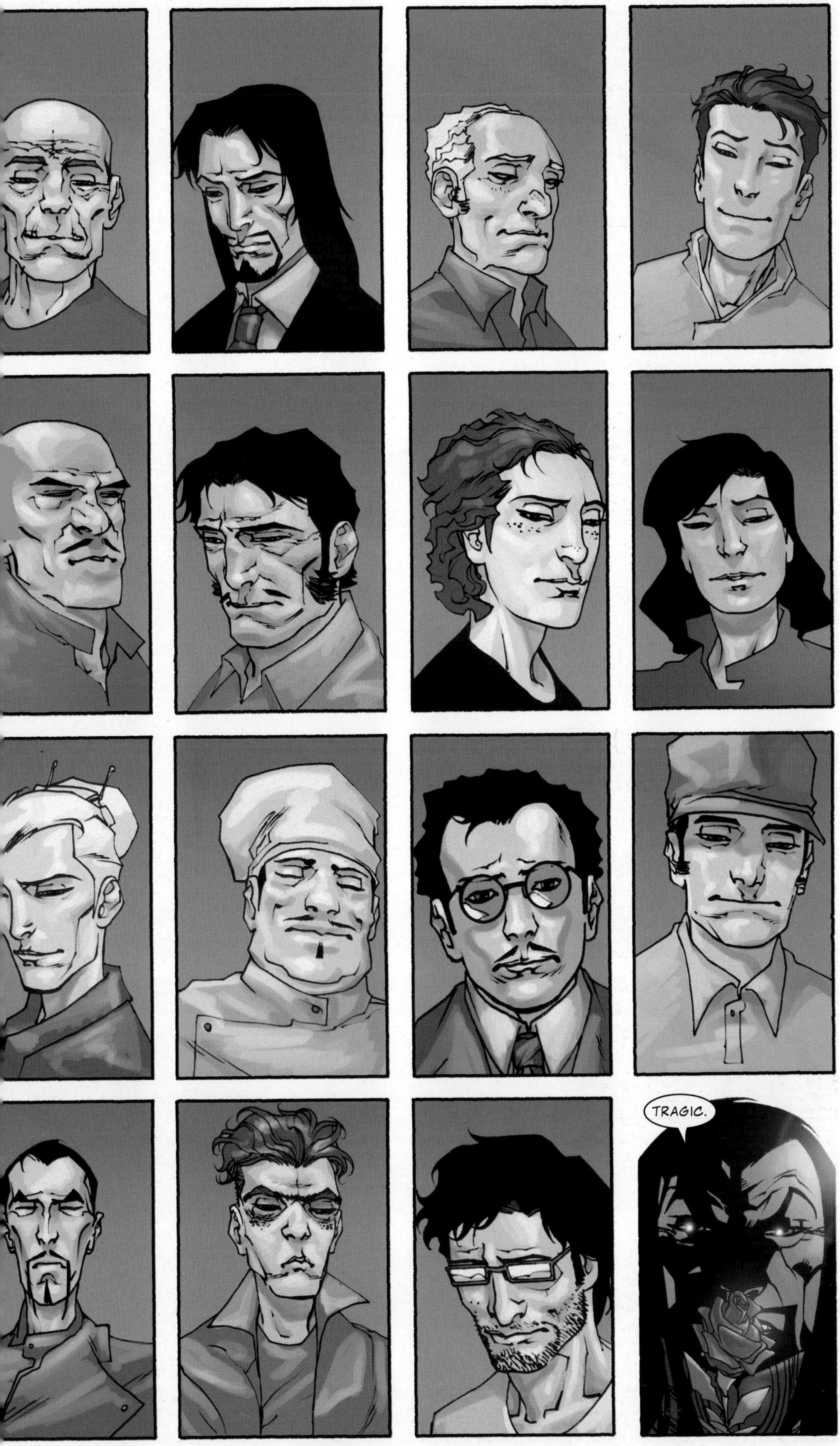
TRAGIC.

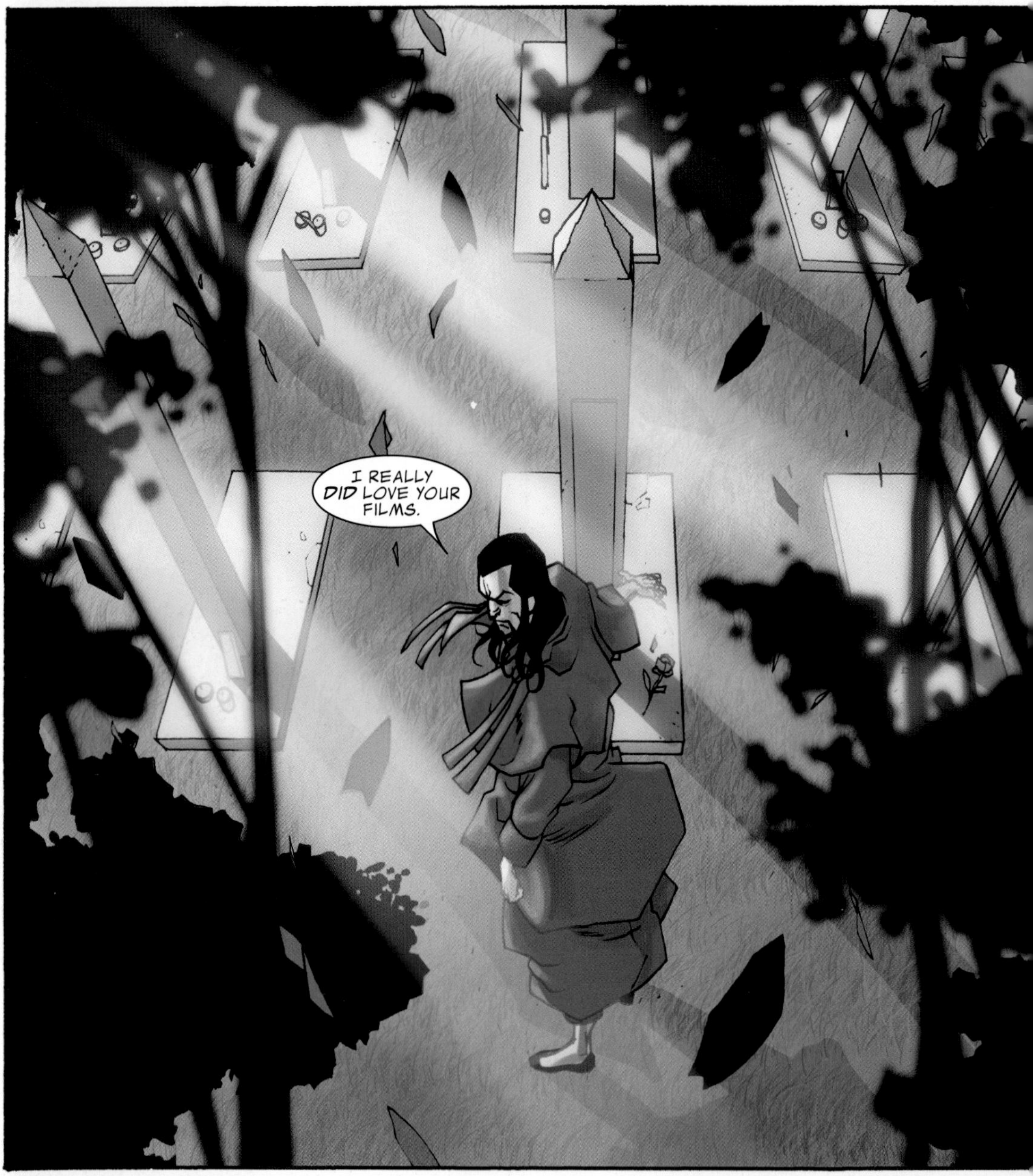
I REALLY DID LOVE YOUR FILMS.

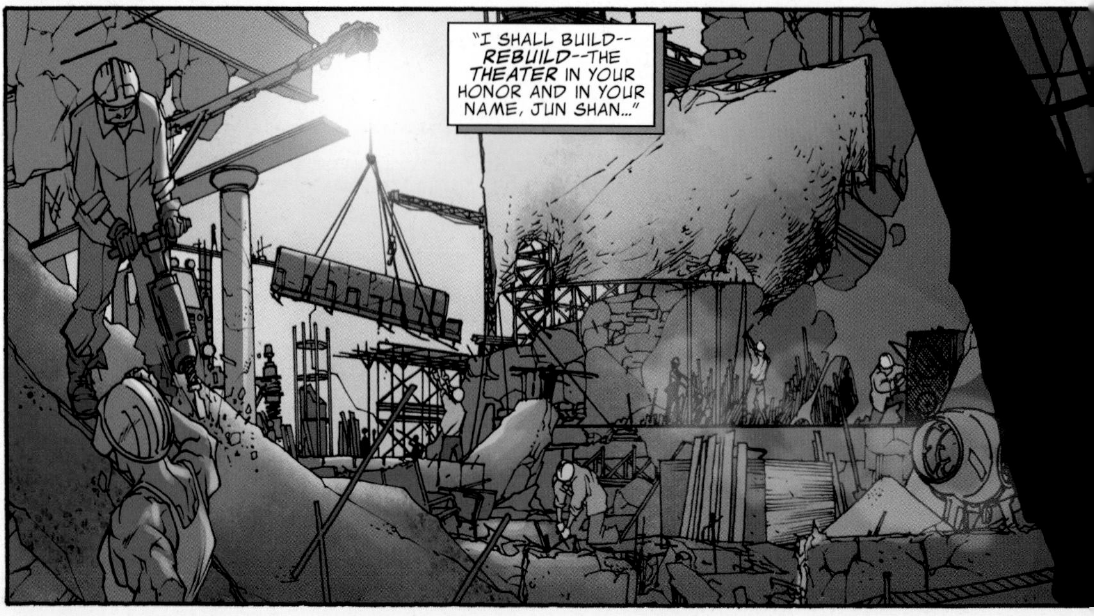
"I SHALL BUILD-- REBUILD--THE THEATER IN YOUR HONOR AND IN YOUR NAME, JUN SHAN..."

JUN SHAN'S LAST WORK WAS MUCH LIKE HIS FIRST.

A STORY ABOUT THE BRAVERY REQUIRED TO STAND UP FOR ONE'S BELIEFS, AND FOR ONE'S INALIENABLE RIGHT TO FREEDOM.

I WAS PROUD TO BE A PART OF IT.

IN THE YEAR SINCE HIS DISAPPEARANCE, THE ABSENCE OF THE MAN HAS BEEN FILLED ONLY BY HIS FILMS.

HIS WONDERFUL, ALIVE, TRUTH-SEEKING FILMS.

HIS STORIES WERE OUR STORIES.

JUN SHAN'S VOICE WAS OUR VOICE.

HE WAS MY HERO AND MY MENTOR.

AND THROUGH HIS BODY OF WORK...THROUGH THE GREAT WORKS THAT DEFINED AND PROPELLED HIS LIFE...

...HE WILL LIVE FOREVER.

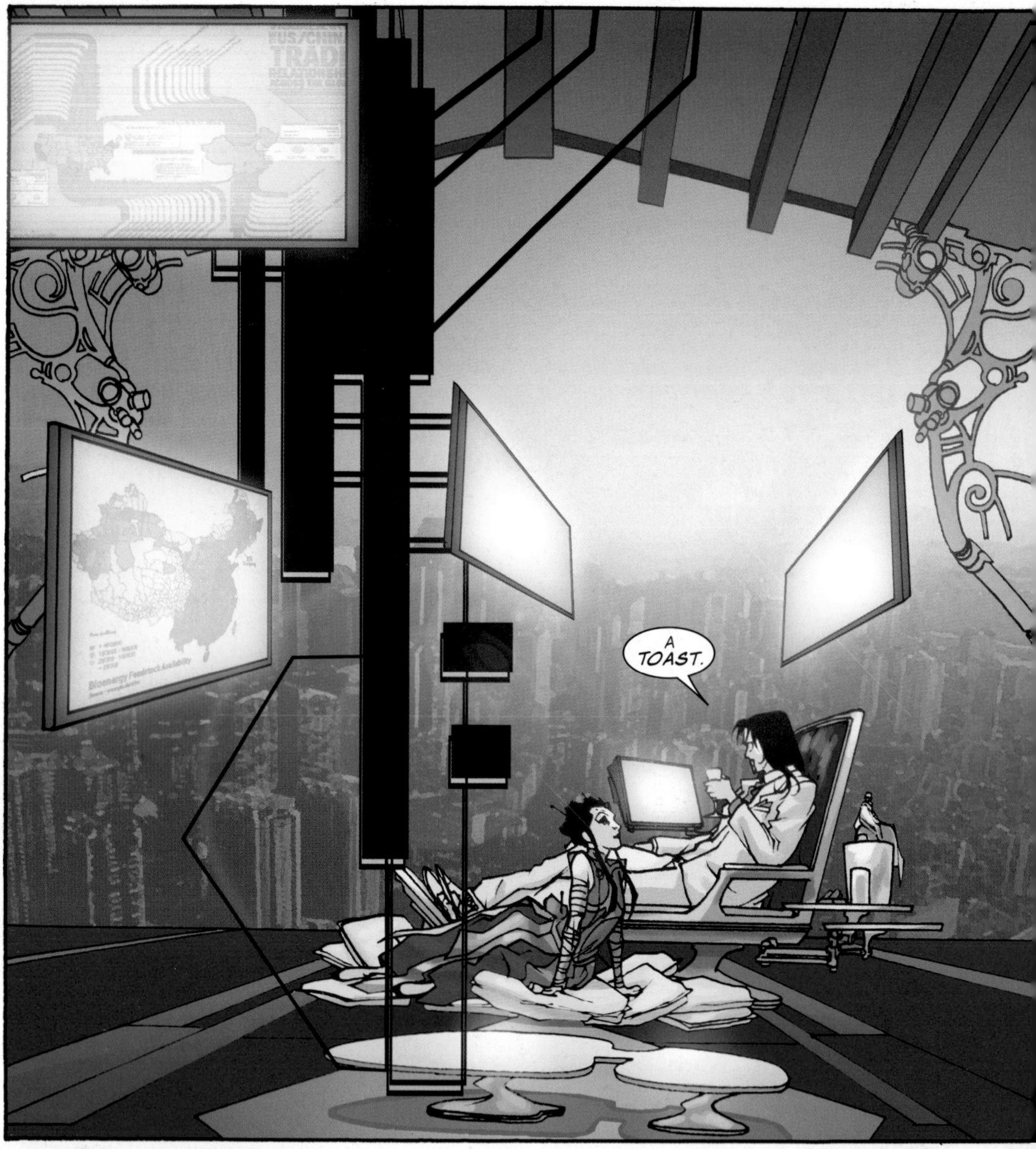
TRADE
Bioenergy Feedstock Availability
A TOAST.

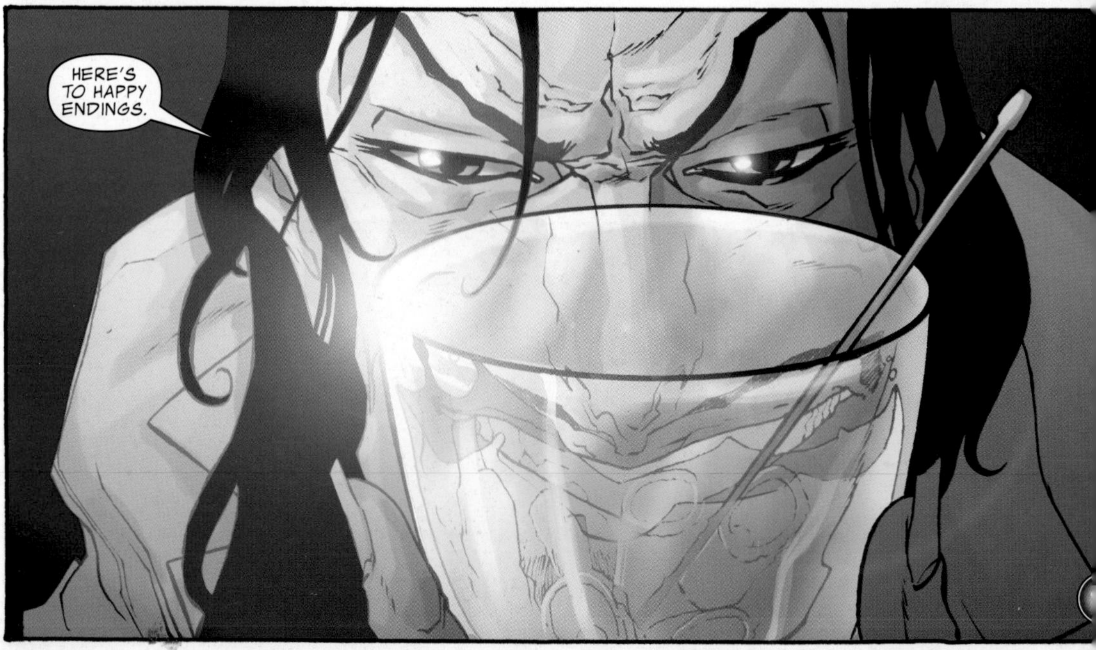
HERE'S TO HAPPY ENDINGS.

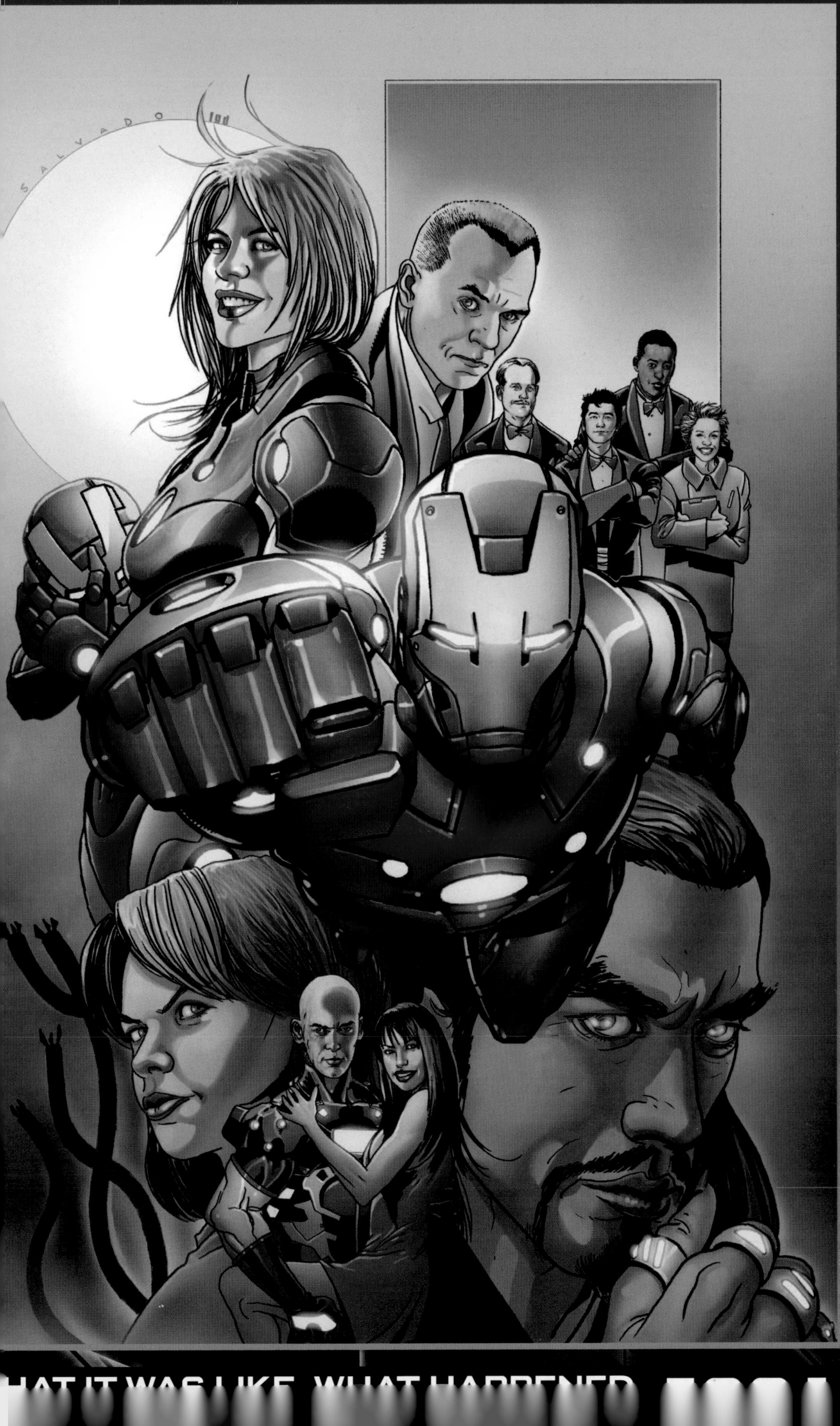

HAT IT WAS LIKE, WHAT HAPPENED

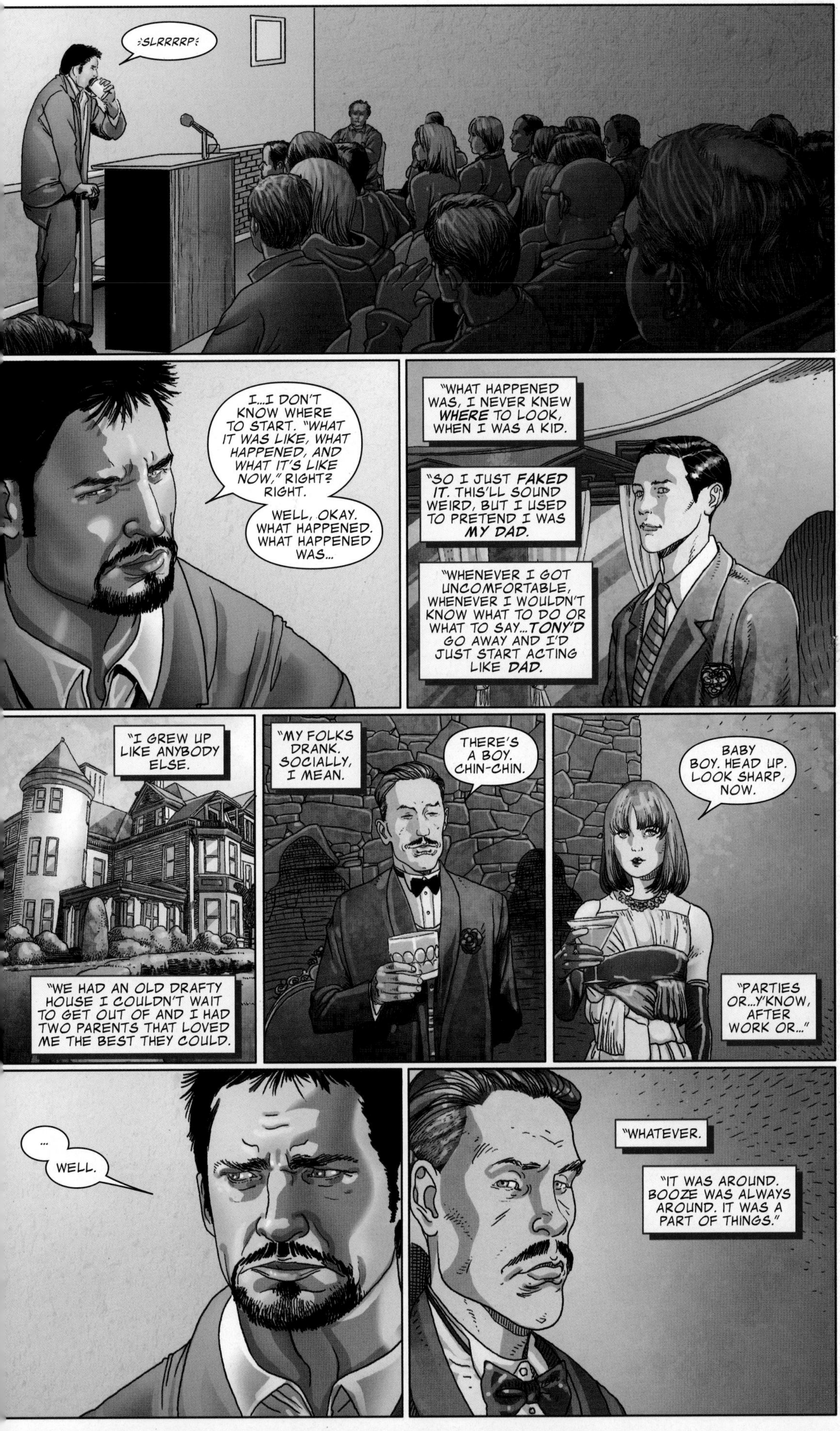

:SLRRRRP:
I...I DON'T KNOW WHERE TO START. "WHAT IT WAS LIKE, WHAT HAPPENED, AND WHAT IT'S LIKE NOW," RIGHT? RIGHT.
WELL, OKAY. WHAT HAPPENED. WHAT HAPPENED WAS...
"WHAT HAPPENED WAS, I NEVER KNEW WHERE TO LOOK, WHEN I WAS A KID.
"SO I JUST FAKED IT. THIS'LL SOUND WEIRD, BUT I USED TO PRETEND I WAS MY DAD.
"WHENEVER I GOT UNCOMFORTABLE, WHENEVER I WOULDN'T KNOW WHAT TO DO OR WHAT TO SAY...TONY'D GO AWAY AND I'D JUST START ACTING LIKE DAD.
"I GREW UP LIKE ANYBODY ELSE.
"WE HAD AN OLD DRAFTY HOUSE I COULDN'T WAIT TO GET OUT OF AND I HAD TWO PARENTS THAT LOVED ME THE BEST THEY COULD.
"MY FOLKS DRANK. SOCIALLY, I MEAN.
THERE'S A BOY. CHIN-CHIN.
BABY BOY. HEAD UP. LOOK SHARP, NOW.
"PARTIES OR...Y'KNOW, AFTER WORK OR..."
... WELL.
"WHATEVER.
"IT WAS AROUND. BOOZE WAS ALWAYS AROUND. IT WAS A PART OF THINGS."

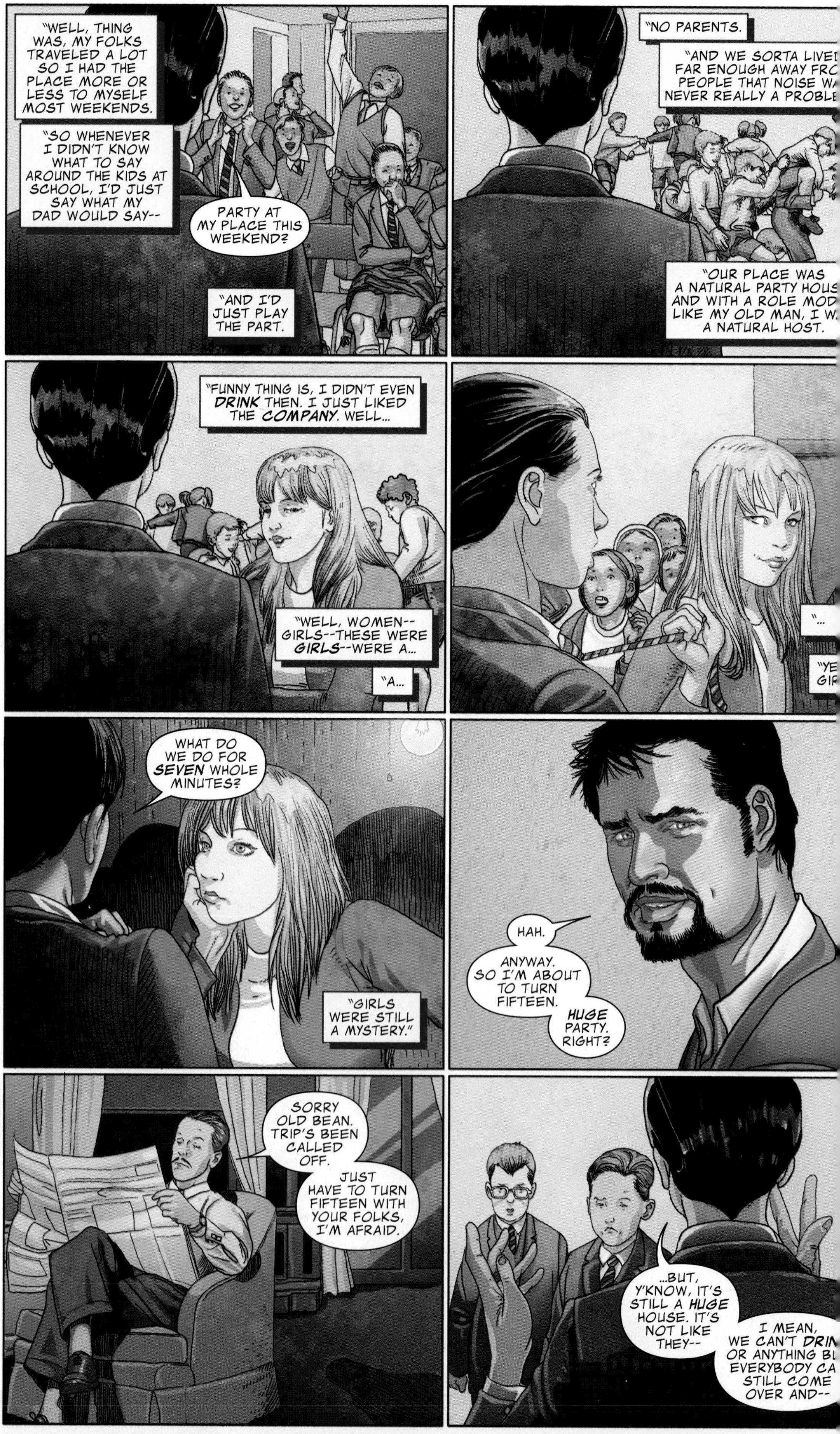
"WELL, THING WAS, MY FOLKS TRAVELED A LOT SO I HAD THE PLACE MORE OR LESS TO MYSELF MOST WEEKENDS.
"SO WHENEVER I DIDN'T KNOW WHAT TO SAY AROUND THE KIDS AT SCHOOL, I'D JUST SAY WHAT MY DAD WOULD SAY--
PARTY AT MY PLACE THIS WEEKEND?
"AND I'D JUST PLAY THE PART.
"NO PARENTS.
"AND WE SORTA LIVEI FAR ENOUGH AWAY FRC PEOPLE THAT NOISE WA NEVER REALLY A PROBLE
"OUR PLACE WAS A NATURAL PARTY HOUS AND WITH A ROLE MOD LIKE MY OLD MAN, I W A NATURAL HOST.
"FUNNY THING IS, I DIDN'T EVEN DRINK THEN. I JUST LIKED THE COMPANY. WELL...
"WELL, WOMEN-- GIRLS--THESE WERE GIRLS--WERE A...
"A...
"...
"YE GIF
WHAT DO WE DO FOR SEVEN WHOLE MINUTES?
"GIRLS WERE STILL A MYSTERY."
HAH.
ANYWAY. SO I'M ABOUT TO TURN FIFTEEN.
HUGE PARTY. RIGHT?
SORRY OLD BEAN. TRIP'S BEEN CALLED OFF.
JUST HAVE TO TURN FIFTEEN WITH YOUR FOLKS, I'M AFRAID.
...BUT, Y'KNOW, IT'S STILL A HUGE HOUSE. IT'S NOT LIKE THEY--
I MEAN, WE CAN'T DRIN OR ANYTHING BU EVERYBODY CA STILL COME OVER AND--

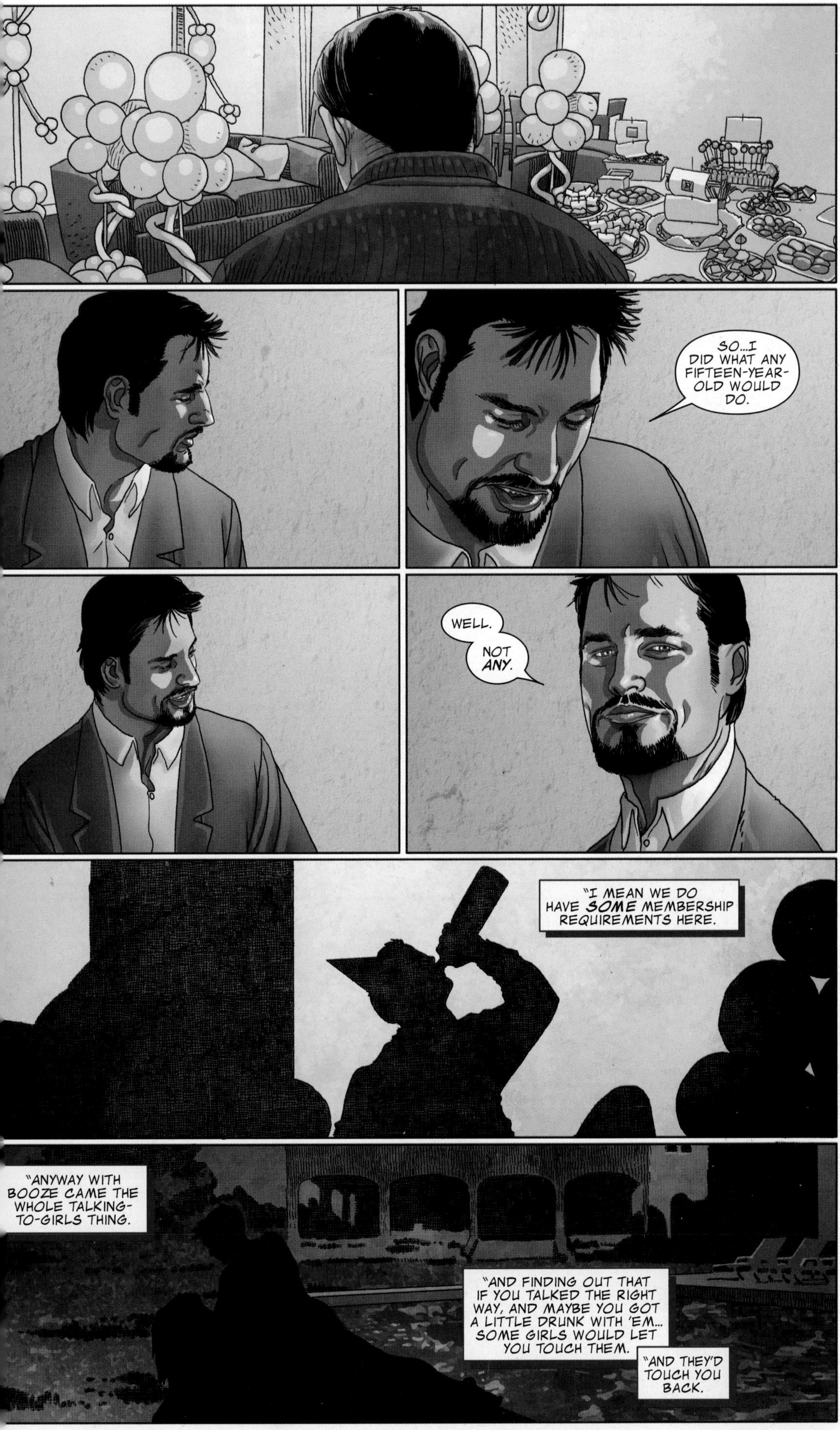

SO...I DID WHAT ANY FIFTEEN-YEAR-OLD WOULD DO.
WELL.
NOT ANY.
"I MEAN WE DO HAVE SOME MEMBERSHIP REQUIREMENTS HERE.
"ANYWAY WITH BOOZE CAME THE WHOLE TALKING-TO-GIRLS THING.
"AND FINDING OUT THAT IF YOU TALKED THE RIGHT WAY, AND MAYBE YOU GOT A LITTLE DRUNK WITH 'EM... SOME GIRLS WOULD LET YOU TOUCH THEM.
"AND THEY'D TOUCH YOU BACK.

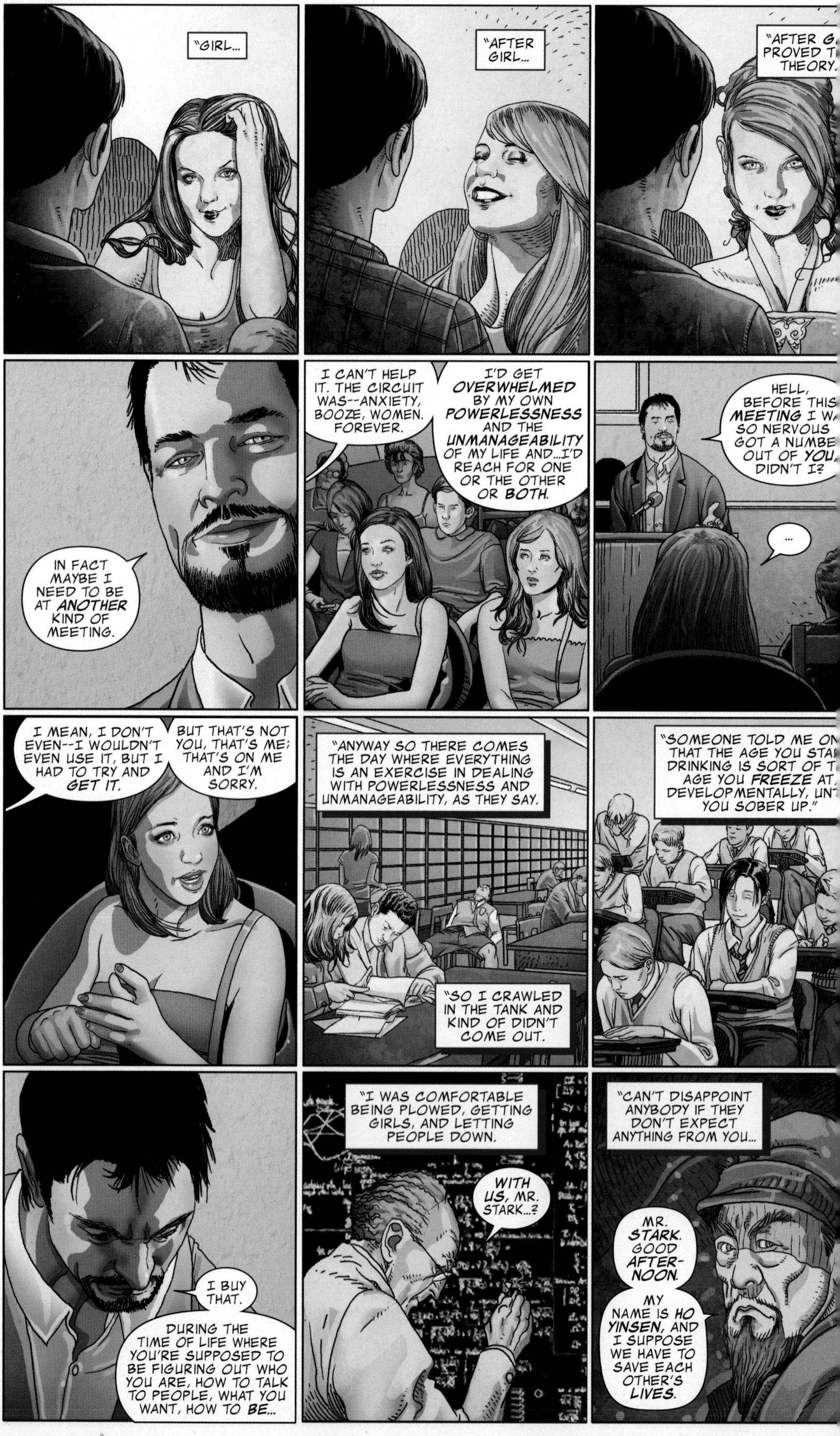
"GIRL...
"AFTER GIRL...
"AFTER G
PROVED T
THEORY.
I CAN'T HELP IT. THE CIRCUIT WAS--ANXIETY, BOOZE, WOMEN. FOREVER.
I'D GET OVERWHELMED BY MY OWN POWERLESSNESS AND THE UNMANAGEABILITY OF MY LIFE AND...I'D REACH FOR ONE OR THE OTHER OR BOTH.
HELL, BEFORE THIS MEETING I W
SO NERVOUS
GOT A NUMBE
OUT OF YOU,
DIDN'T I?
...
IN FACT MAYBE I NEED TO BE AT ANOTHER KIND OF MEETING.
I MEAN, I DON'T EVEN--I WOULDN'T EVEN USE IT, BUT I HAD TO TRY AND GET IT.
BUT THAT'S NOT YOU, THAT'S ME; THAT'S ON ME AND I'M SORRY.
"ANYWAY SO THERE COMES THE DAY WHERE EVERYTHING IS AN EXERCISE IN DEALING WITH POWERLESSNESS AND UNMANAGEABILITY, AS THEY SAY.
"SO I CRAWLED IN THE TANK AND KIND OF DIDN'T COME OUT.
"SOMEONE TOLD ME ON
THAT THE AGE YOU STAR
DRINKING IS SORT OF T
AGE YOU FREEZE AT,
DEVELOPMENTALLY, UNT
YOU SOBER UP."
I BUY THAT.
DURING THE TIME OF LIFE WHERE YOU'RE SUPPOSED TO BE FIGURING OUT WHO YOU ARE, HOW TO TALK TO PEOPLE, WHAT YOU WANT, HOW TO BE...
"I WAS COMFORTABLE BEING PLOWED, GETTING GIRLS, AND LETTING PEOPLE DOWN.
WITH US, MR. STARK...?
"CAN'T DISAPPOINT ANYBODY IF THEY DON'T EXPECT ANYTHING FROM YOU...
MR. STARK. GOOD AFTER-NOON.
MY NAME IS HO YINSEN, AND I SUPPOSE WE HAVE TO SAVE EACH OTHER'S LIVES.

I...AH...SO A LITTLE WHILE AFTER SCHOOL, I GO INTO THE FAMILY BUSINESS AND FIND MYSELF KIND OF *AMBUSHED.*

"I THOUGHT I KNEW THE JOB BETTER THAN THEY DID, AND THEY WERE GONNA MAKE ME PAY FOR IT. YOU KNOW HOW IT GOES.

I GOT...PARTNERED UP WITH THIS OLD GUY ON THIS ONE PARTICULAR PROJECT.

"SORT OF A MATTER OF LIFE AND DEATH FOR US BOTH.

"WE HAD THESE... *REALLY...OVER-ZEALOUS...* MICROMANAGERS WATCHING OVER US CONSTANTLY.

"THEY WANTED US TO DO THINGS ONE WAY, BUT WE WANTED TO DO THINGS *OUR* WAY, THERE WAS ALL THIS SECRECY AND HIDING...

AND I HADN'T BEEN SOBER AT THIS LONG A STRETCH SINCE HIGH SCHOOL.

"IT WAS...

"IT WAS THE FIRST REAL TEST OF MY PROFESSIONAL LIFE. IT *SUCKED.*

"BUT WE DUG IN TOGETHER, THE OLD GUY AND ME, AND FIGURED OUT HOW TO MAKE IT WORK IN SPITE OF EVERYTHING...

AND WE ENDED UP ON TOP OF THE OTHER GUYS AND RAN THE SHOW.

"FOR THE FIRST TIME IN MY LIFE, I FOUND SOMETHING I LOVED DOING. I FOUND A...A *CALLING,* I GUESS.

"YOU'D THINK I'D HAVE MADE THE LINK BETWEEN *NOT DRINKING* AND *FINDING A PURPOSE IN LIFE,* BUT THAT WOULDN'T OCCUR TO ME FOR A WHILE.

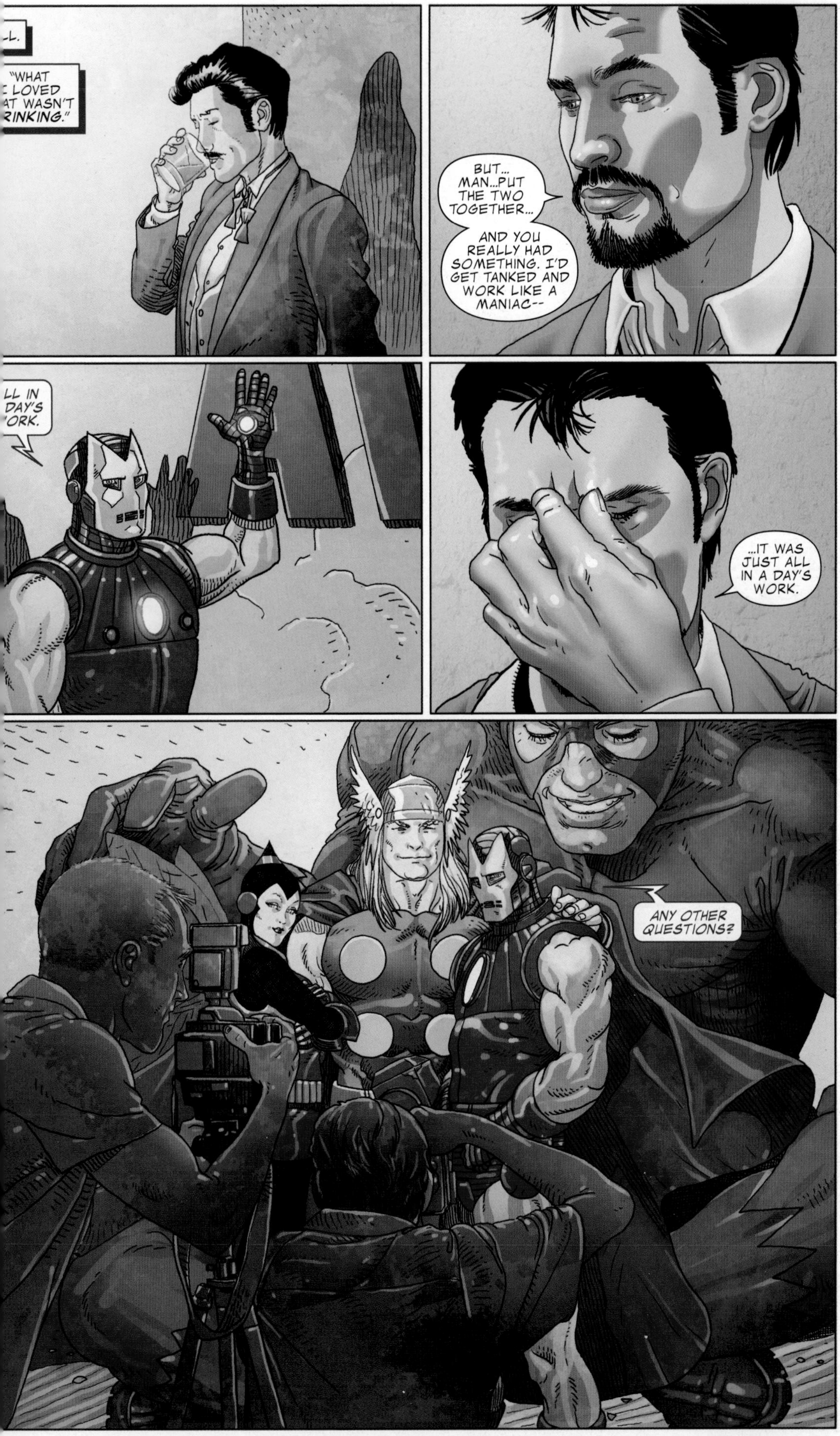
-L.
"WHAT
C LOVED
AT WASN'T
RINKING."
BUT... MAN...PUT THE TWO TOGETHER...
AND YOU REALLY HAD SOMETHING. I'D GET TANKED AND WORK LIKE A MANIAC--
LL IN DAY'S WORK.
...IT WAS JUST ALL IN A DAY'S WORK.
ANY OTHER QUESTIONS?

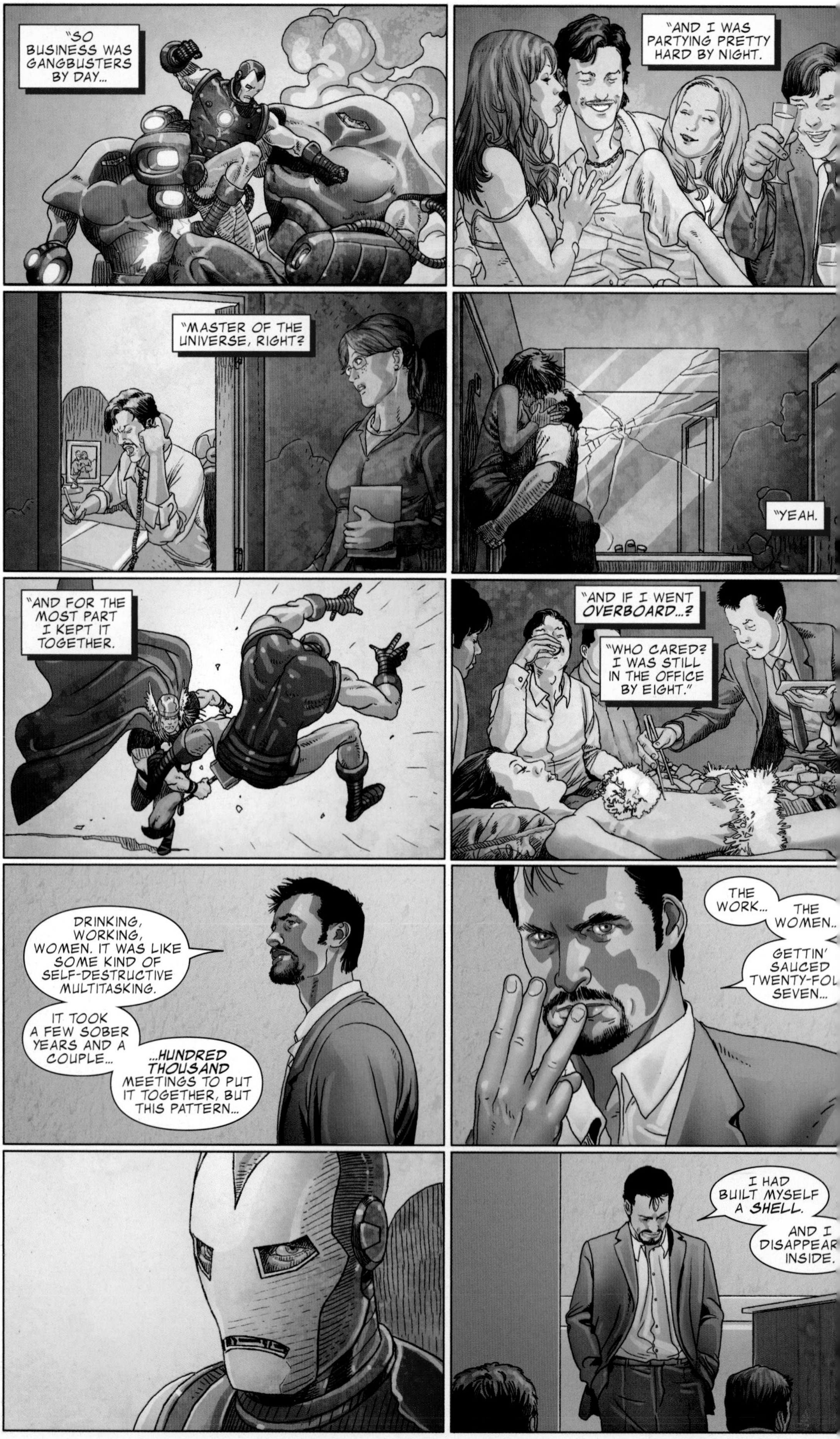
"SO BUSINESS WAS GANGBUSTERS BY DAY...
"AND I WAS PARTYING PRETTY HARD BY NIGHT.
"MASTER OF THE UNIVERSE, RIGHT?
"YEAH.
"AND FOR THE MOST PART I KEPT IT TOGETHER.
"AND IF I WENT OVERBOARD...?
"WHO CARED? I WAS STILL IN THE OFFICE BY EIGHT."
DRINKING, WORKING, WOMEN. IT WAS LIKE SOME KIND OF SELF-DESTRUCTIVE MULTITASKING.
IT TOOK A FEW SOBER YEARS AND A COUPLE...
...HUNDRED THOUSAND MEETINGS TO PUT IT TOGETHER, BUT THIS PATTERN...
THE WORK...
THE WOMEN...
GETTIN' SAUCED TWENTY-FO
SEVEN...
I HAD BUILT MYSELF A SHELL.
AND I DISAPPEAR
INSIDE.

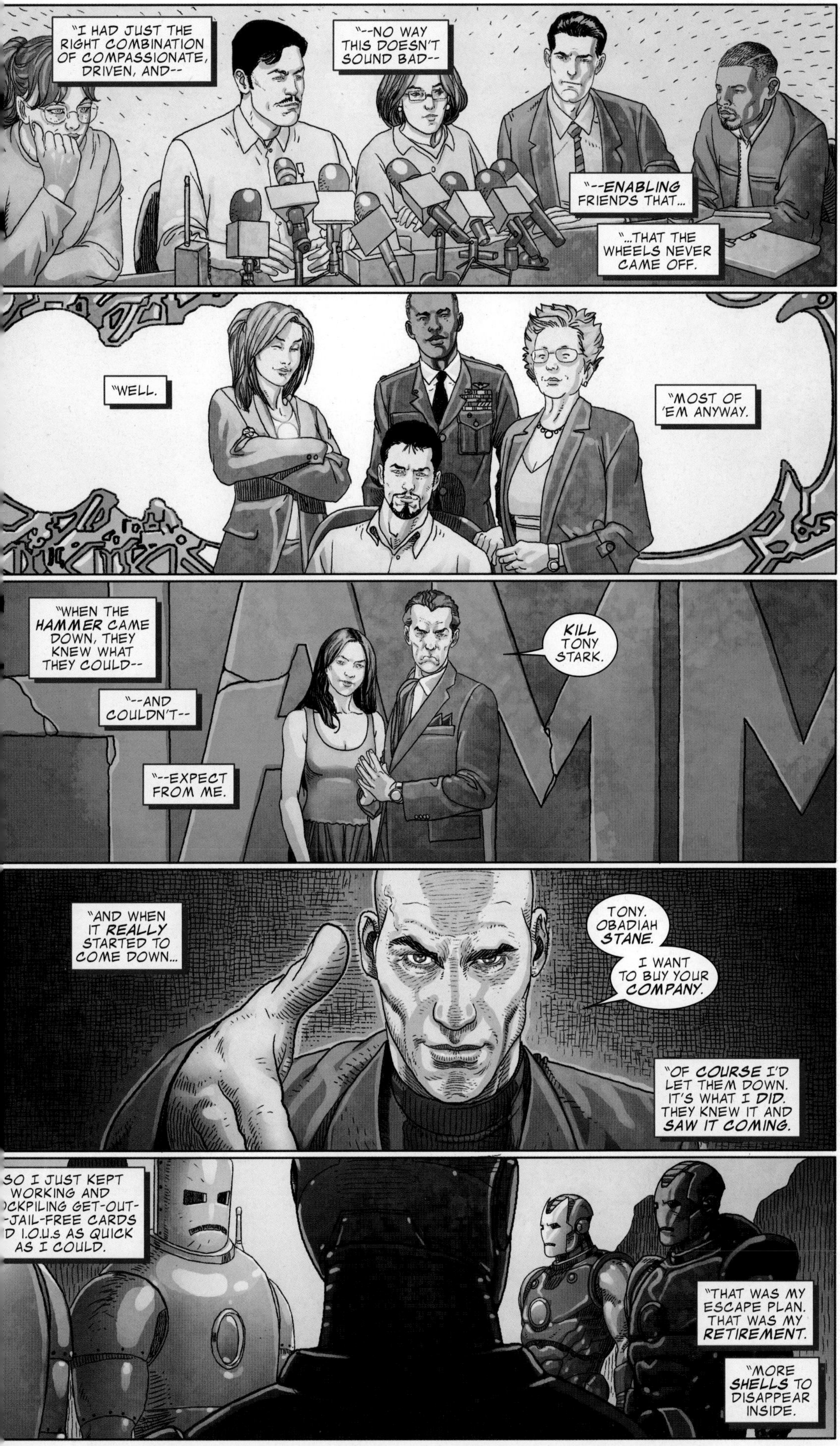
"I HAD JUST THE RIGHT COMBINATION OF COMPASSIONATE, DRIVEN, AND--
"--NO WAY THIS DOESN'T SOUND BAD--
"--ENABLING FRIENDS THAT...
"...THAT THE WHEELS NEVER CAME OFF.
"WELL.
"MOST OF 'EM ANYWAY.
"WHEN THE HAMMER CAME DOWN, THEY KNEW WHAT THEY COULD--
"--AND COULDN'T--
"--EXPECT FROM ME.
KILL TONY STARK.
"AND WHEN IT REALLY STARTED TO COME DOWN...
TONY. OBADIAH STANE.
I WANT TO BUY YOUR COMPANY.
"OF COURSE I'D LET THEM DOWN. IT'S WHAT I DID. THEY KNEW IT AND SAW IT COMING.
SO I JUST KEPT WORKING AND OCKPILING GET-OUT- -JAIL-FREE CARDS D I.O.U.s AS QUICK AS I COULD.
"THAT WAS MY ESCAPE PLAN. THAT WAS MY RETIREMENT.
"MORE SHELLS TO DISAPPEAR INSIDE.

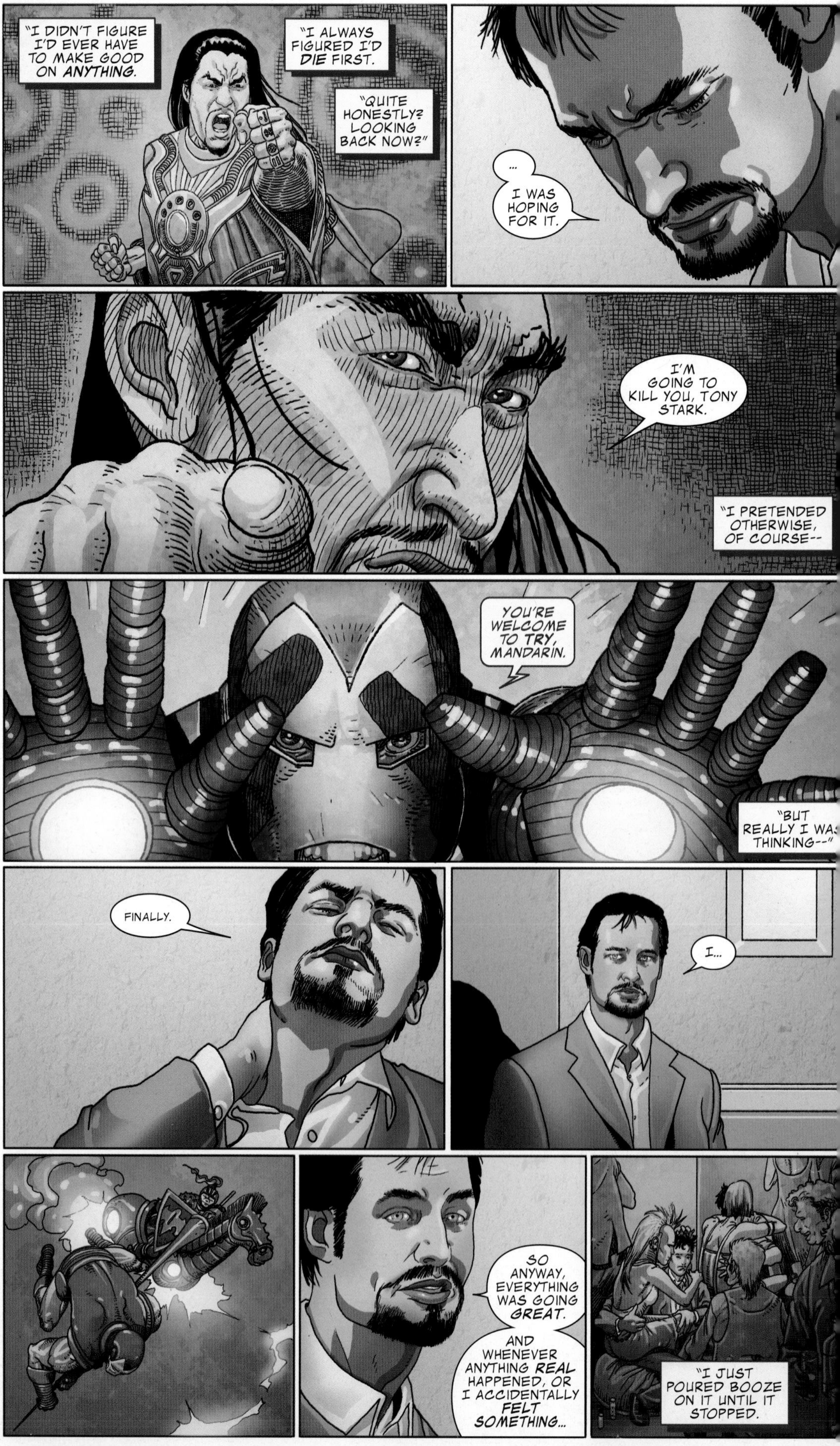
"I DIDN'T FIGURE I'D EVER HAVE TO MAKE GOOD ON ANYTHING.
"I ALWAYS FIGURED I'D DIE FIRST.
"QUITE HONESTLY? LOOKING BACK NOW?"
... I WAS HOPING FOR IT.
I'M GOING TO KILL YOU, TONY STARK.
"I PRETENDED OTHERWISE, OF COURSE--
YOU'RE WELCOME TO TRY, MANDARIN.
"BUT REALLY I WAS THINKING--"
FINALLY.
I...
SO ANYWAY, EVERYTHING WAS GOING GREAT.
AND WHENEVER ANYTHING REAL HAPPENED, OR I ACCIDENTALLY FELT SOMETHING...
"I JUST POURED BOOZE ON IT UNTIL IT STOPPED.

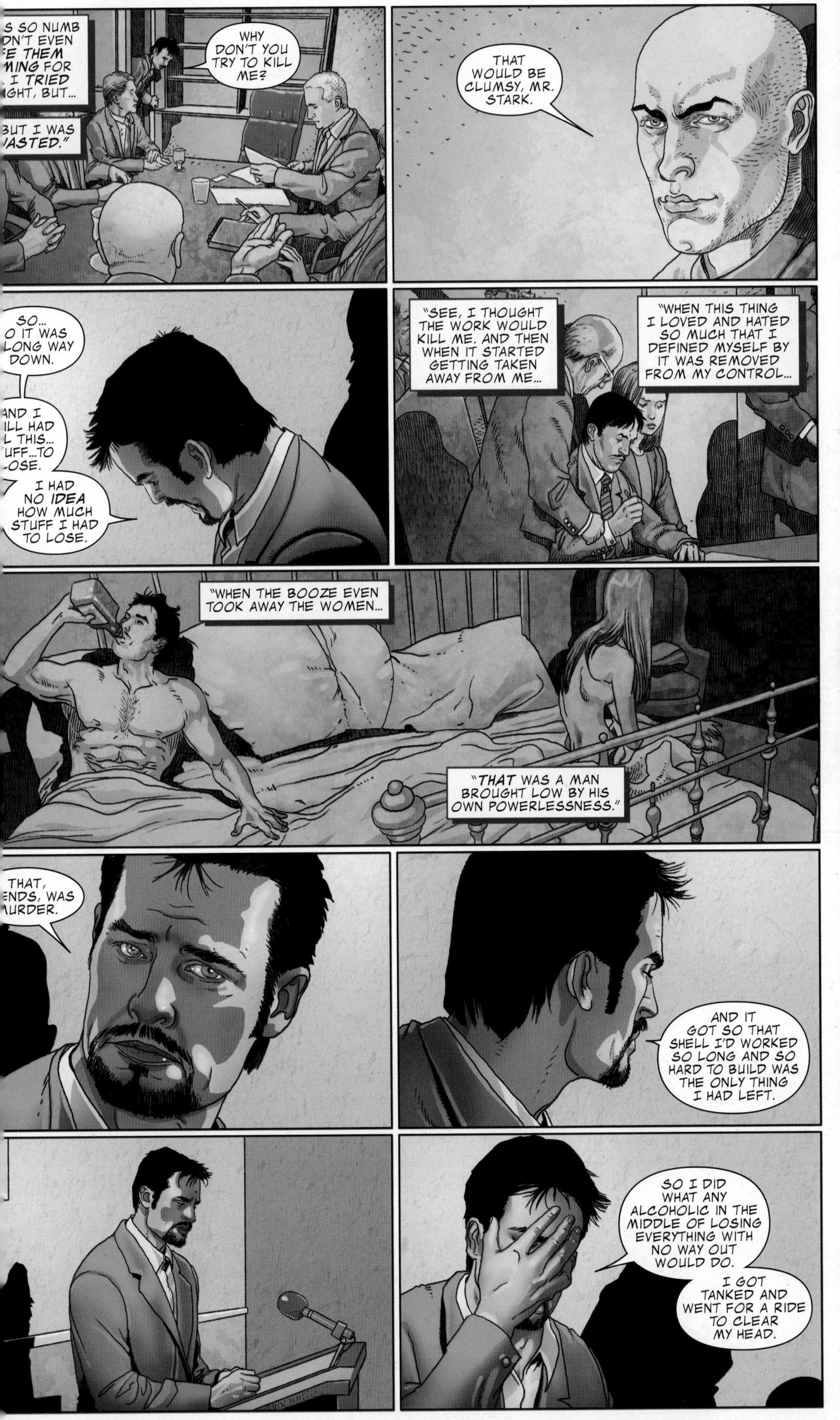

S SO NUMB DN'T EVEN FE THEM MING FOR I TRIED GHT, BUT...
BUT I WAS WASTED."
WHY DON'T YOU TRY TO KILL ME?
THAT WOULD BE CLUMSY, MR. STARK.
SO... O IT WAS LONG WAY DOWN.
AND I ILL HAD L THIS... UFF...TO OSE.
I HAD NO IDEA HOW MUCH STUFF I HAD TO LOSE.
"SEE, I THOUGHT THE WORK WOULD KILL ME. AND THEN WHEN IT STARTED GETTING TAKEN AWAY FROM ME...
"WHEN THIS THING I LOVED AND HATED SO MUCH THAT I DEFINED MYSELF BY IT WAS REMOVED FROM MY CONTROL...
"WHEN THE BOOZE EVEN TOOK AWAY THE WOMEN...
"THAT WAS A MAN BROUGHT LOW BY HIS OWN POWERLESSNESS."
THAT, ENDS, WAS URDER.
AND IT GOT SO THAT SHELL I'D WORKED SO LONG AND SO HARD TO BUILD WAS THE ONLY THING I HAD LEFT.
SO I DID WHAT ANY ALCOHOLIC IN THE MIDDLE OF LOSING EVERYTHING WITH NO WAY OUT WOULD DO.
I GOT TANKED AND WENT FOR A RIDE TO CLEAR MY HEAD.

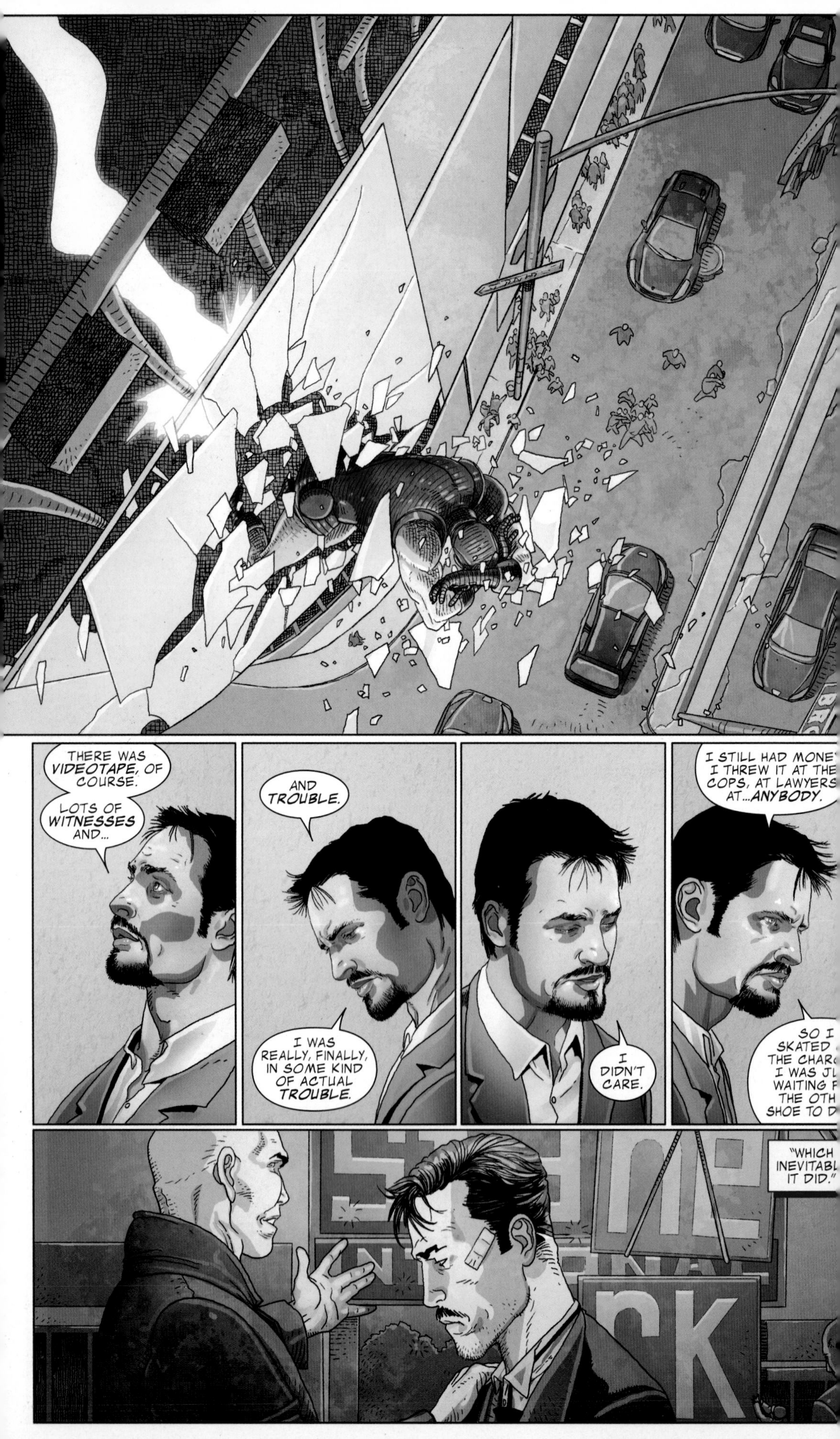
THERE WAS VIDEOTAPE, OF COURSE.
LOTS OF WITNESSES AND...
AND TROUBLE.
I WAS REALLY, FINALLY, IN SOME KIND OF ACTUAL TROUBLE.
I DIDN'T CARE.
I STILL HAD MONE I THREW IT AT THE COPS, AT LAWYERS AT...ANYBODY.
SO I SKATED THE CHARG I WAS JU WAITING F THE OTH SHOE TO D
"WHICH INEVITABL IT DID."

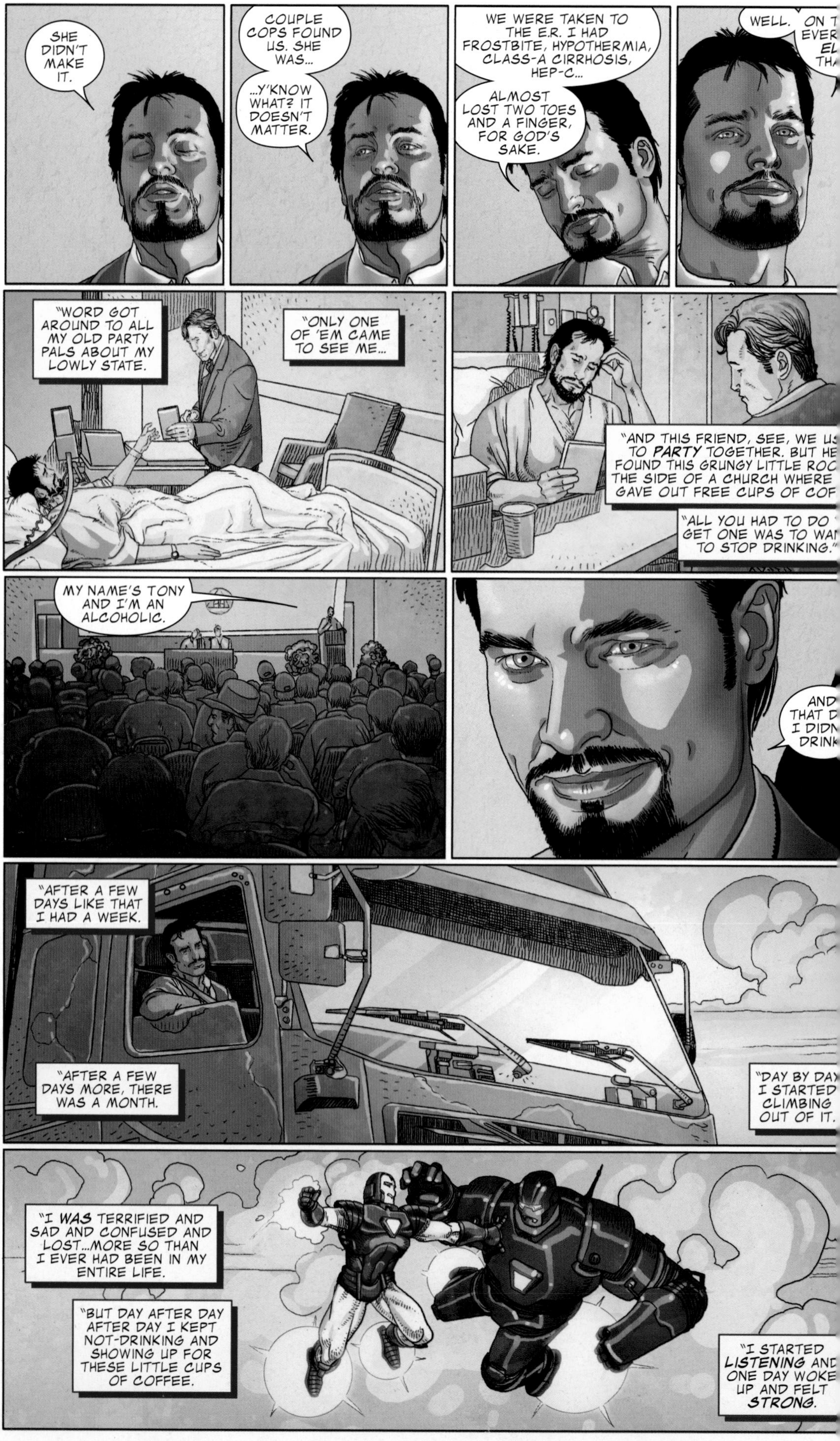

SHE DIDN'T MAKE IT.
COUPLE COPS FOUND US. SHE WAS...
...Y'KNOW WHAT? IT DOESN'T MATTER.
WE WERE TAKEN TO THE E.R. I HAD FROSTBITE, HYPOTHERMIA, CLASS-A CIRRHOSIS, HEP-C...
ALMOST LOST TWO TOES AND A FINGER, FOR GOD'S SAKE.
WELL.
ON T EVER EL THA
"WORD GOT AROUND TO ALL MY OLD PARTY PALS ABOUT MY LOWLY STATE.
"ONLY ONE OF 'EM CAME TO SEE ME...
"AND THIS FRIEND, SEE, WE US TO PARTY TOGETHER. BUT HE FOUND THIS GRUNGY LITTLE ROC THE SIDE OF A CHURCH WHERE GAVE OUT FREE CUPS OF COF
"ALL YOU HAD TO DO GET ONE WAS TO WA TO STOP DRINKING."
MY NAME'S TONY AND I'M AN ALCOHOLIC.
AND THAT D I DIDN DRINK
"AFTER A FEW DAYS LIKE THAT I HAD A WEEK.
"AFTER A FEW DAYS MORE, THERE WAS A MONTH.
"DAY BY DAY I STARTED CLIMBING OUT OF IT.
"I WAS TERRIFIED AND SAD AND CONFUSED AND LOST...MORE SO THAN I EVER HAD BEEN IN MY ENTIRE LIFE.
"BUT DAY AFTER DAY AFTER DAY I KEPT NOT-DRINKING AND SHOWING UP FOR THESE LITTLE CUPS OF COFFEE.
"I STARTED LISTENING AND ONE DAY WOKE UP AND FELT STRONG.

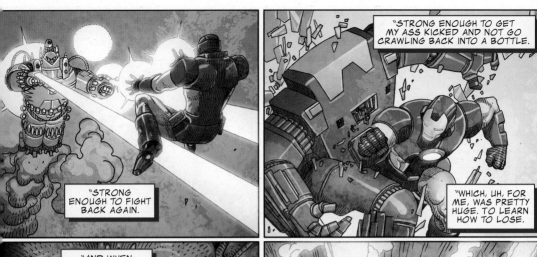

"STRONG ENOUGH TO FIGHT BACK AGAIN.

"STRONG ENOUGH TO GET MY ASS KICKED AND NOT GO CRAWLING BACK INTO A BOTTLE.

"WHICH, UH, FOR ME, WAS PRETTY HUGE. TO LEARN HOW TO LOSE.

"AND WHEN LIFE HAS GOTTEN WEIRD--

"--BELIEVE ME YOU HAVE NO IDEA *HOW* WEIRD--

"--I HANDLED IT. SOBER.

"I LEARNED HOW TO *SHARE*. HOW TO *PLAY WELL* WITH OTHERS.

"I EVEN MANAGED TO HAVE A [REL]-ATIONSHIP OR TWO THAT WASN'T COMPLETELY [AN]D TOTALLY TOXICALLY UNHEALTHY OR SO-CASUAL-AS-TO-BE-ANONYMOUS.

"ALMOST.

"[G]RADUALLY I [CA]ME TO REALIZE... [I] KEPT COMING [FO]R THE FREE [C]OFFEE AND [L]ISTENING...

"I COULD HANDLE NO MATTER *WHAT* WEIRD CURVE BALL CAME MY WAY.

"I COULD REBUILD, REINVENT, REDO.

STARK SOLUTIONS

"RE-EVERYTHING. EVERYTHING I LOST I COULD FIND AGAIN.

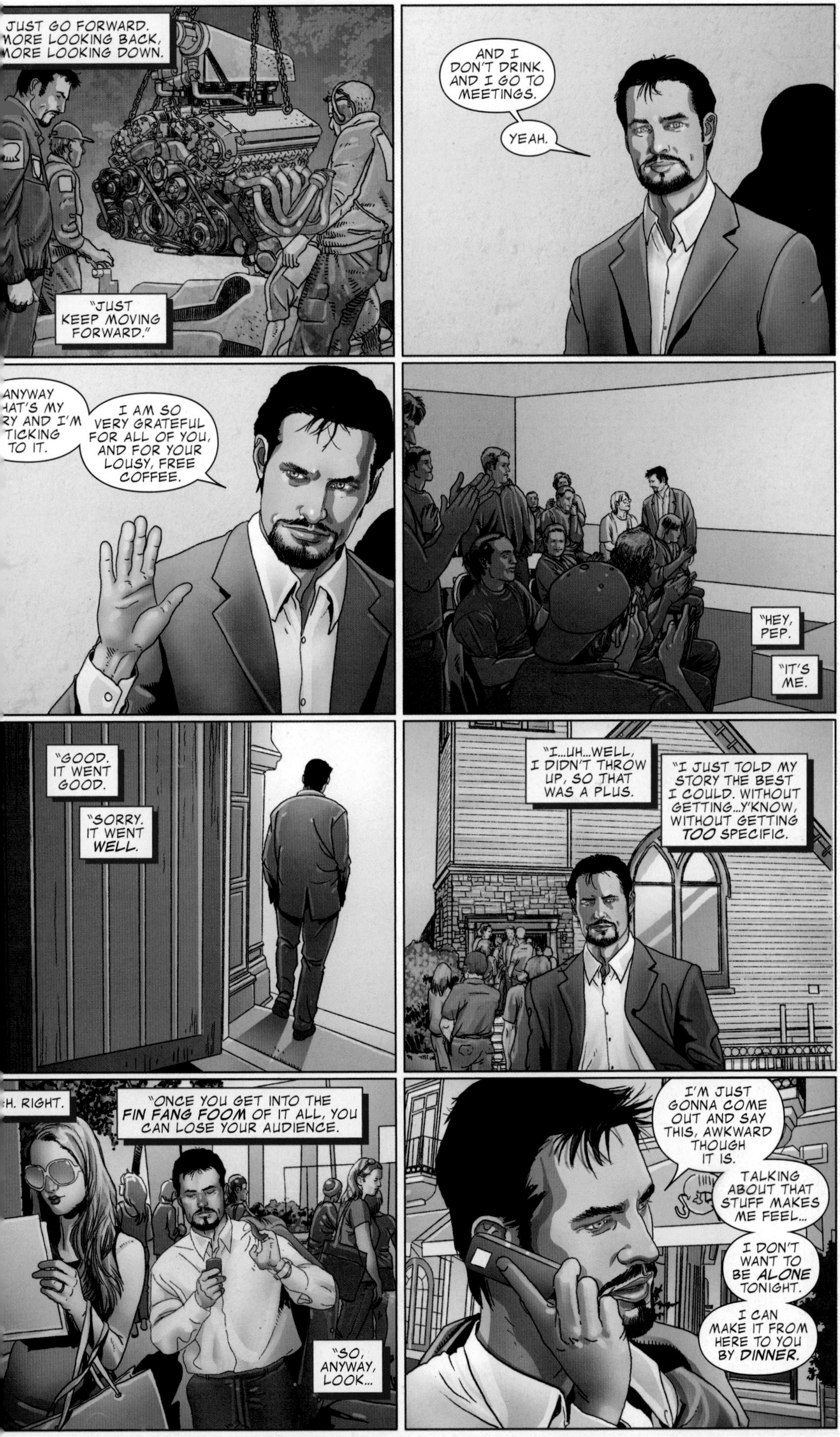
JUST GO FORWARD.
MORE LOOKING BACK,
MORE LOOKING DOWN.
"JUST KEEP MOVING FORWARD."
AND I DON'T DRINK. AND I GO TO MEETINGS.
YEAH.
ANYWAY HAT'S MY RY AND I'M TICKING TO IT.
I AM SO VERY GRATEFUL FOR ALL OF YOU, AND FOR YOUR LOUSY, FREE COFFEE.
"HEY, PEP.
"IT'S ME.
"GOOD. IT WENT GOOD.
"SORRY. IT WENT WELL.
"I...UH...WELL, I DIDN'T THROW UP, SO THAT WAS A PLUS.
"I JUST TOLD MY STORY THE BEST I COULD. WITHOUT GETTING...Y'KNOW, WITHOUT GETTING TOO SPECIFIC.
H. RIGHT.
"ONCE YOU GET INTO THE FIN FANG FOOM OF IT ALL, YOU CAN LOSE YOUR AUDIENCE.
"SO, ANYWAY, LOOK...
I'M JUST GONNA COME OUT AND SAY THIS, AWKWARD THOUGH IT IS.
TALKING ABOUT THAT STUFF MAKES ME FEEL...
I DON'T WANT TO BE ALONE TONIGHT.
I CAN MAKE IT FROM HERE TO YOU BY DINNER.

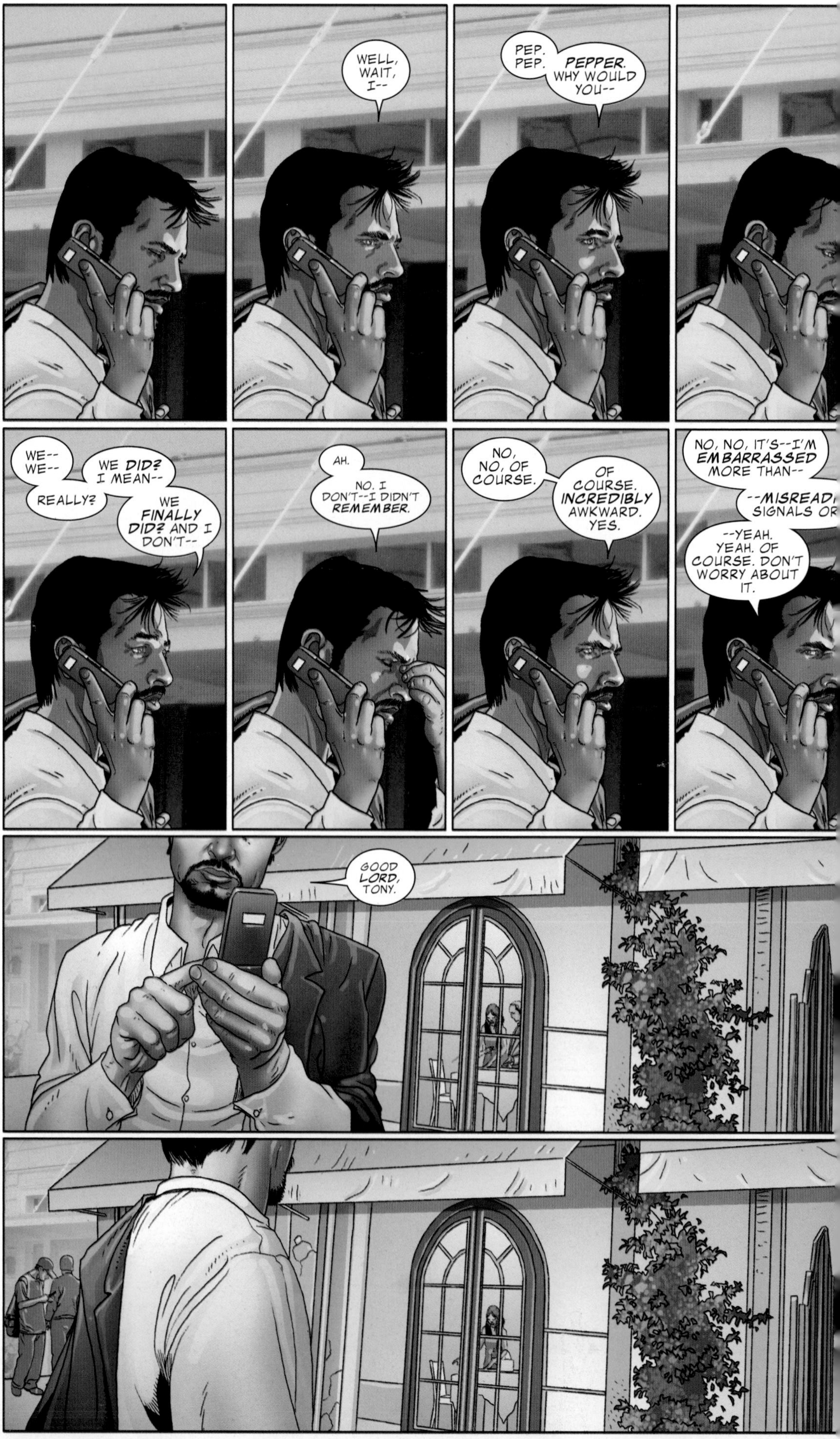
WELL, WAIT, I--
PEP. PEP.
PEPPER. WHY WOULD YOU--
WE-- WE--
WE DID? I MEAN--
REALLY?
WE FINALLY DID? AND I DON'T--
AH.
NO. I DON'T--I DIDN'T REMEMBER.
NO, NO, OF COURSE.
OF COURSE. INCREDIBLY AWKWARD. YES.
NO, NO, IT'S--I'M EMBARRASSED MORE THAN--
--YEAH. YEAH. OF COURSE. DON'T WORRY ABOUT IT.
GOOD LORD, TONY.

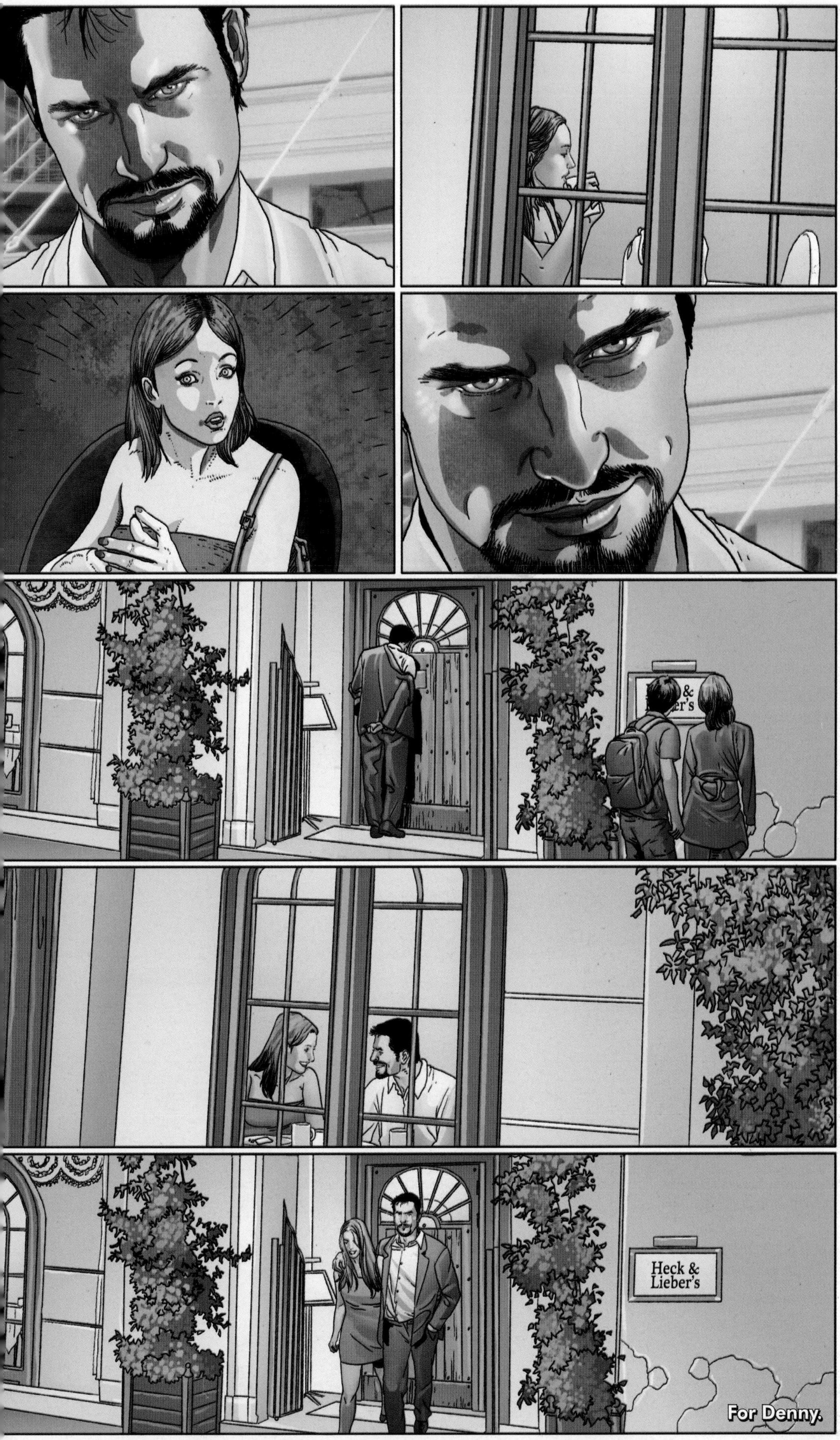
Heck &
Lieber's
For Denny.

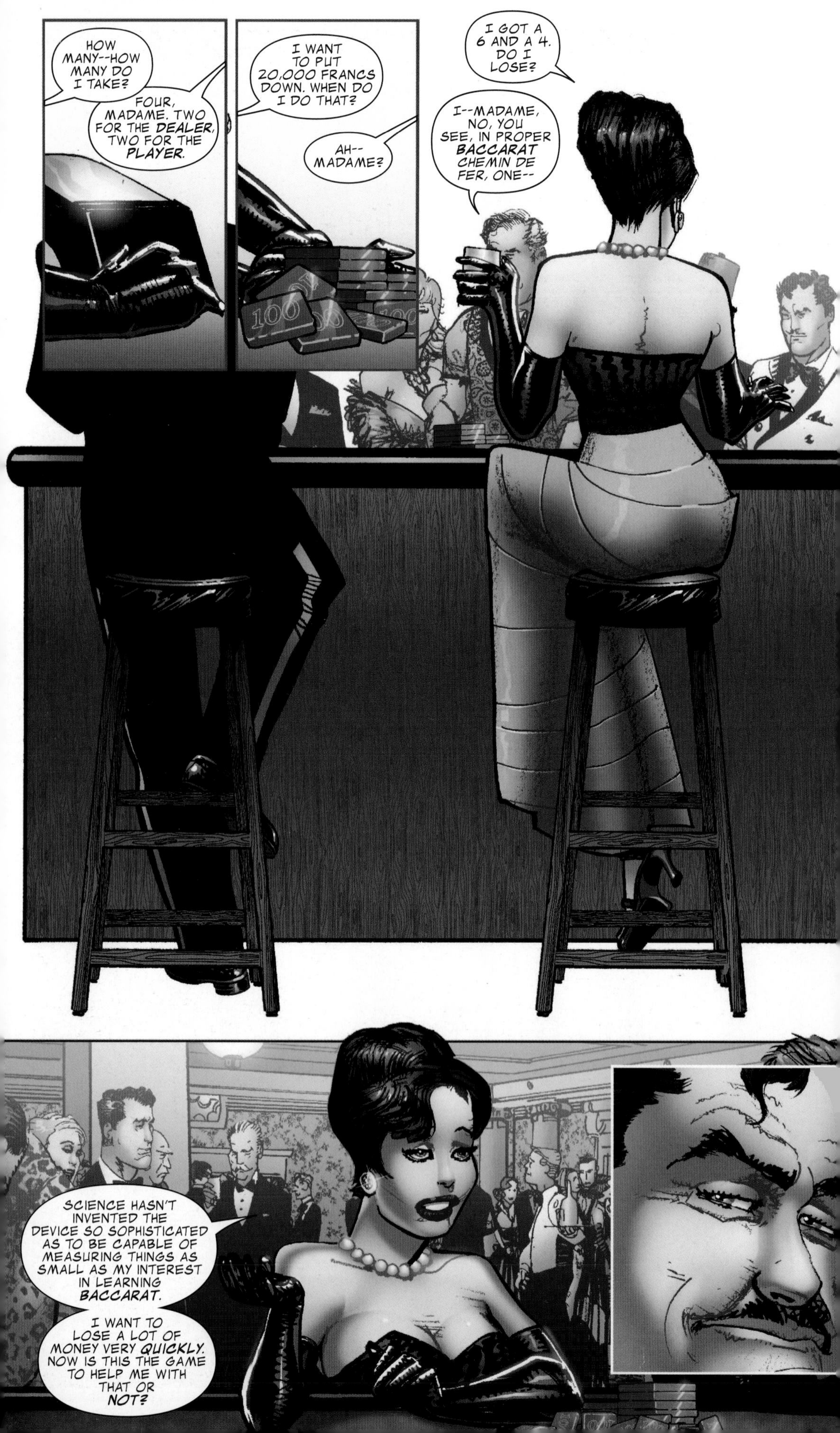
HOW MANY--HOW MANY DO I TAKE?
FOUR, MADAME. TWO FOR THE DEALER, TWO FOR THE PLAYER.
I WANT TO PUT 20,000 FRANCS DOWN. WHEN DO I DO THAT?
AH-- MADAME?
I GOT A 6 AND A 4. DO I LOSE?
I--MADAME, NO, YOU SEE, IN PROPER BACCARAT CHEMIN DE FER, ONE--
SCIENCE HASN'T INVENTED THE DEVICE SO SOPHISTICATED AS TO BE CAPABLE OF MEASURING THINGS AS SMALL AS MY INTEREST IN LEARNING BACCARAT.
I WANT TO LOSE A LOT OF MONEY VERY QUICKLY. NOW IS THIS THE GAME TO HELP ME WITH THAT OR NOT?

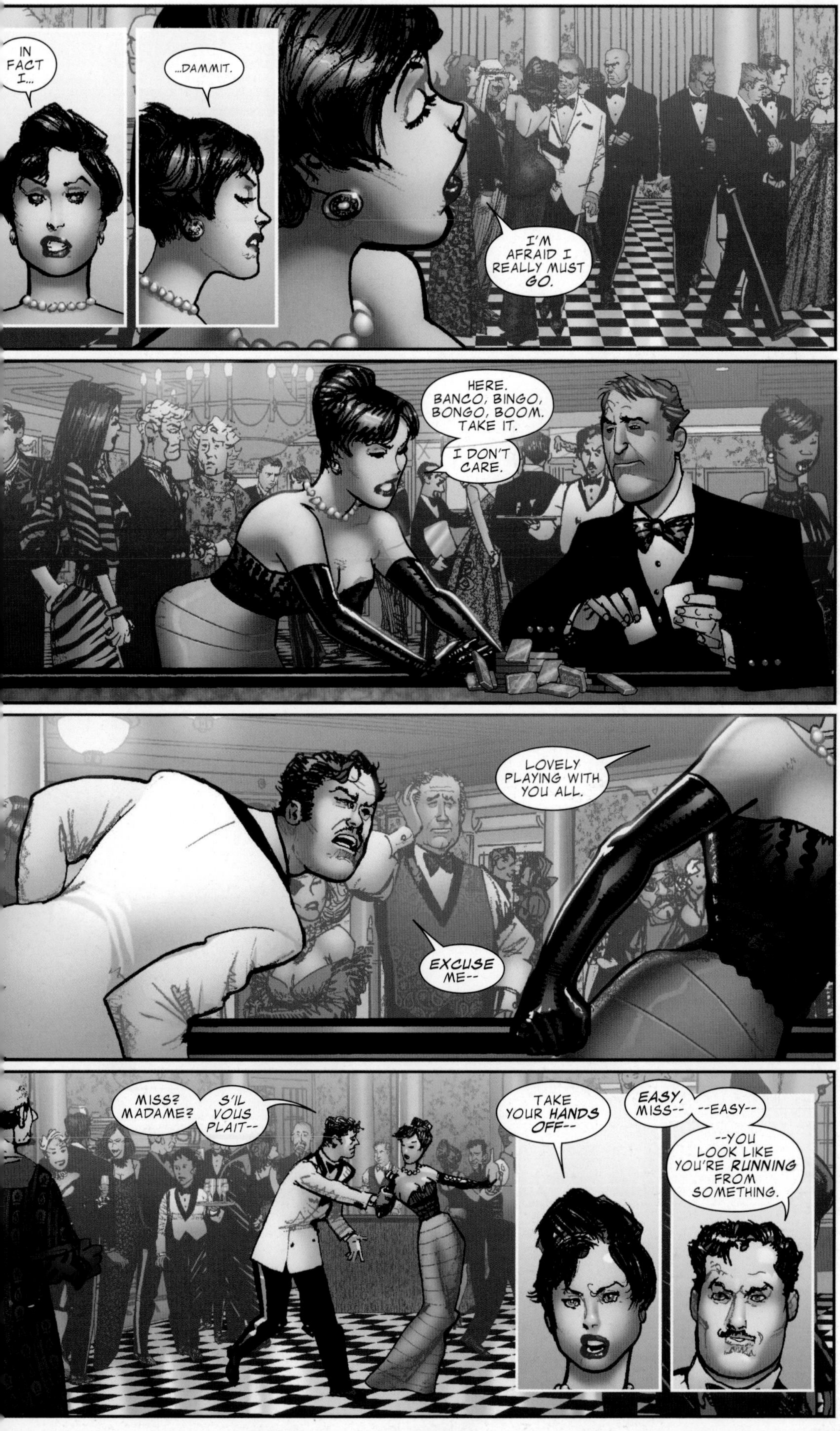

IN FACT I...
...DAMMIT.
I'M AFRAID I REALLY MUST GO.
HERE. BANCO, BINGO, BONGO, BOOM. TAKE IT.
I DON'T CARE.
LOVELY PLAYING WITH YOU ALL.
EXCUSE ME--
MISS? MADAME?
S'IL VOUS PLAIT--
TAKE YOUR HANDS OFF--
EASY, MISS--
--EASY--
--YOU LOOK LIKE YOU'RE RUNNING FROM SOMETHING.

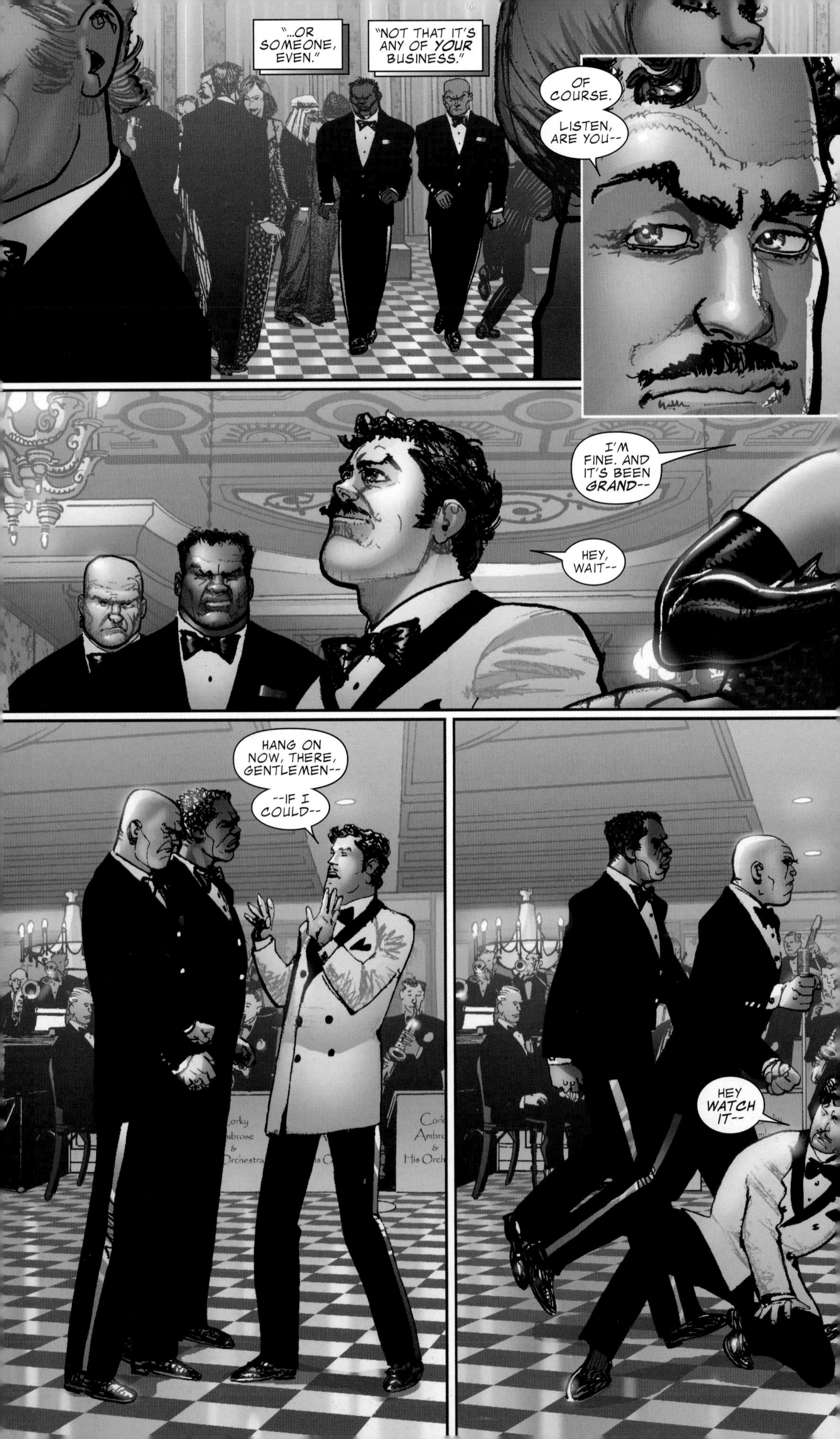
"...OR SOMEONE, EVEN."
"NOT THAT IT'S ANY OF YOUR BUSINESS."
OF COURSE.
LISTEN, ARE YOU--
I'M FINE. AND IT'S BEEN GRAND--
HEY, WAIT--
HANG ON NOW, THERE, GENTLEMEN--
--IF I COULD--
HEY WATCH IT--

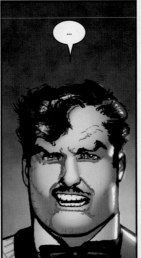

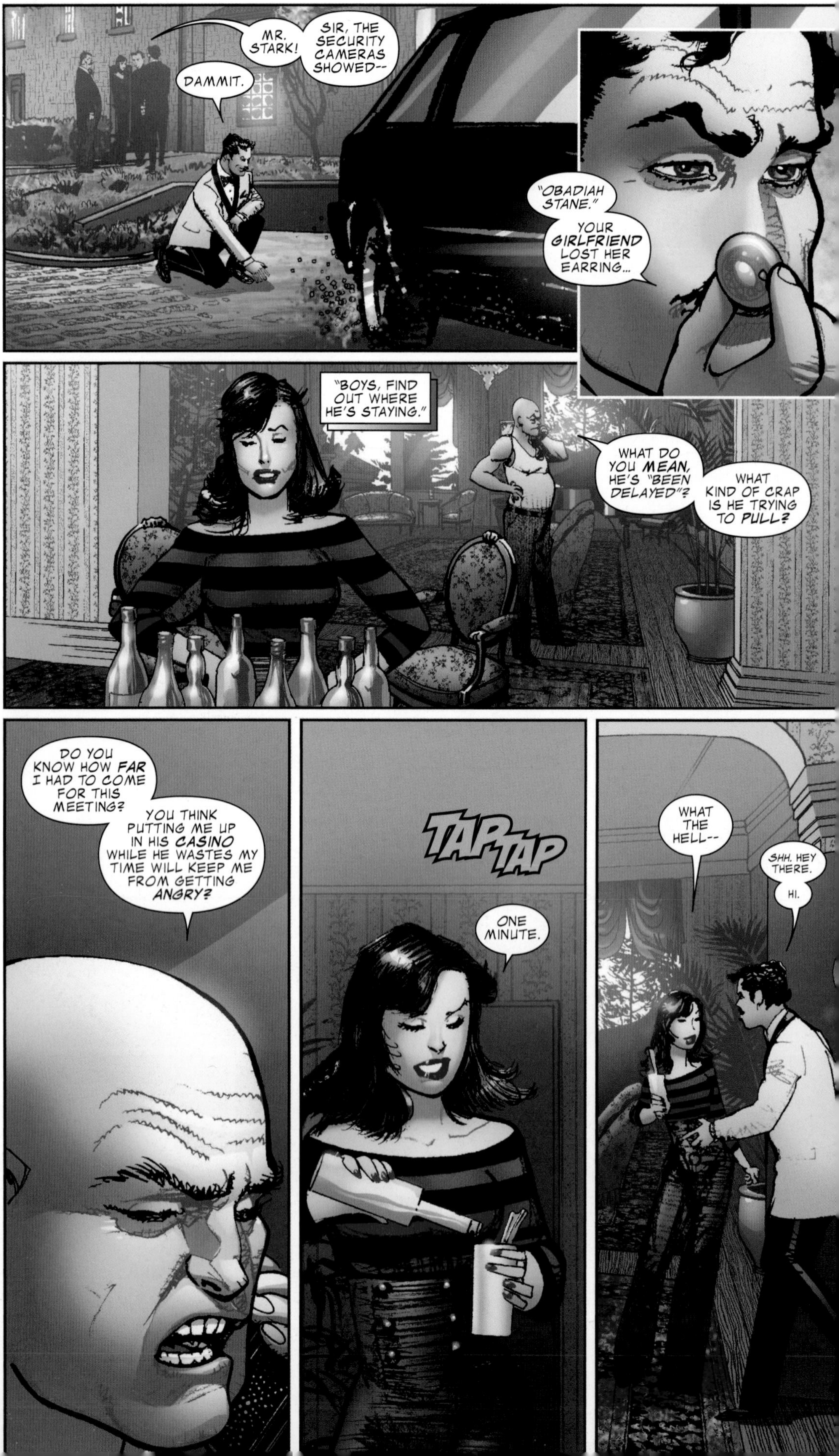
MR. STARK!
SIR, THE SECURITY CAMERAS SHOWED--
DAMMIT.
"OBADIAH STANE."
YOUR GIRLFRIEND LOST HER EARRING...
"BOYS, FIND OUT WHERE HE'S STAYING."
WHAT DO YOU MEAN, HE'S "BEEN DELAYED"?
WHAT KIND OF CRAP IS HE TRYING TO PULL?
DO YOU KNOW HOW FAR I HAD TO COME FOR THIS MEETING?
YOU THINK PUTTING ME UP IN HIS CASINO WHILE HE WASTES MY TIME WILL KEEP ME FROM GETTING ANGRY?
TAP TAP
ONE MINUTE.
WHAT THE HELL--
SHH. HEY THERE.
HI.

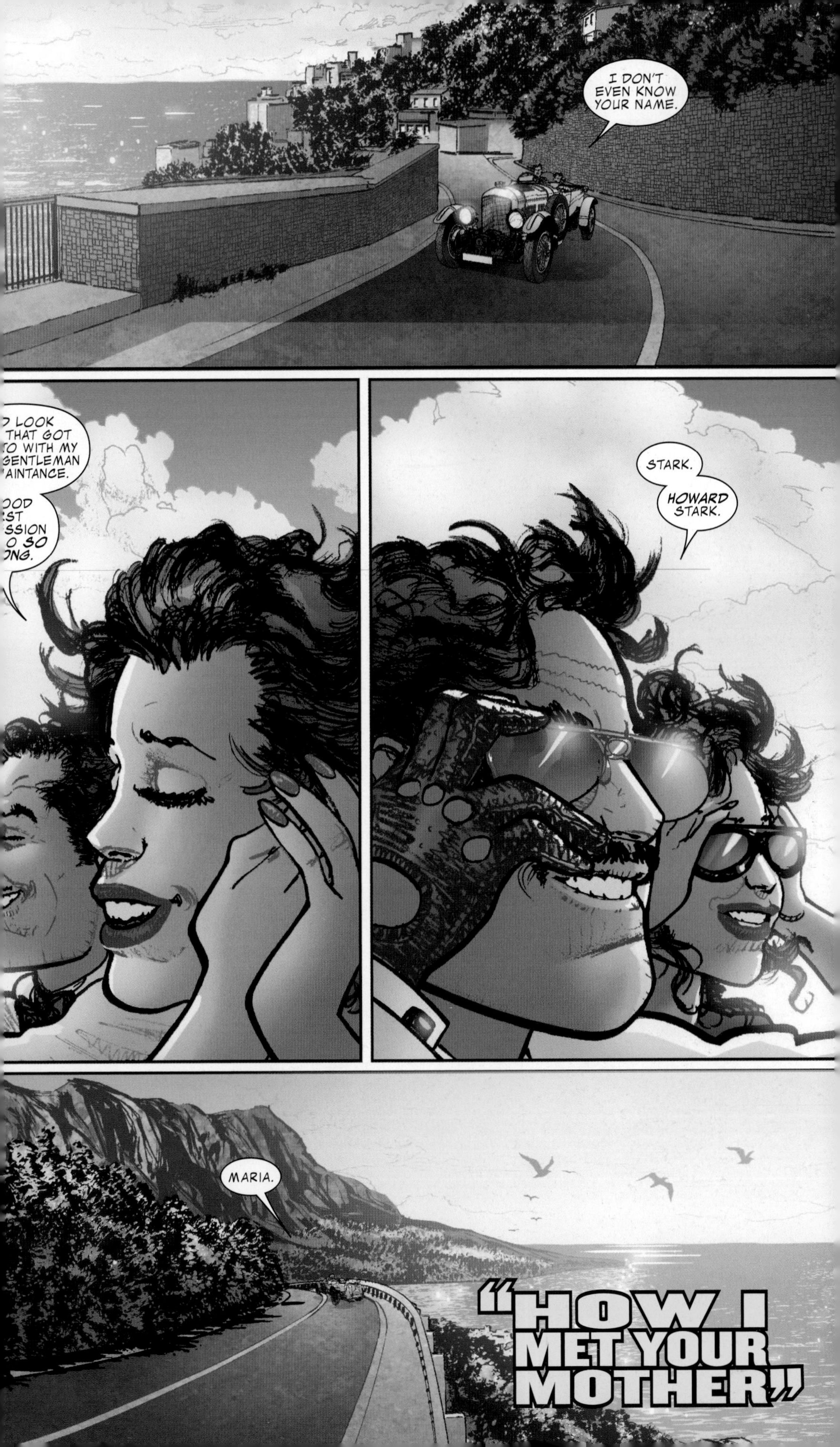

I DON'T EVEN KNOW YOUR NAME.
LOOK THAT GOT TO WITH MY GENTLEMAN AINTANCE.
OOD ST SSION O SO NG.
STARK.
HOWARD STARK.
MARIA.
"HOW I MET YOUR MOTHER"

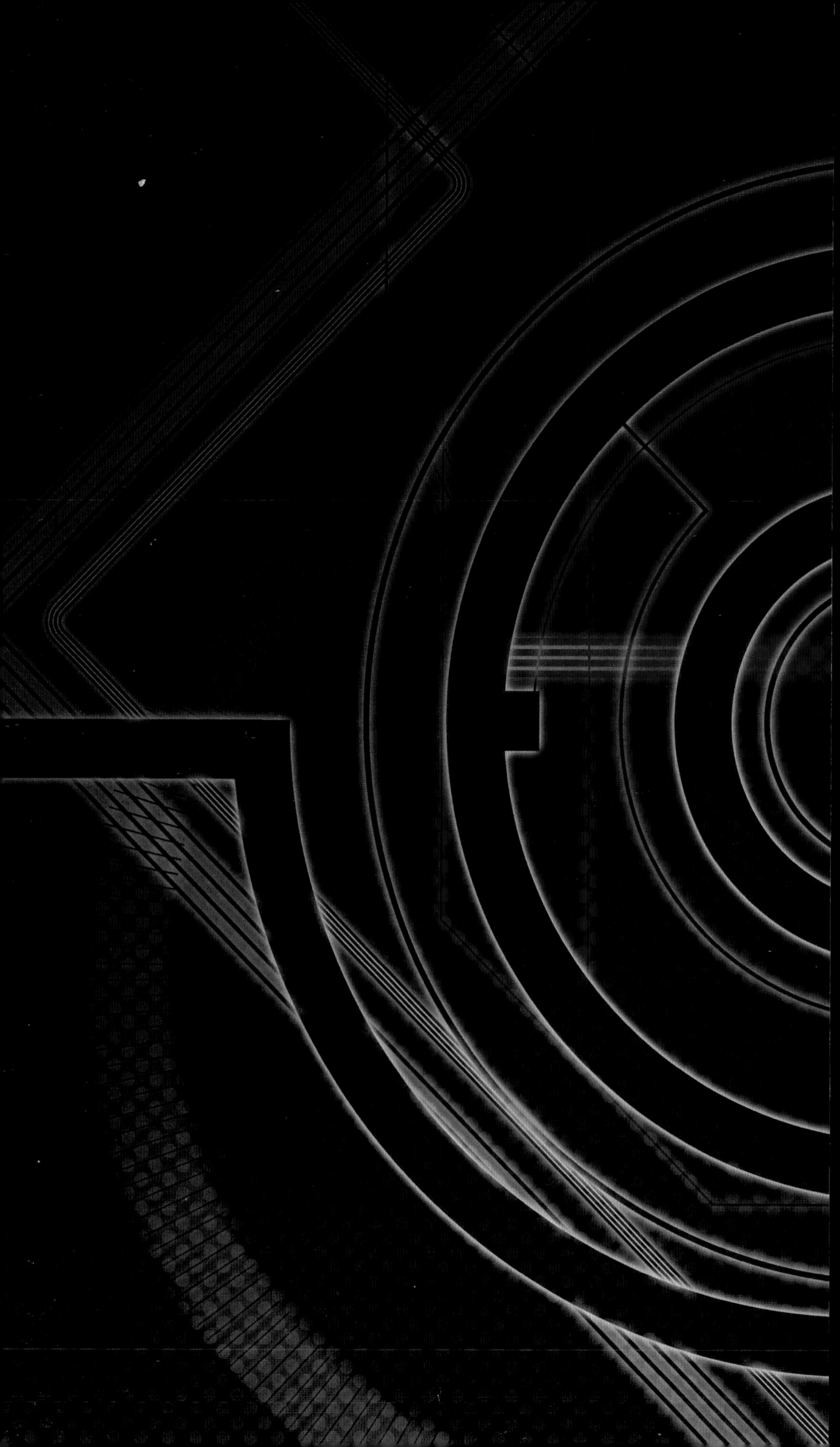

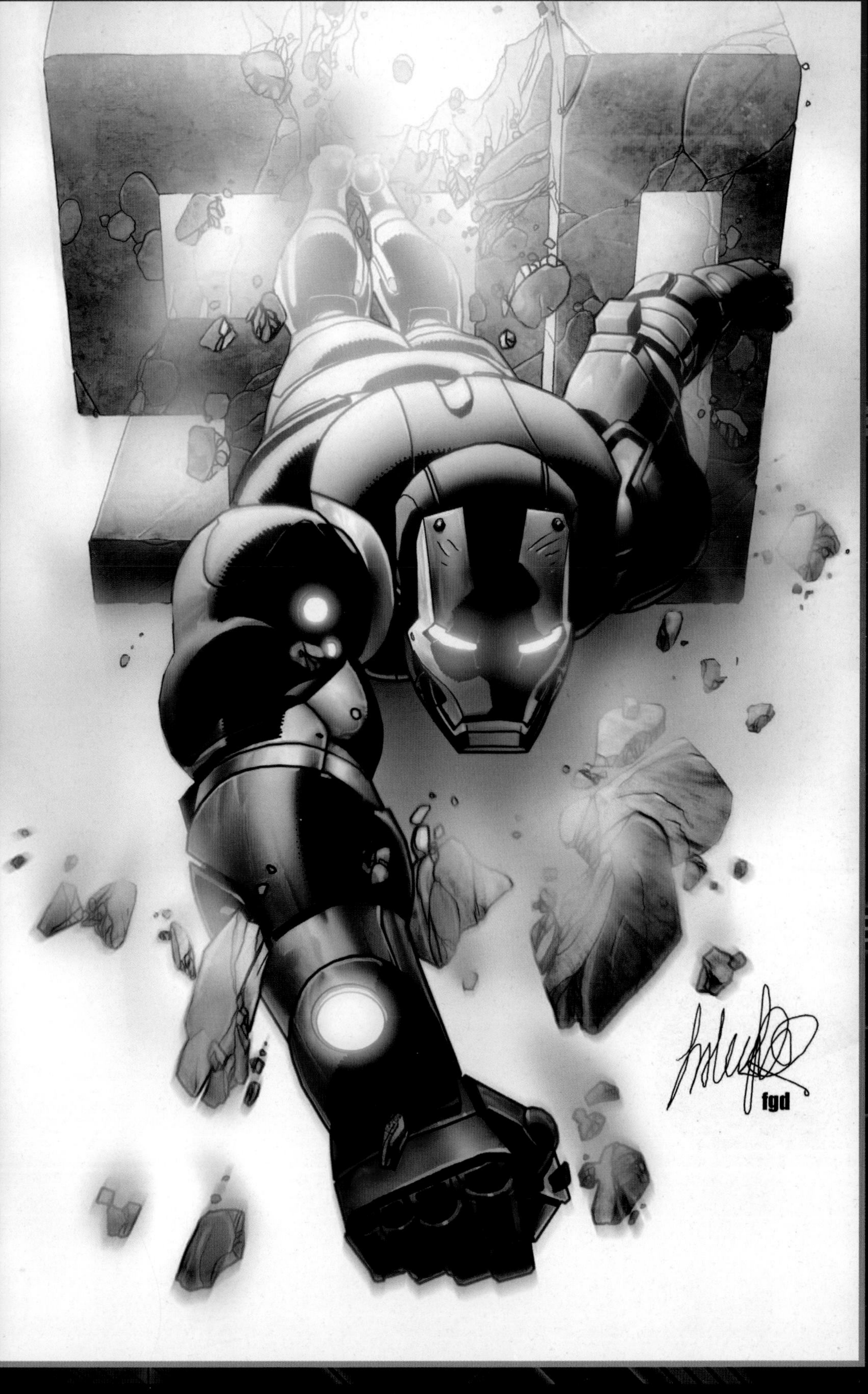
fgd

THE NEW IRON AGE 500

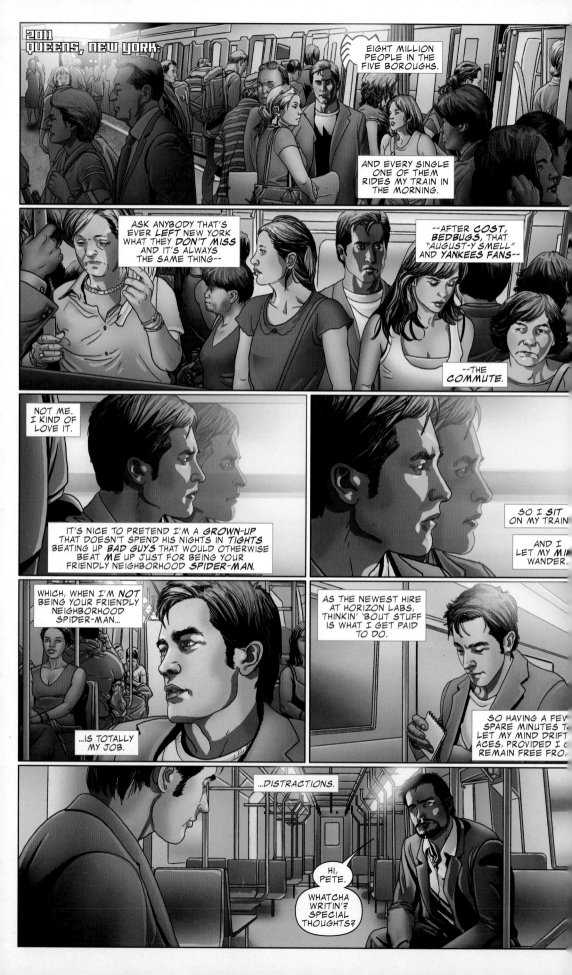

2011
QUEENS, NEW YORK:

EIGHT MILLION PEOPLE IN THE FIVE BOROUGHS.

AND EVERY SINGLE ONE OF THEM RIDES MY TRAIN IN THE MORNING.

ASK ANYBODY THAT'S EVER *LEFT* NEW YORK WHAT THEY *DON'T MISS* AND IT'S ALWAYS THE SAME THING--

--AFTER *COST*, *BEDBUGS*, THAT "*AUGUST-Y SMELL*" AND *YANKEES FANS*--

--THE *COMMUTE*.

NOT ME. I KIND OF *LOVE* IT.

IT'S NICE TO PRETEND I'M A *GROWN-UP* THAT DOESN'T SPEND HIS NIGHTS IN *TIGHTS* BEATING UP *BAD GUYS* THAT WOULD OTHERWISE BEAT *ME* UP JUST FOR BEING YOUR FRIENDLY NEIGHBORHOOD *SPIDER-MAN*.

SO I SIT ON MY TRAIN

AND I LET MY MI[N]D WANDER.

WHICH, WHEN I'M *NOT* BEING YOUR FRIENDLY NEIGHBORHOOD SPIDER-MAN...

...IS TOTALLY MY JOB.

AS THE NEWEST HIRE AT HORIZON LABS, THINKIN' 'BOUT STUFF IS WHAT I GET PAID TO DO.

SO HAVING A FEW SPARE MINUTES T[O] LET MY MIND DRIFT [PL]ACES, PROVIDED I C[AN] REMAIN FREE FRO[M]...

...DISTRACTIONS.

HI, PETE.

WHATCHA WRITIN'? SPECIAL THOUGHTS?

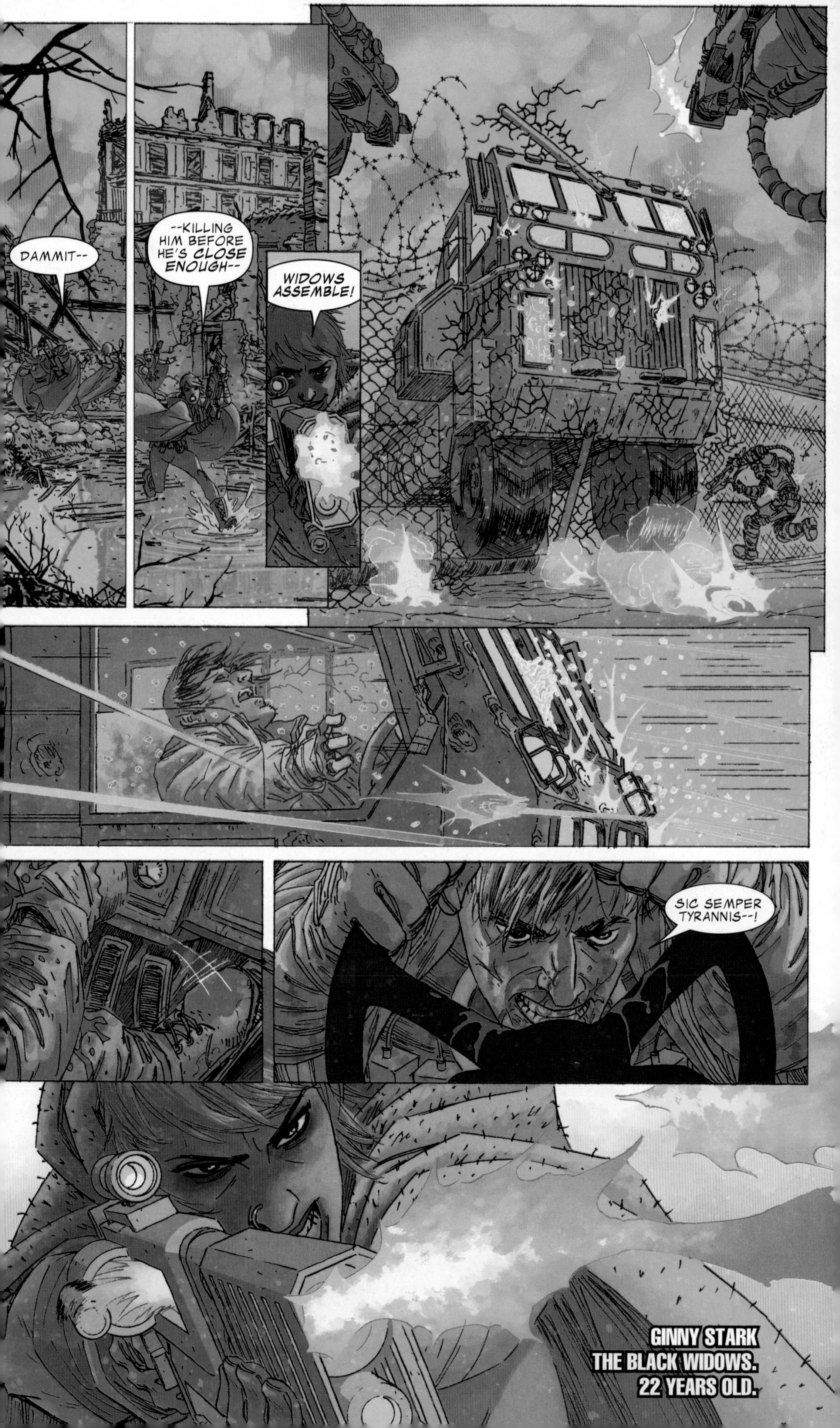
DAMMIT--
--KILLING HIM BEFORE HE'S CLOSE ENOUGH--
WIDOWS ASSEMBLE!
SIC SEMPER TYRANNIS--!
GINNY STARK
THE BLACK WIDOWS.
22 YEARS OLD.

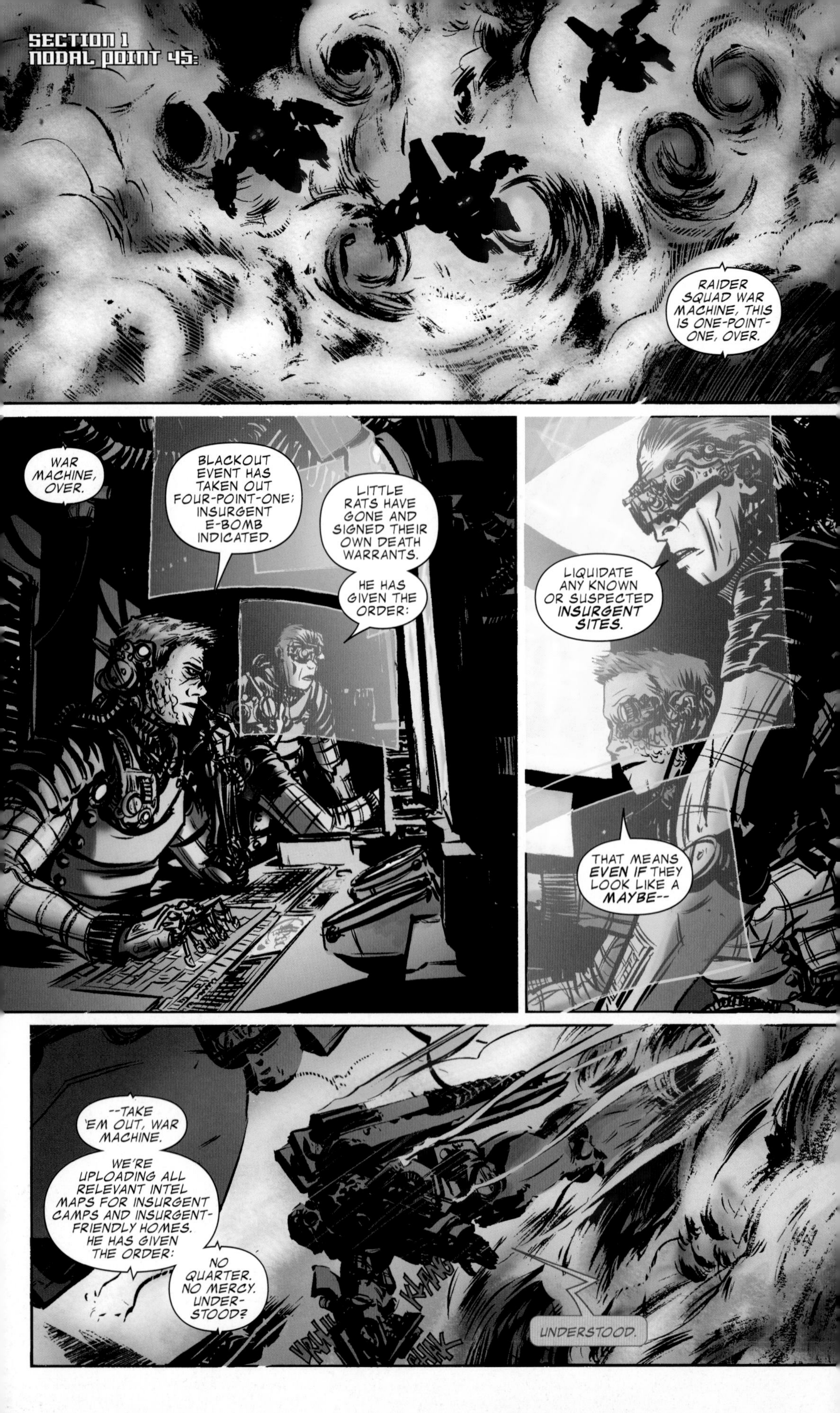
SECTION 1
NODAL POINT 45:
RAIDER SQUAD WAR MACHINE, THIS IS ONE-POINT-ONE, OVER.
WAR MACHINE, OVER.
BLACKOUT EVENT HAS TAKEN OUT FOUR-POINT-ONE; INSURGENT E-BOMB INDICATED.
LITTLE RATS HAVE GONE AND SIGNED THEIR OWN DEATH WARRANTS.
HE HAS GIVEN THE ORDER:
LIQUIDATE ANY KNOWN OR SUSPECTED INSURGENT SITES.
THAT MEANS EVEN IF THEY LOOK LIKE A MAYBE--
--TAKE 'EM OUT, WAR MACHINE.
WE'RE UPLOADING ALL RELEVANT INTEL MAPS FOR INSURGENT CAMPS AND INSURGENT-FRIENDLY HOMES. HE HAS GIVEN THE ORDER:
NO QUARTER. NO MERCY. UNDER-STOOD?
UNDERSTOOD.

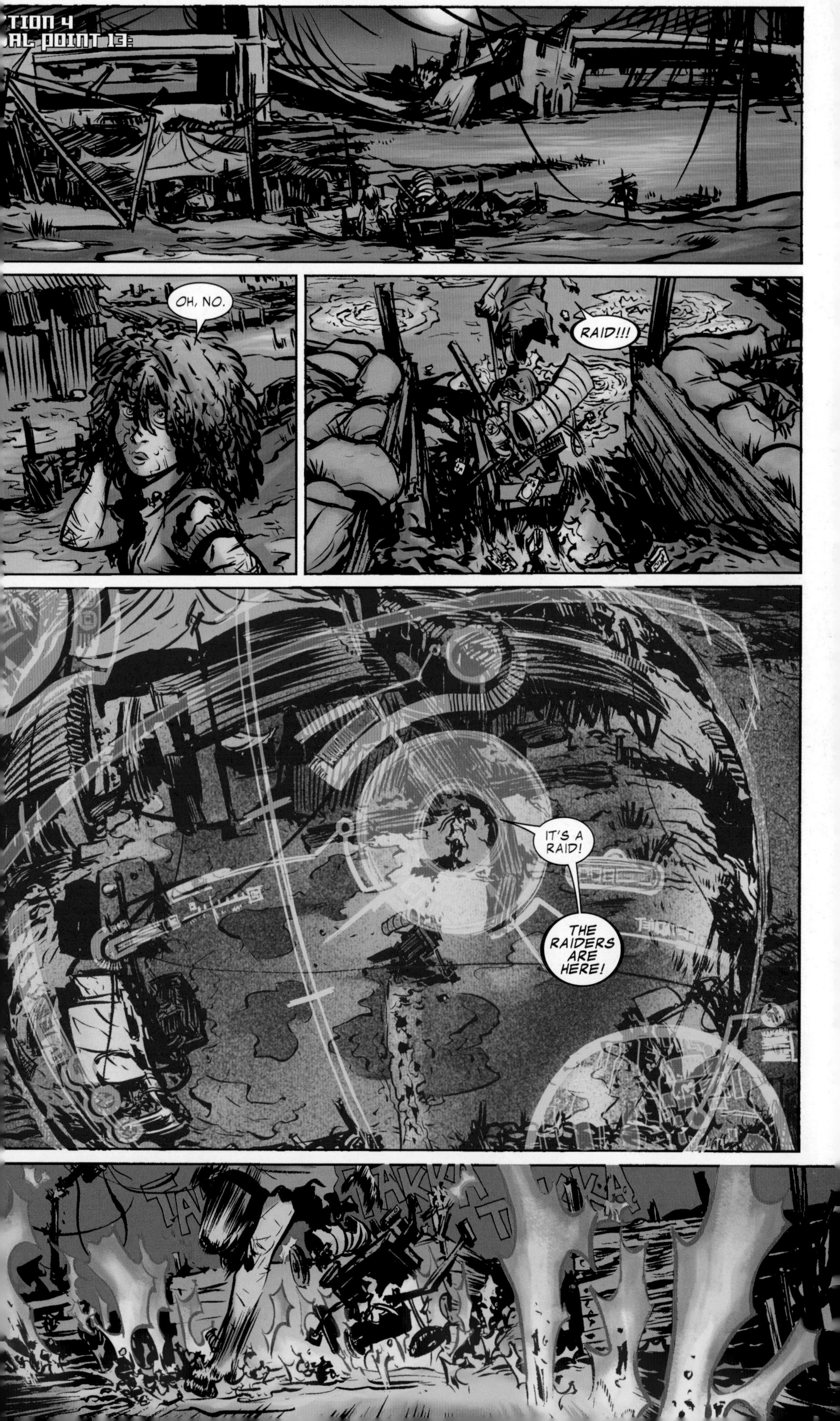
TION 4
AL POINT 13:
OH, NO.
RAID!!!
IT'S A RAID!
THE RAIDERS ARE HERE!

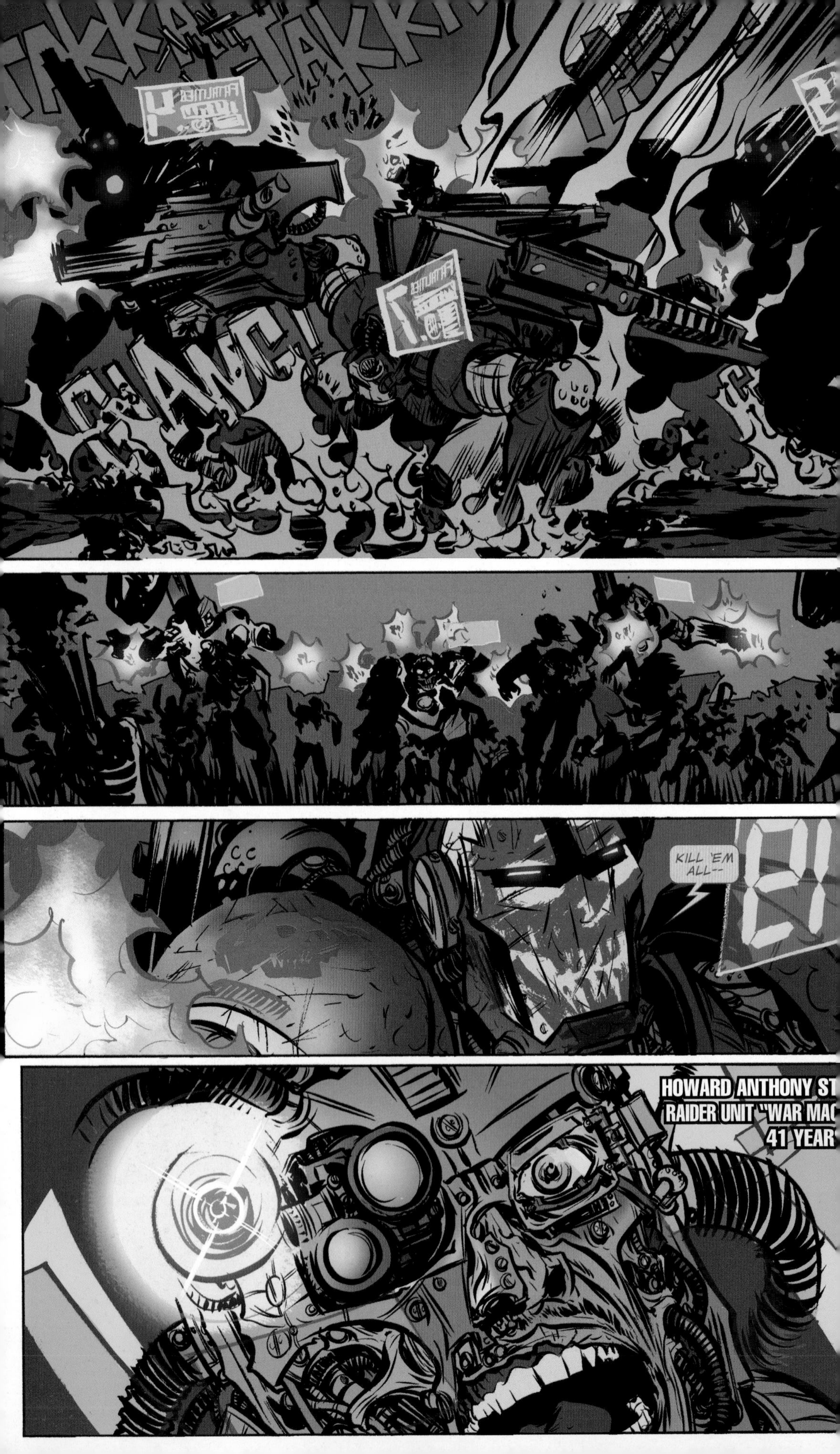
TAKKA TAKKA
FATALITIES 4
FATALITIES 7
BLAM!
KILL 'EM ALL--
HOWARD ANTHONY ST
RAIDER UNIT "WAR MAC
41 YEAR

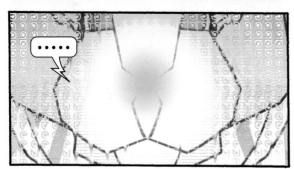

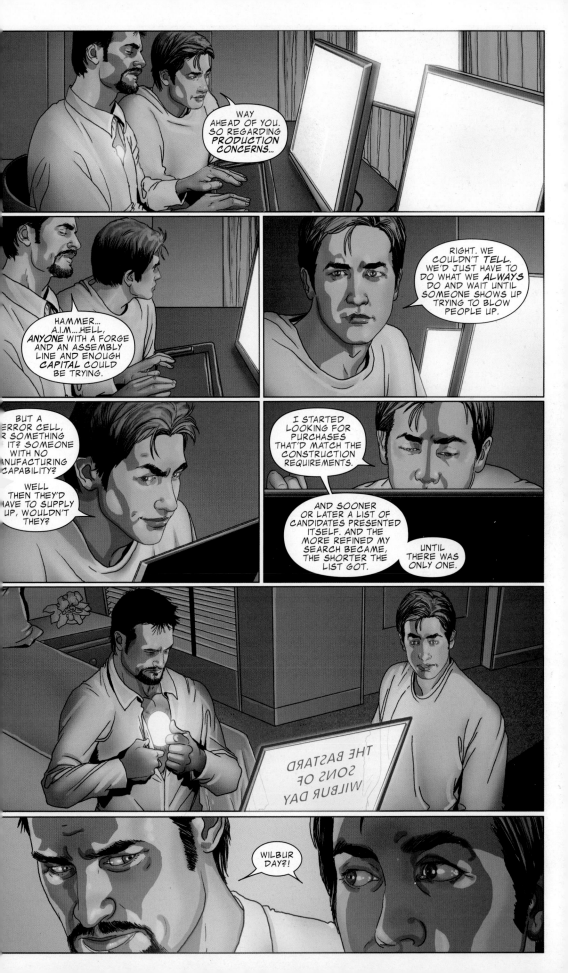

REMEMBER THE SPIDER.

REMEMBER THE SPIDER.

UM-- GINNY?

EMEMBER THE IDER, STARTING HER WEB AND CRAWLING UP...

GINNY, YOU'RE TALKING TO YOURSELF.

REMEMBER THE-- HANG ON--

OKAY. SORRY.

"REMEMBER THE SPIDER." LITTLE MNEMONIC DEVICE TO REMEMBER THE CIRCUIT SEQUENCING.

I DON'T--I DON'T KNOW WHAT THOSE WORDS MEAN.

A SHORT THING THAT HELPS YOU REMEMBER A LONG THING.

THE SPIDER SHAPE IS THE KEY. SEE?

AH, SO IT'S LIKE--

PERIMETER BREACH-- INCOMING--THIS IS NOT A DRILL--

OH NO--

RAIDERS--

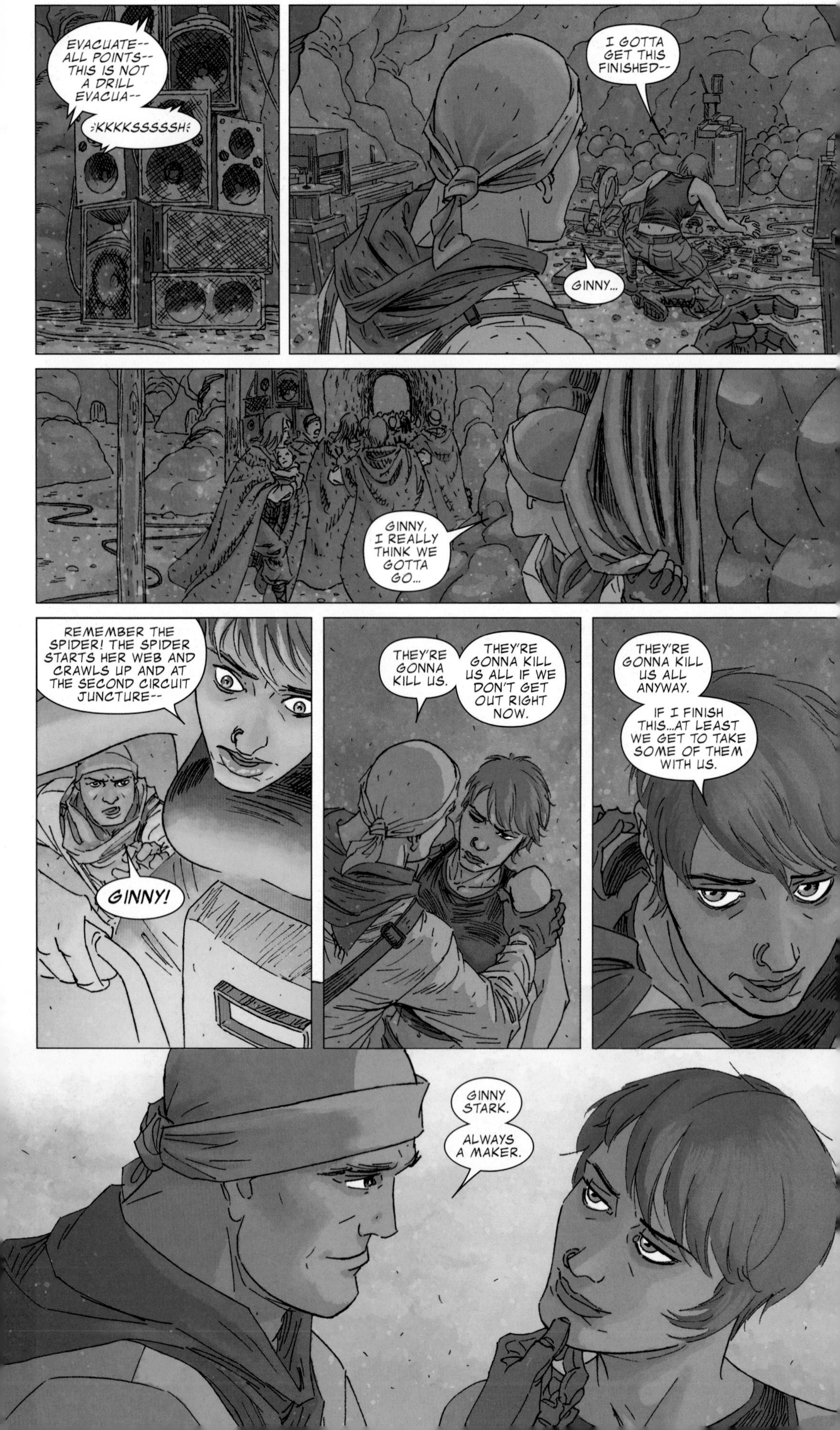
EVACUATE-- ALL POINTS-- THIS IS NOT A DRILL EVACUA--
KKKKSSSSSH
I GOTTA GET THIS FINISHED--
GINNY...
GINNY, I REALLY THINK WE GOTTA GO...
REMEMBER THE SPIDER! THE SPIDER STARTS HER WEB AND CRAWLS UP AND AT THE SECOND CIRCUIT JUNCTURE--
GINNY!
THEY'RE GONNA KILL US.
THEY'RE GONNA KILL US ALL IF WE DON'T GET OUT RIGHT NOW.
THEY'RE GONNA KILL US ALL ANYWAY.
IF I FINISH THIS...AT LEAST WE GET TO TAKE SOME OF THEM WITH US.
GINNY STARK.
ALWAYS A MAKER.

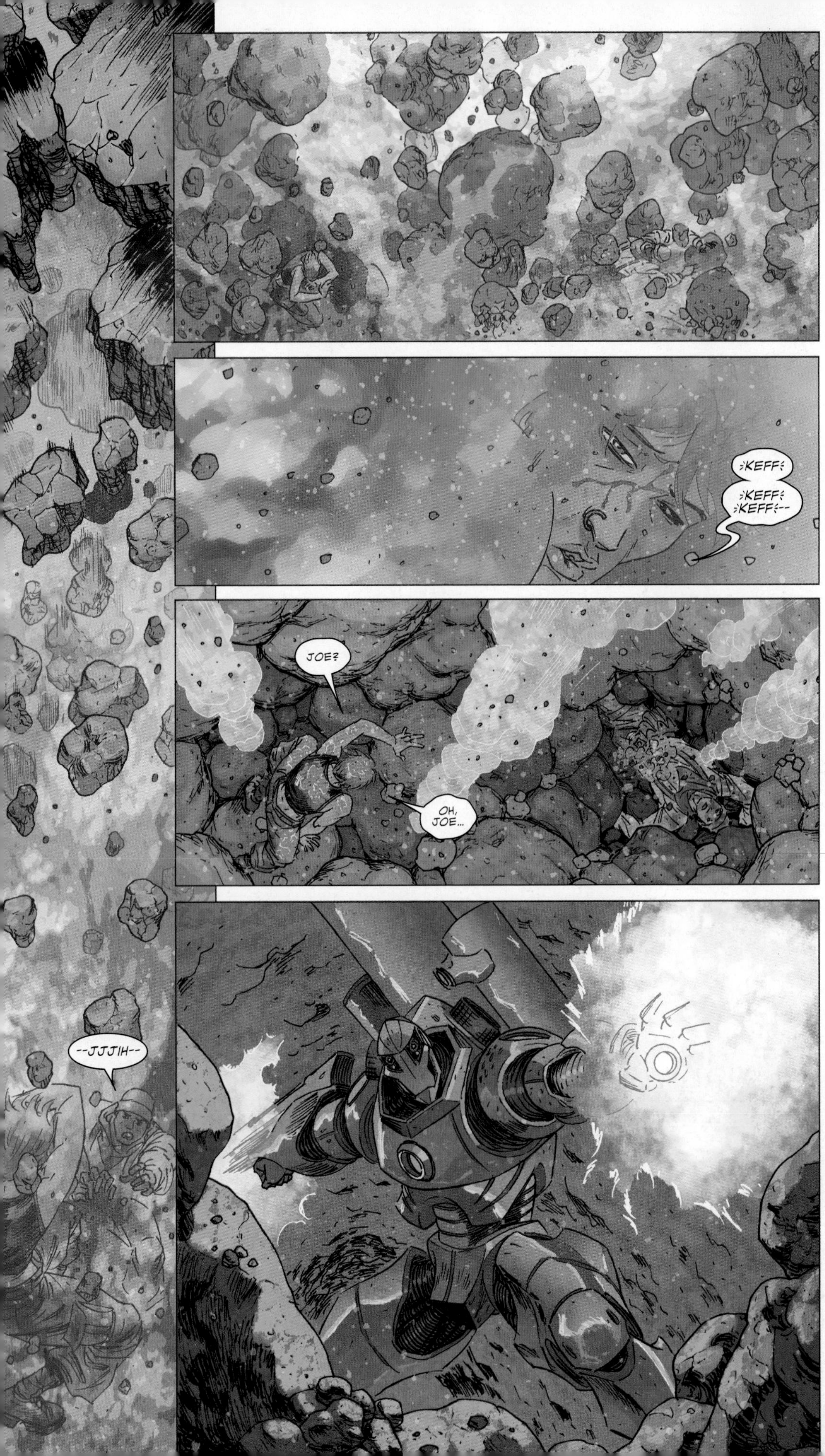
KEFF
KEFF
KEFF--
JOE?
OH, JOE...
--JJJIH--

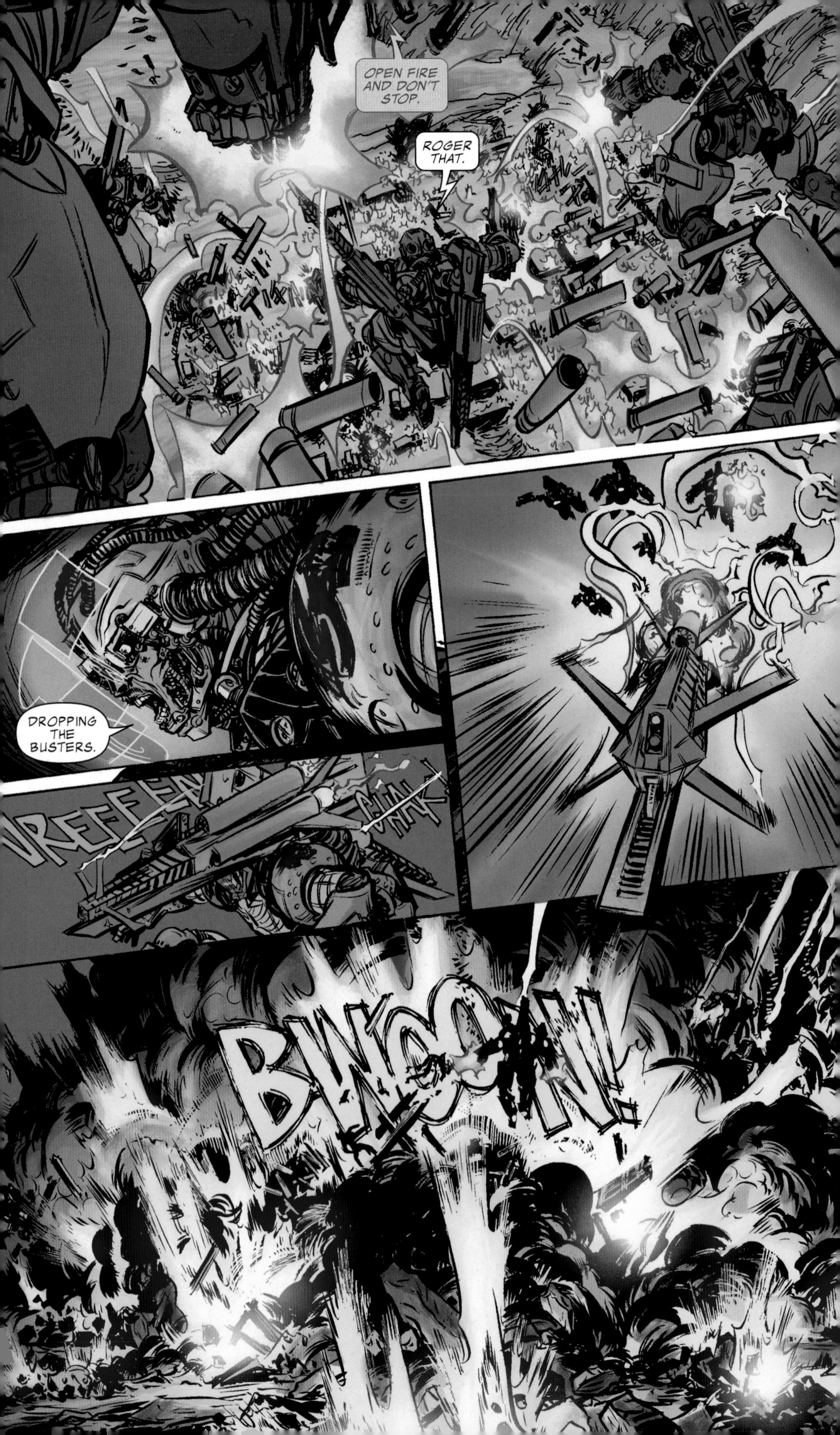
OPEN FIRE AND DON'T STOP.
ROGER THAT.
DROPPING THE BUSTERS.
VREEEEN
CHUNK
BWOOM!

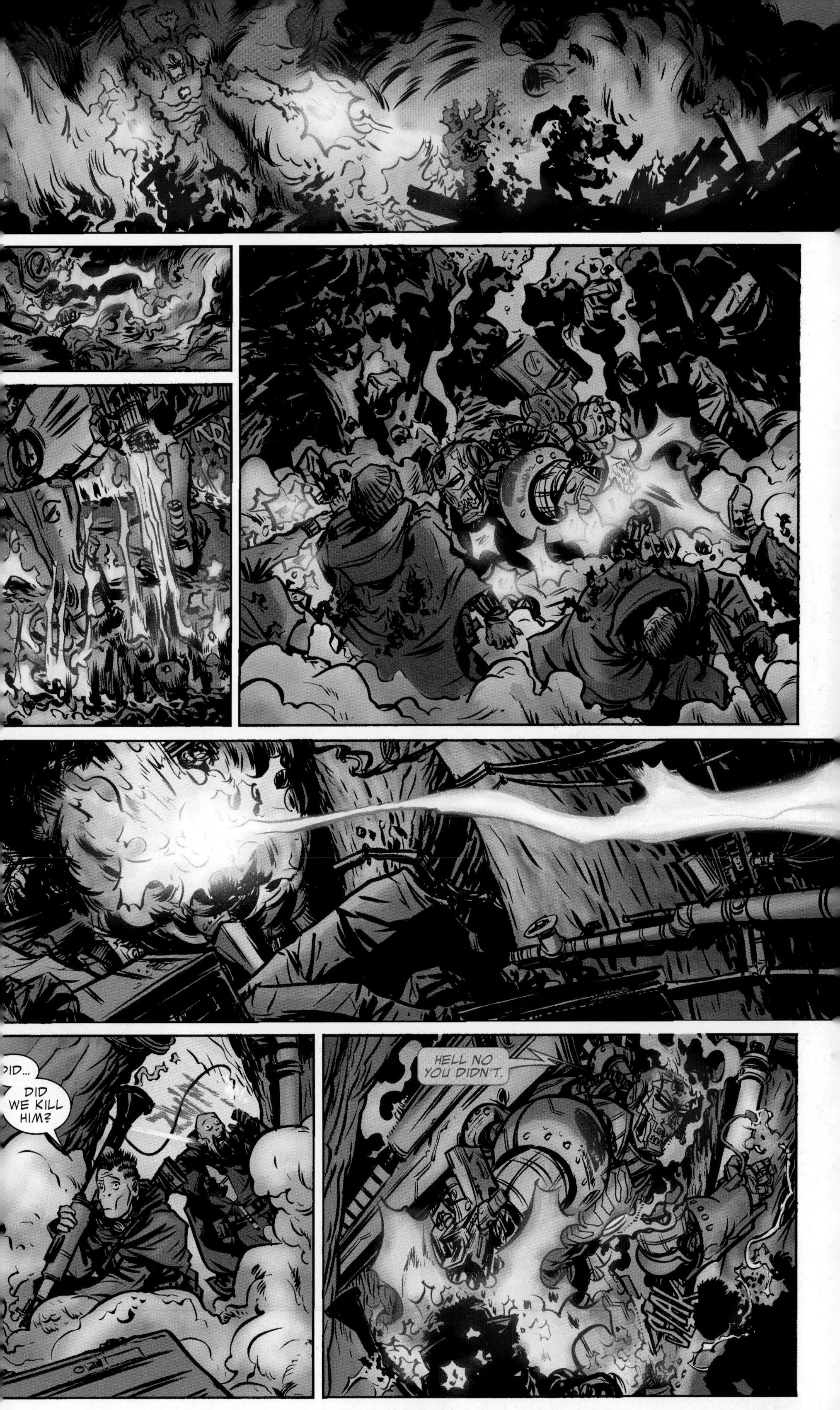
DID...
DID WE KILL HIM?
HELL NO YOU DIDN'T.

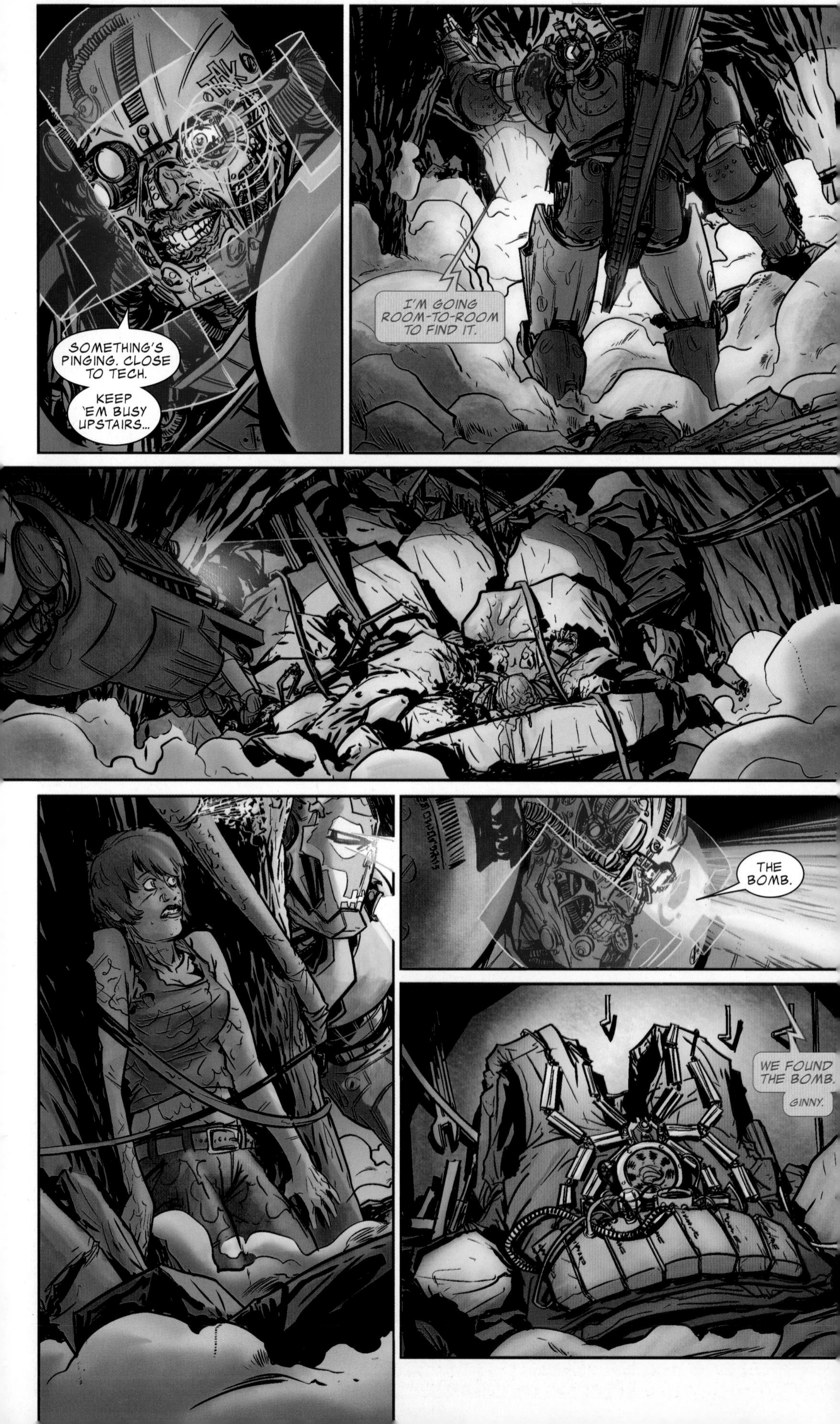
SOMETHING'S PINGING. CLOSE TO TECH.
KEEP 'EM BUSY UPSTAIRS...
I'M GOING ROOM-TO-ROOM TO FIND IT.
THE BOMB.
WE FOUND THE BOMB.
GINNY.

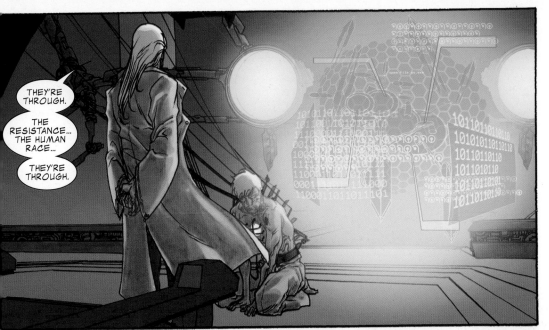

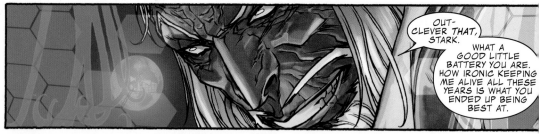

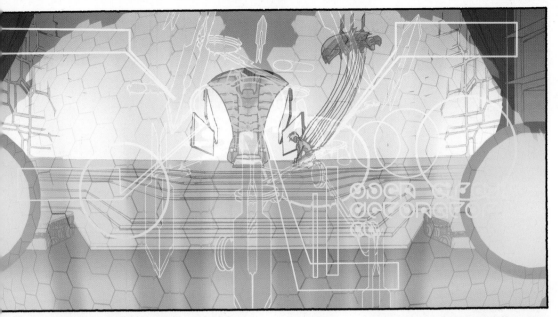

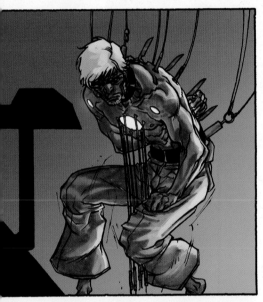

I...

...REMEMBER...

"REMEMBER THE SPIDER."

OH, GOD, GINNY...I...I REMEMBER NOW.

GINNY. HOWARD.

DON'T LET ME BE TOO LATE.

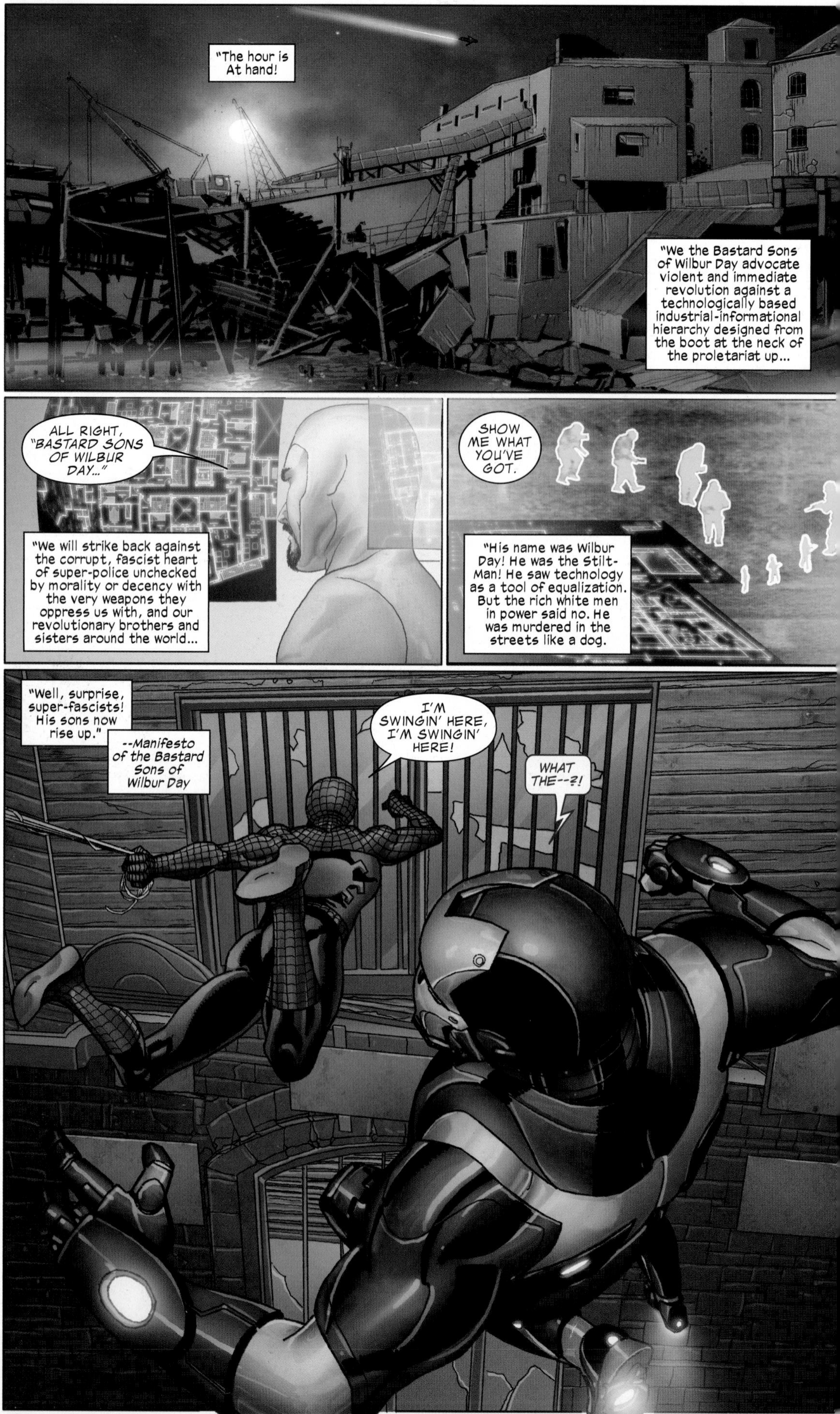
"The hour is At hand!
"We the Bastard Sons of Wilbur Day advocate violent and immediate revolution against a technologically based industrial-informational hierarchy designed from the boot at the neck of the proletariat up...
ALL RIGHT, "BASTARD SONS OF WILBUR DAY..."
"We will strike back against the corrupt, fascist heart of super-police unchecked by morality or decency with the very weapons they oppress us with, and our revolutionary brothers and sisters around the world...
SHOW ME WHAT YOU'VE GOT.
"His name was Wilbur Day! He was the Stilt-Man! He saw technology as a tool of equalization. But the rich white men in power said no. He was murdered in the streets like a dog.
"Well, surprise, super-fascists! His sons now rise up."
--Manifesto of the Bastard Sons of Wilbur Day
I'M SWINGIN' HERE, I'M SWINGIN' HERE!
WHAT THE--?!

THE CHARADE
S DONE, DAD.
ET'S MAKE IT
-OOK GOOD.

RUN, GIRL. MAKE IT LOOK GOOD.

GOOD.

GOOD GIRL.

JEEZ, DAD--

--TRUST ME--

JUST LIKE I TAUGHT YOU--

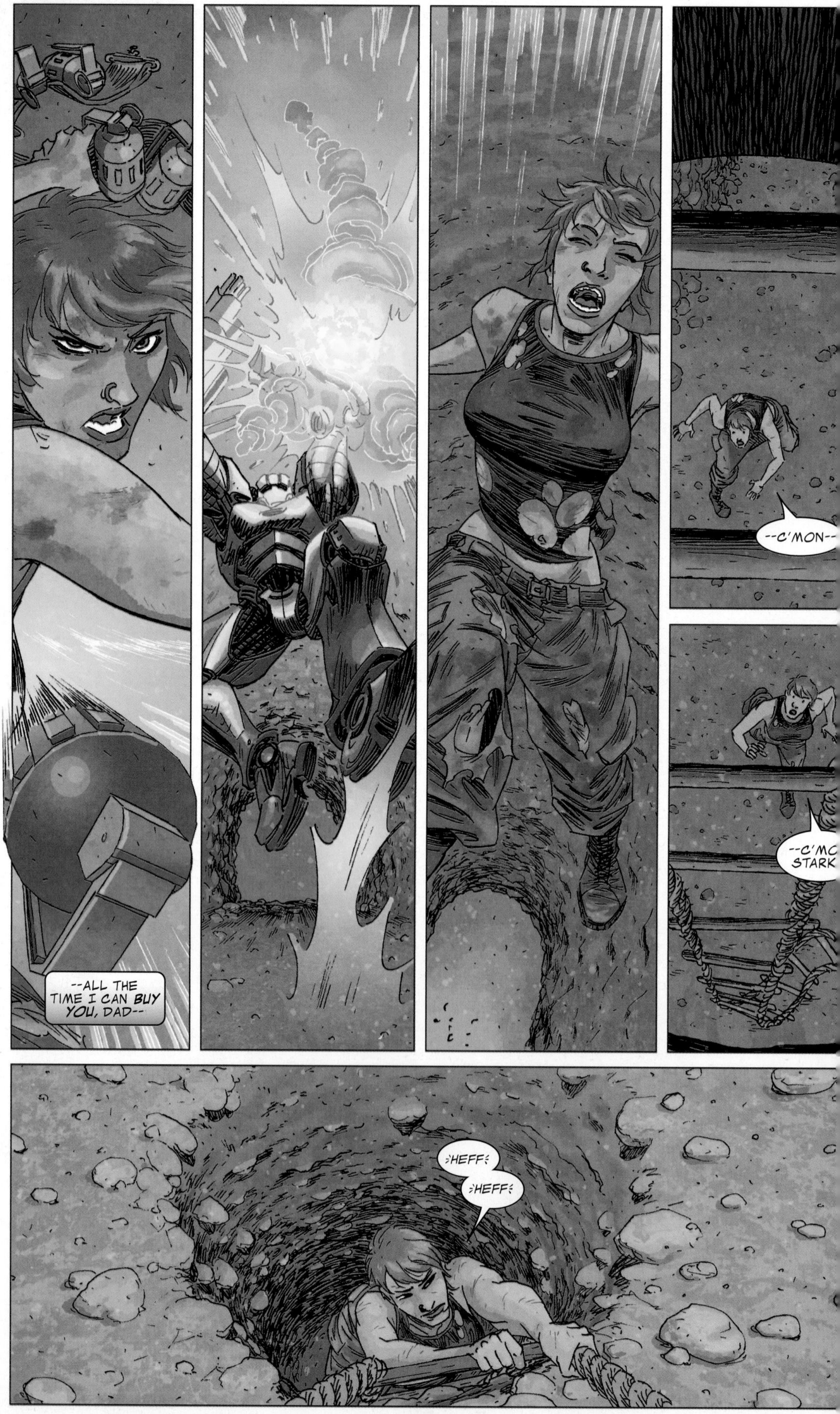

--ALL THE TIME I CAN BUY YOU, DAD--
--C'MON--
--C'MO STARK
HEFF
HEFF

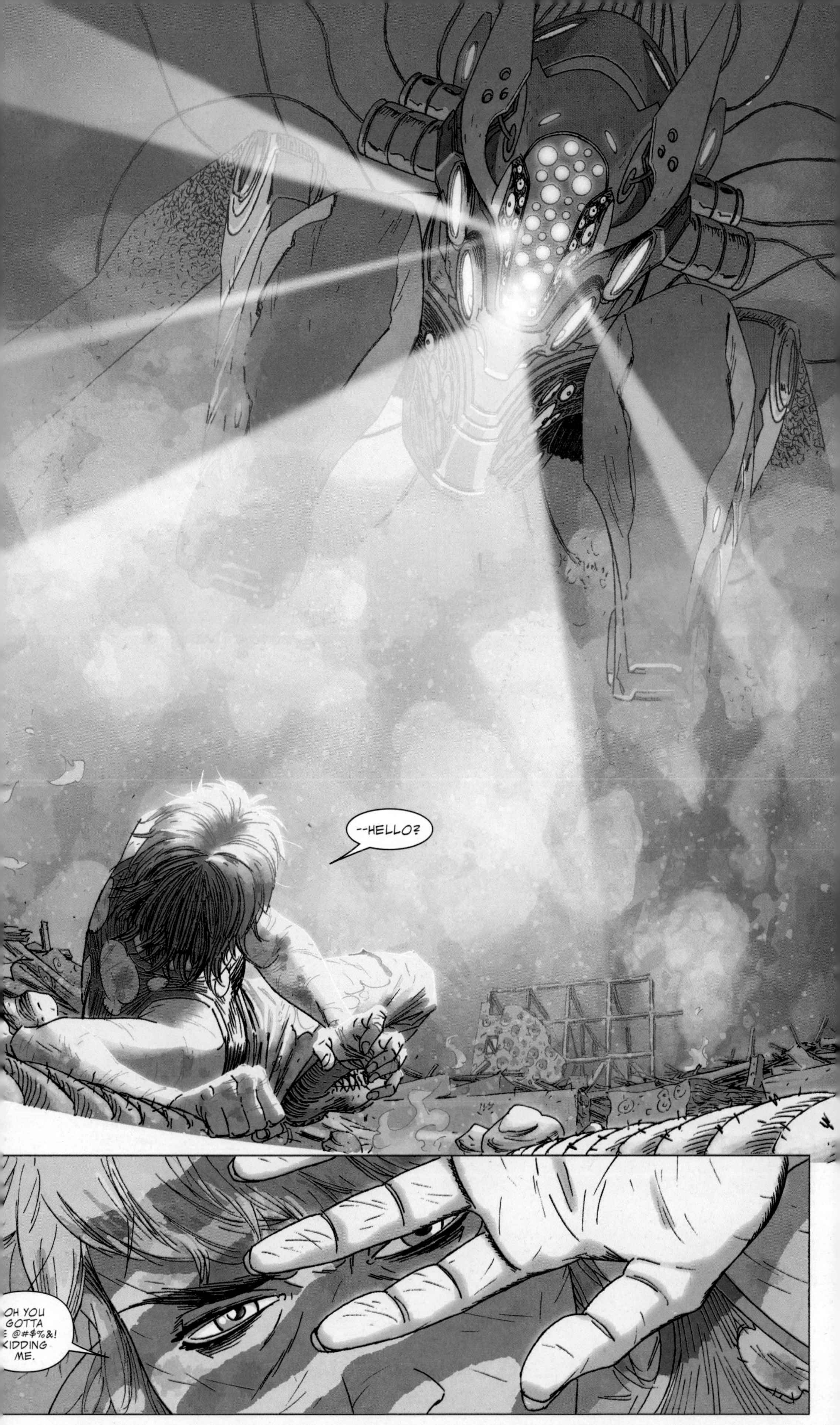

--HELLO?
OH YOU GOTTA E @#$%&! KIDDING ME.

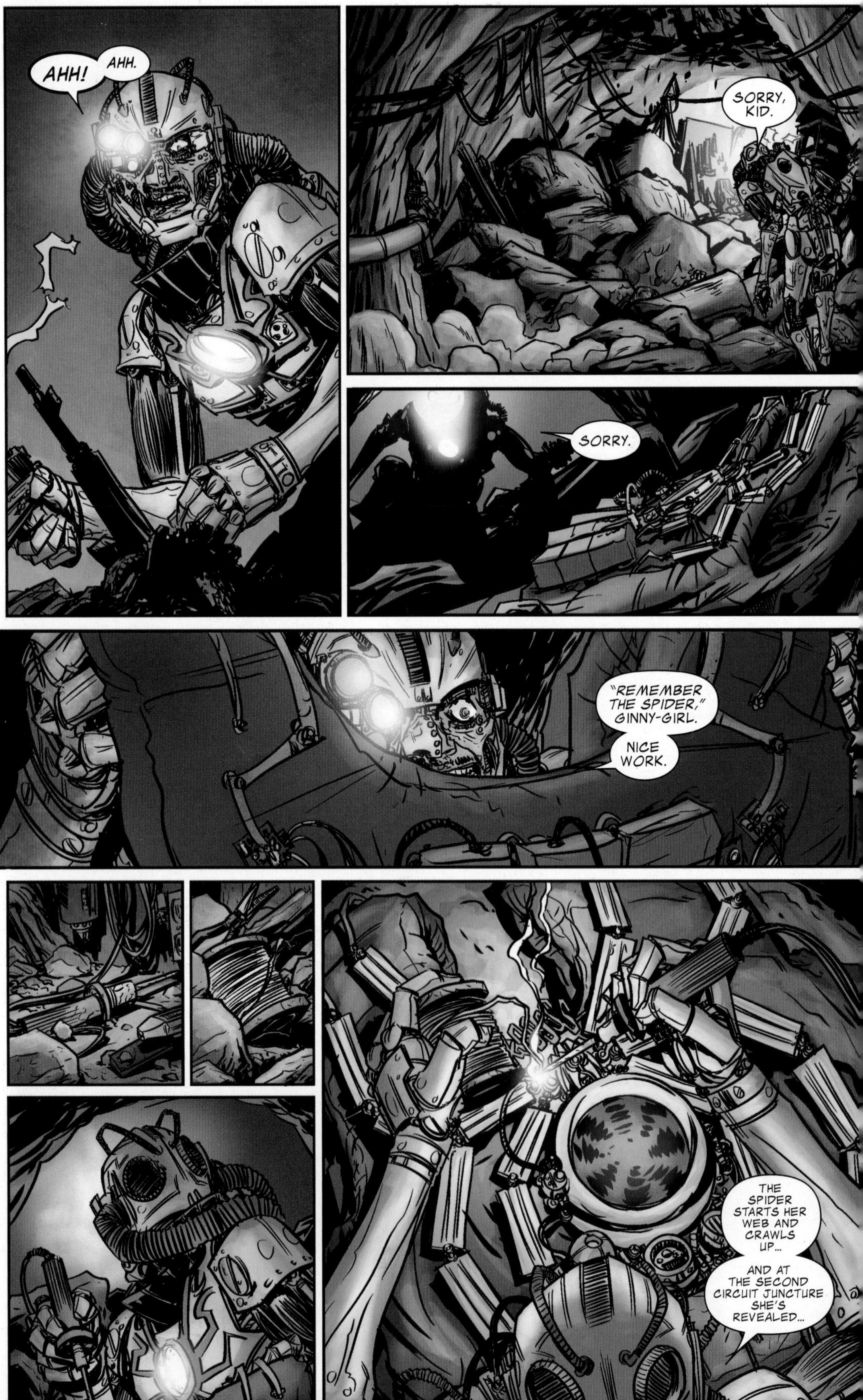
AHH!
AHH.
SORRY, KID.
SORRY.
"REMEMBER THE SPIDER," GINNY-GIRL.
NICE WORK.
THE SPIDER STARTS HER WEB AND CRAWLS UP...
AND AT THE SECOND CIRCUIT JUNCTURE SHE'S REVEALED...

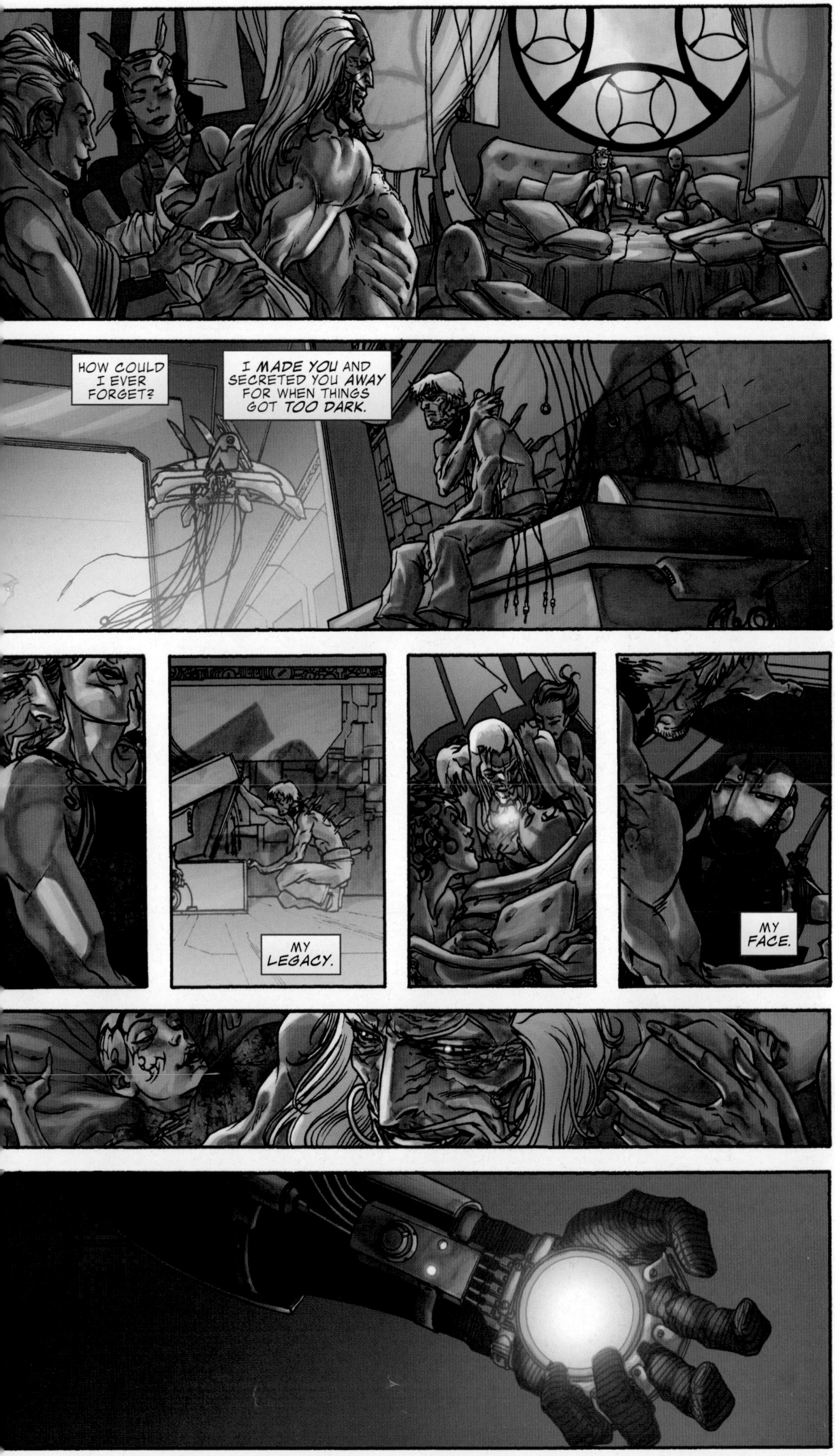

HOW COULD I EVER FORGET?
I MADE YOU AND SECRETED YOU AWAY FOR WHEN THINGS GOT TOO DARK.
MY LEGACY.
MY FACE.

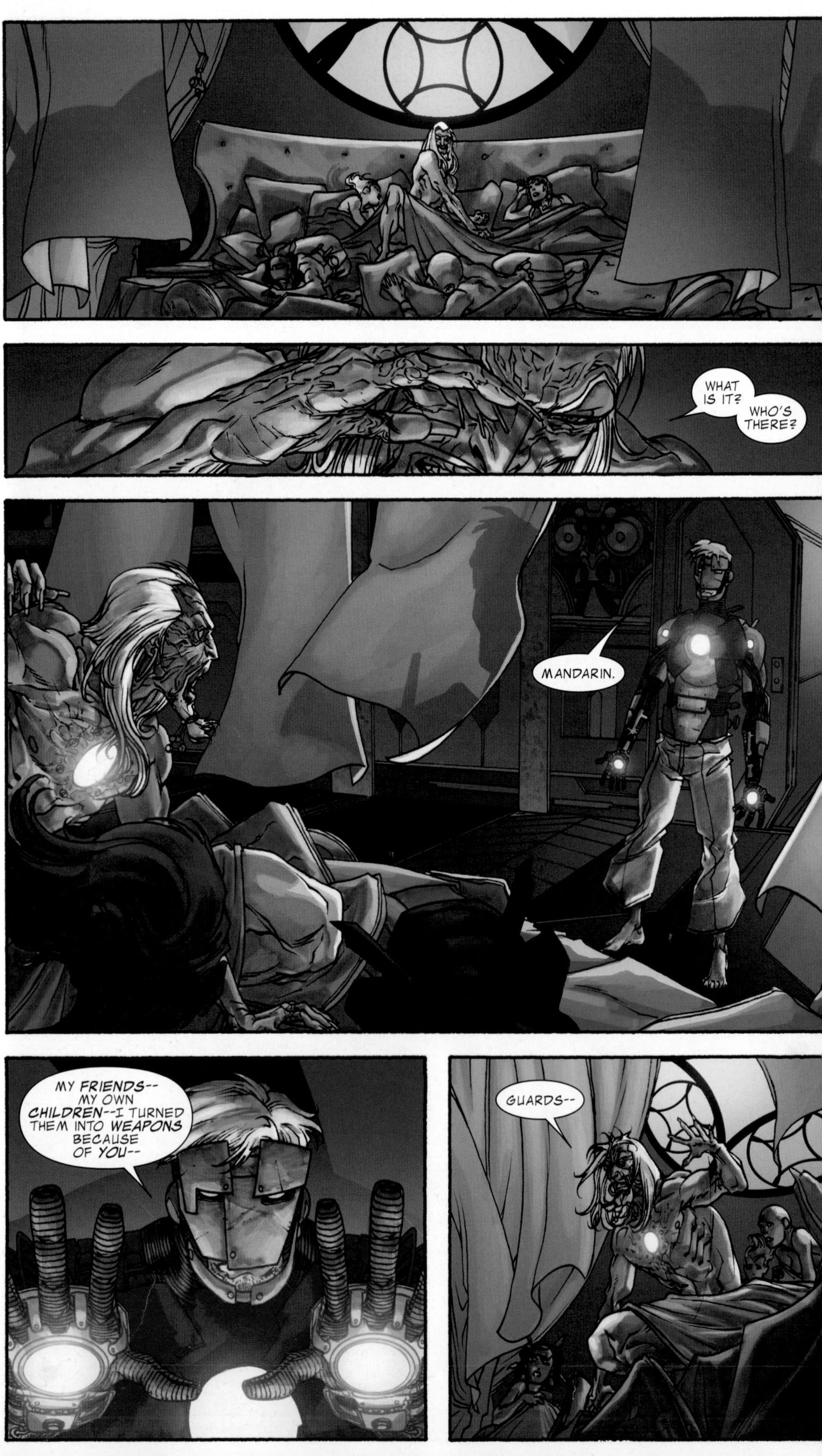
WHAT IS IT? WHO'S THERE?
MANDARIN.
MY FRIENDS-- MY OWN CHILDREN--I TURNED THEM INTO WEAPONS BECAUSE OF YOU--
GUARDS--

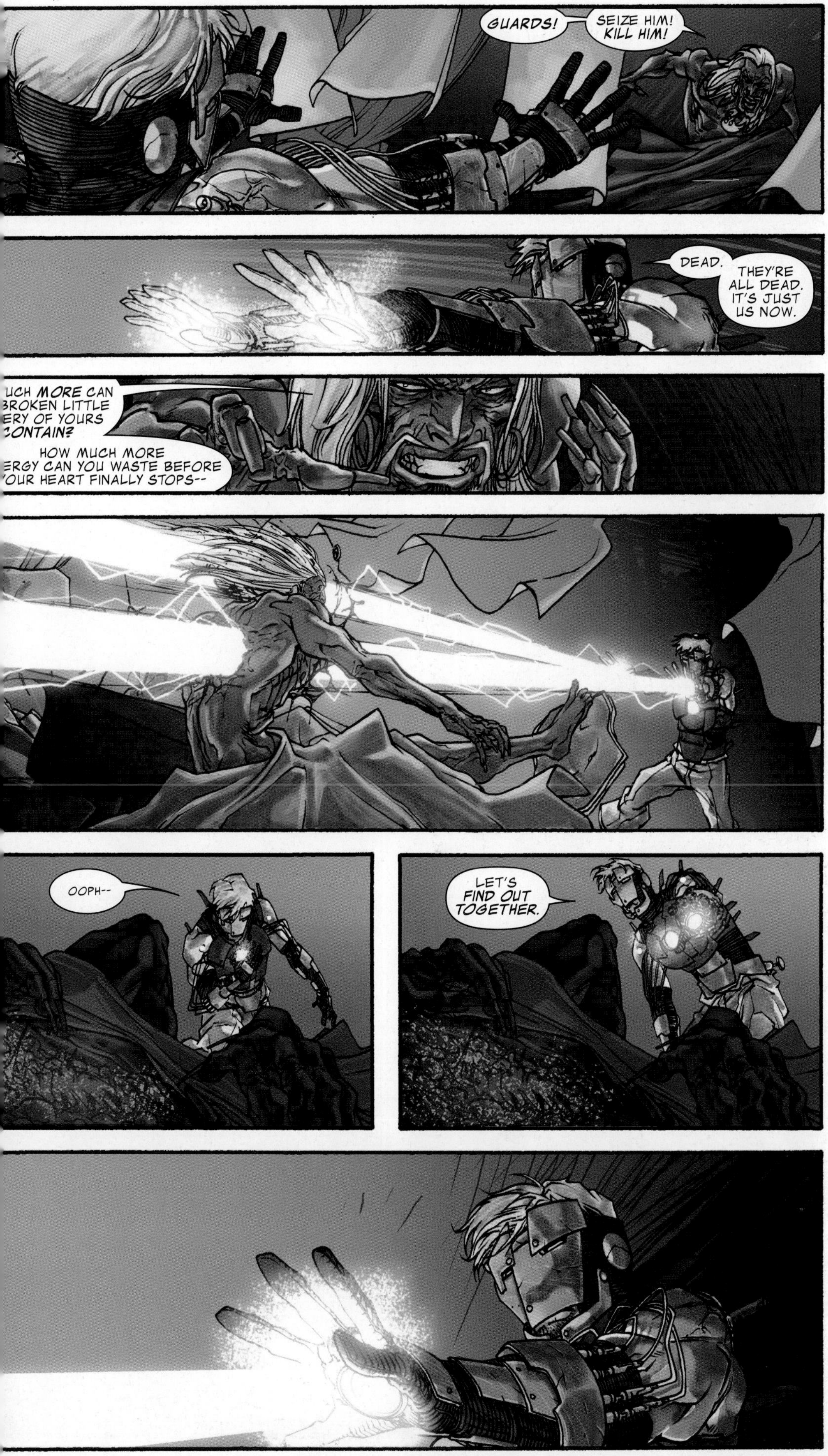
GUARDS!
SEIZE HIM! KILL HIM!
DEAD.
THEY'RE ALL DEAD. IT'S JUST US NOW.
UCH MORE CAN BROKEN LITTLE ERY OF YOURS CONTAIN?
HOW MUCH MORE ERGY CAN YOU WASTE BEFORE OUR HEART FINALLY STOPS--
OOPH--
LET'S FIND OUT TOGETHER.

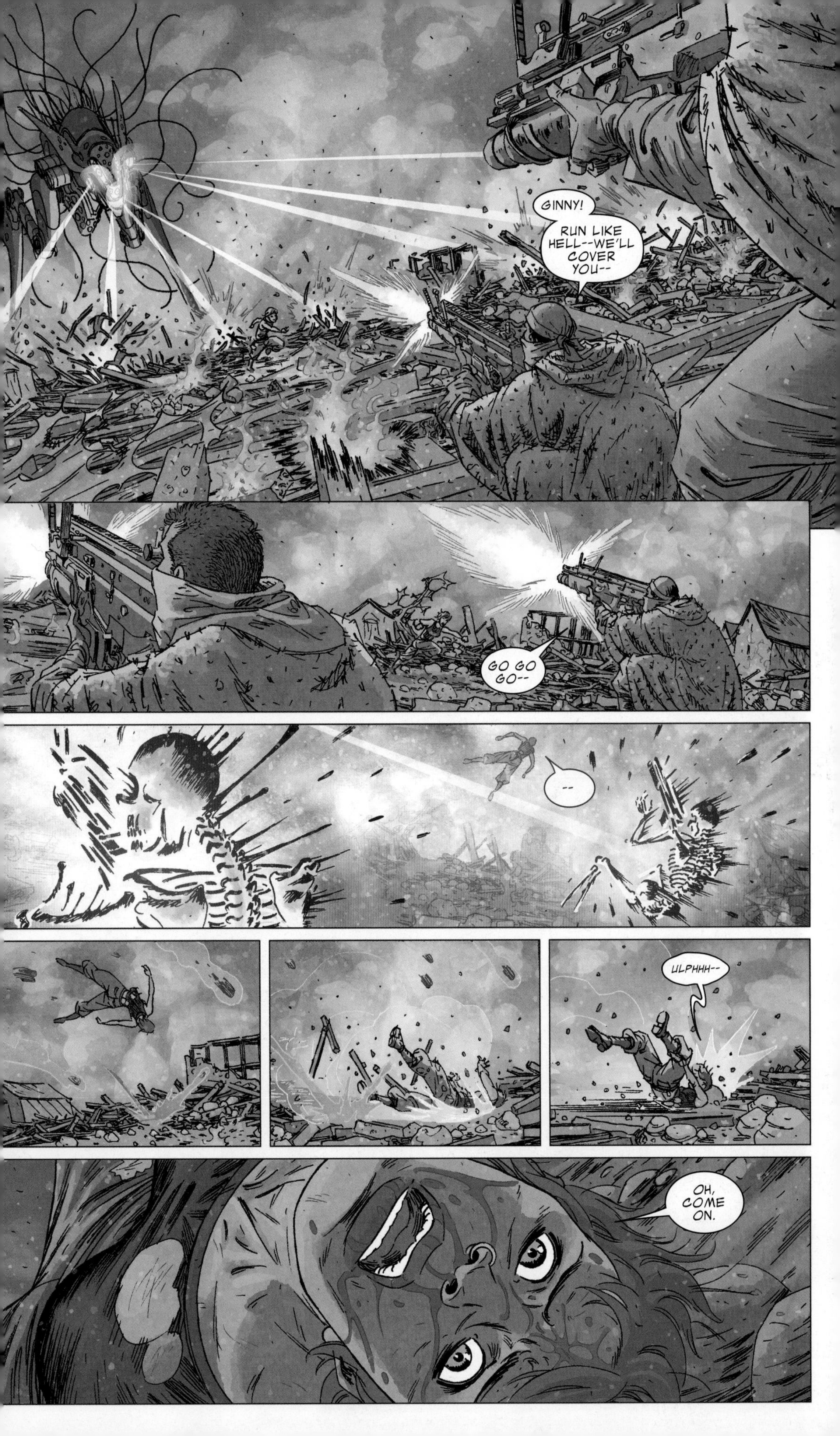
GINNY!
RUN LIKE HELL--WE'LL COVER YOU--
GO GO GO--
--
ULPHHH--
OH, COME ON.

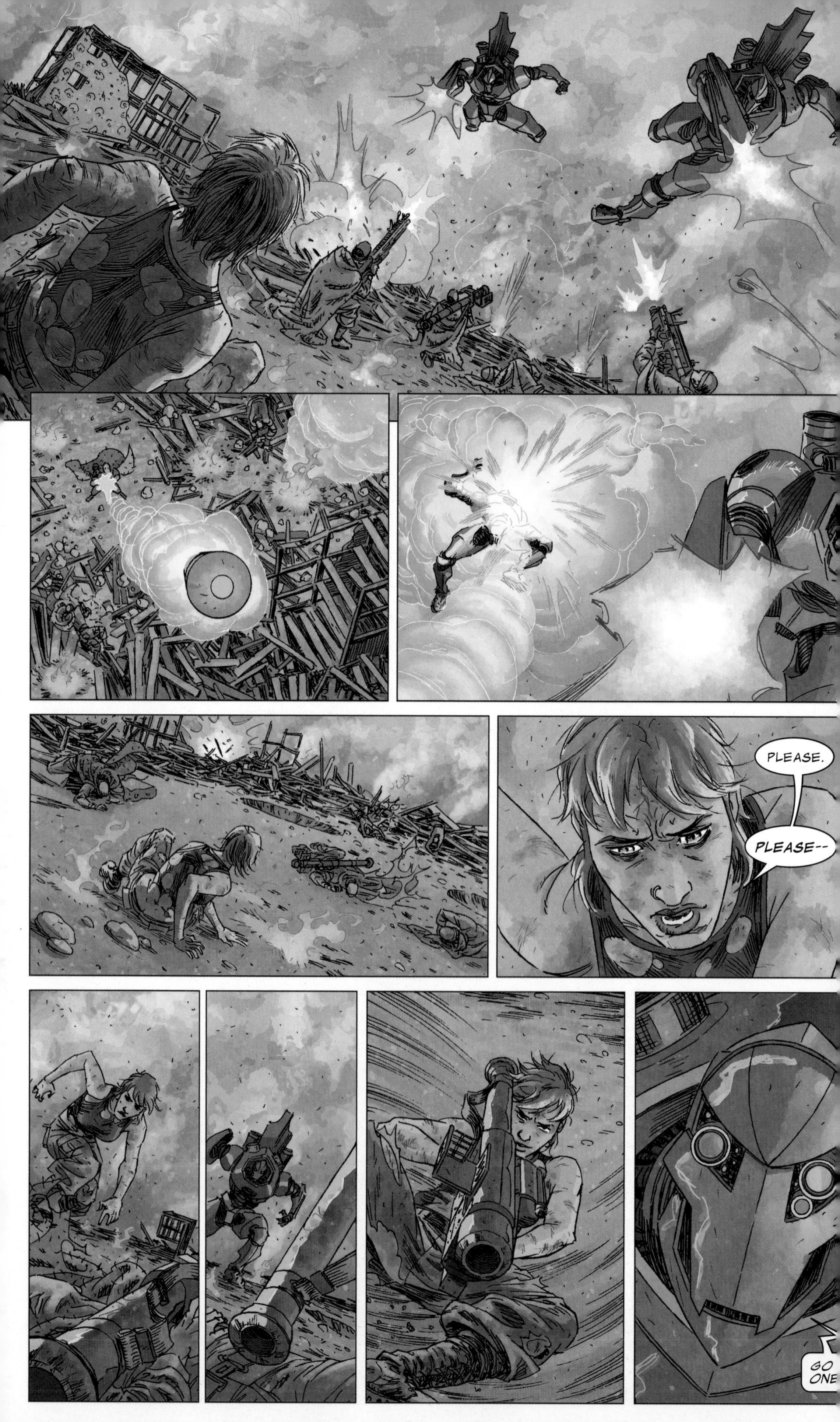
PLEASE.
PLEASE--
GO
ONE

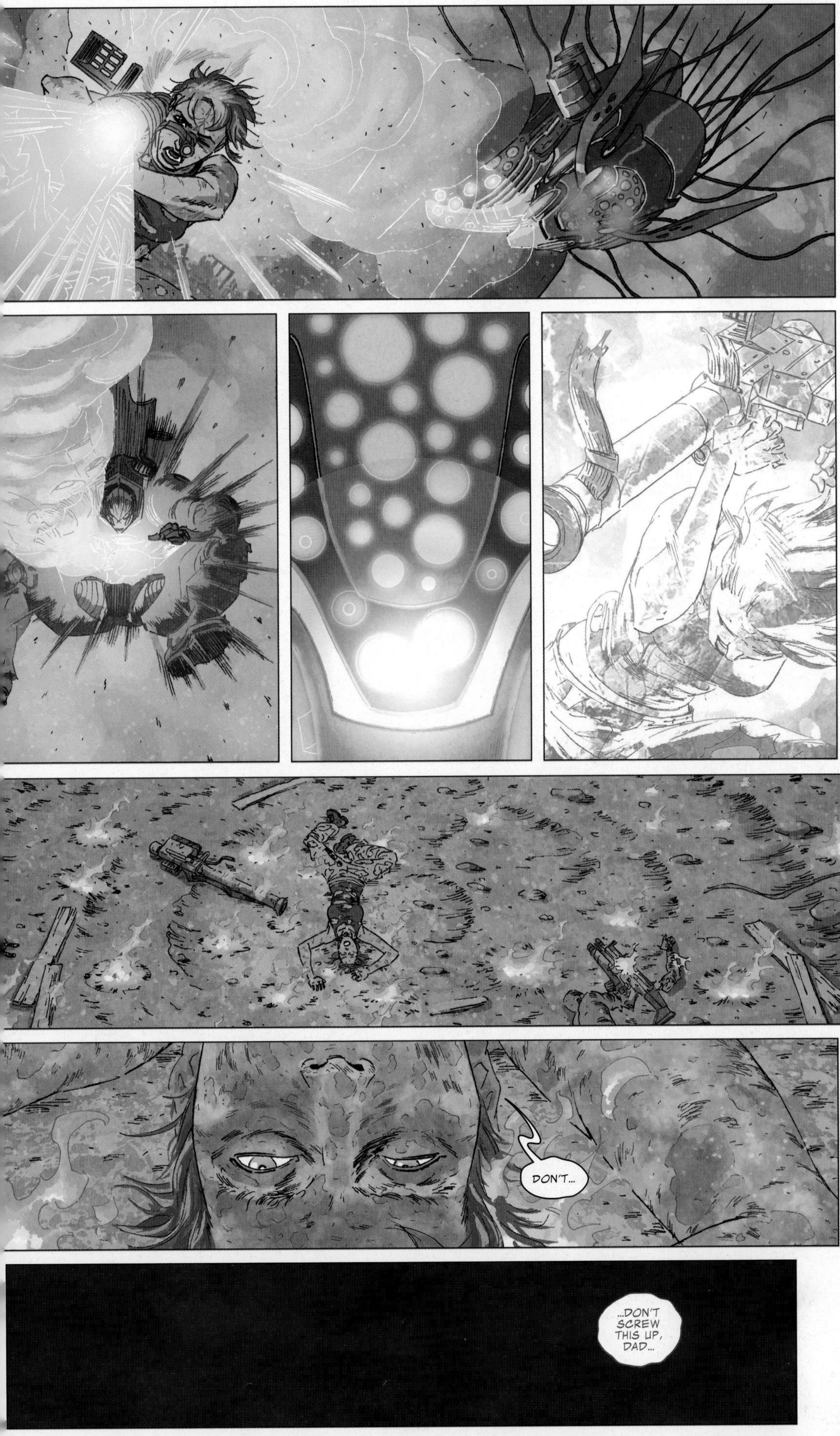
DON'T...
...DON'T SCREW THIS UP, DAD...

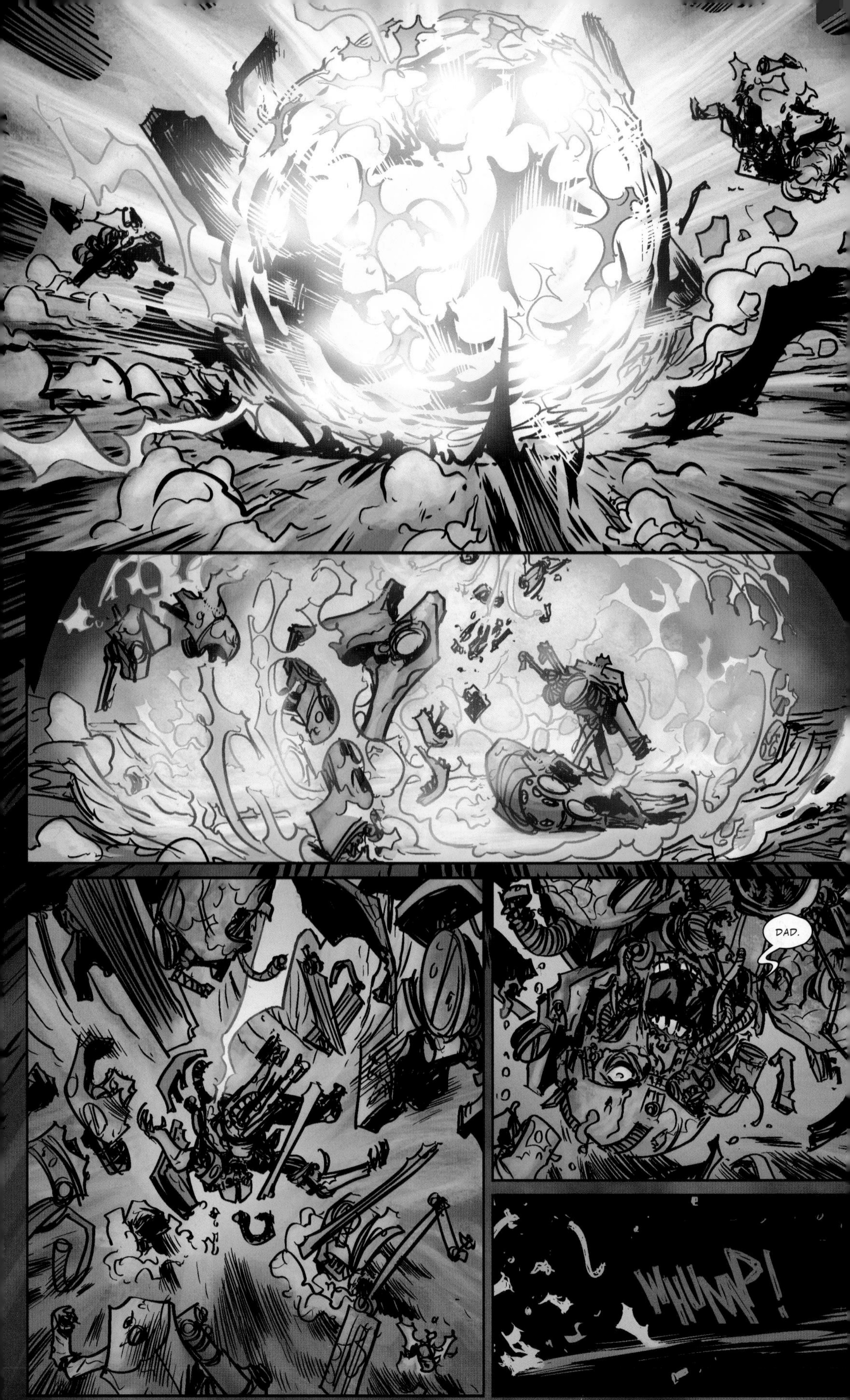
DAD.
WHUMP!

OOPH.

C'MON, OLD MAN. ALMOST FINISHED.

TOOK ME A WHILE TO REMEMBER AFTER EVERYTHING YOU *DID* TO ME, MANDARIN.

SHOCK. TORTURE.

BUT I REMEMBERED. DIDN'T I?

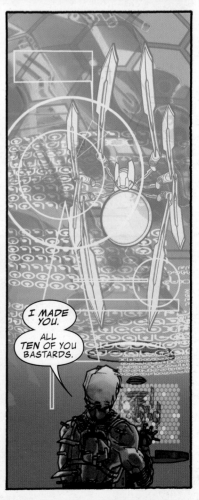

I MADE YOU.

ALL TEN OF YOU BASTARDS.

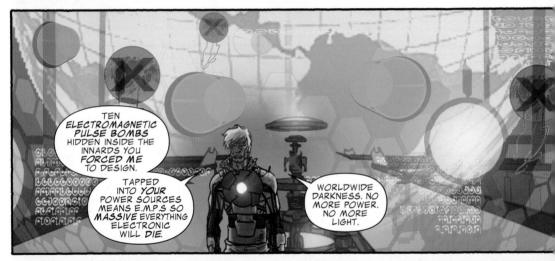

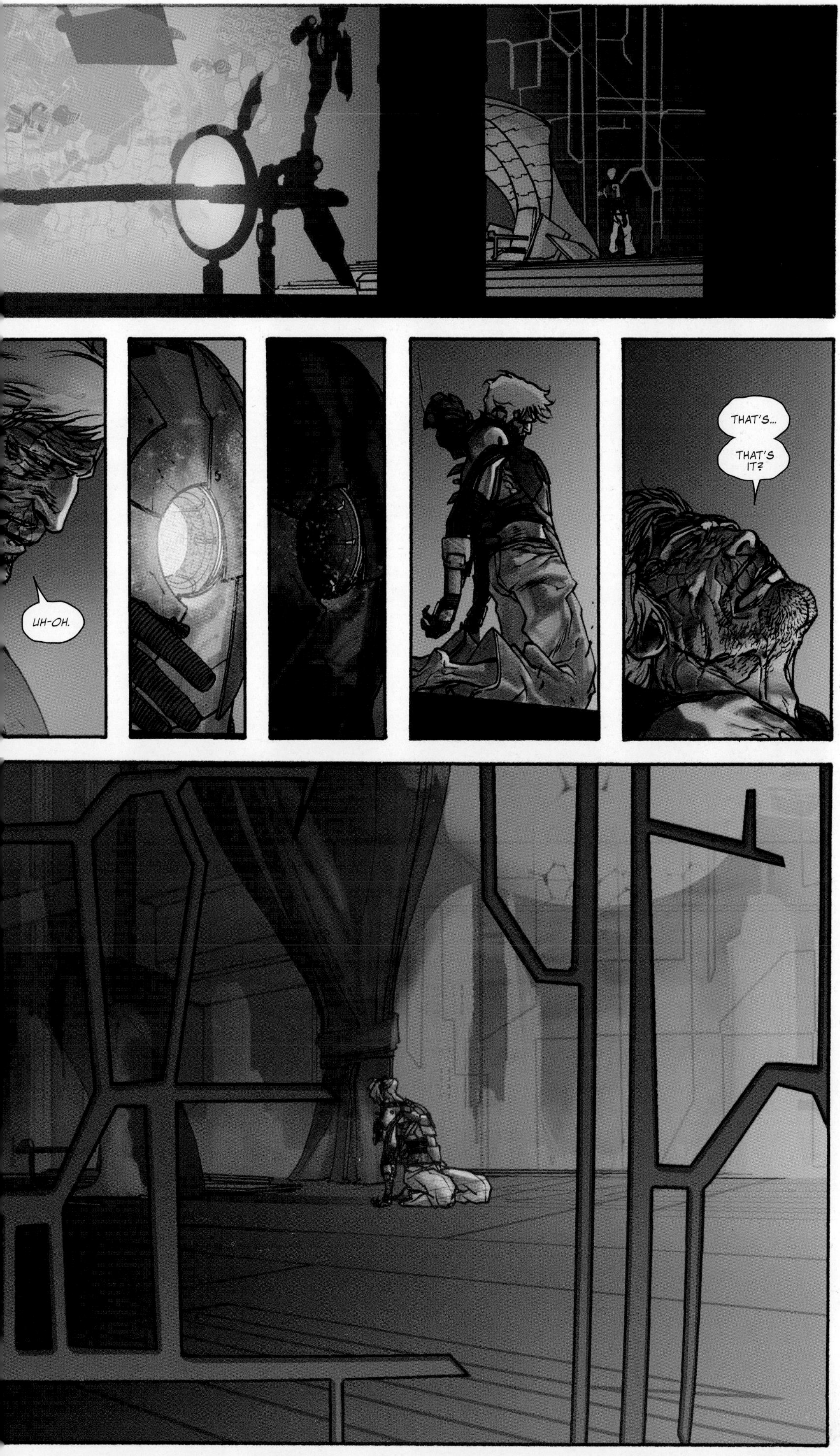
UH-OH.
THAT'S...
THAT'S IT?

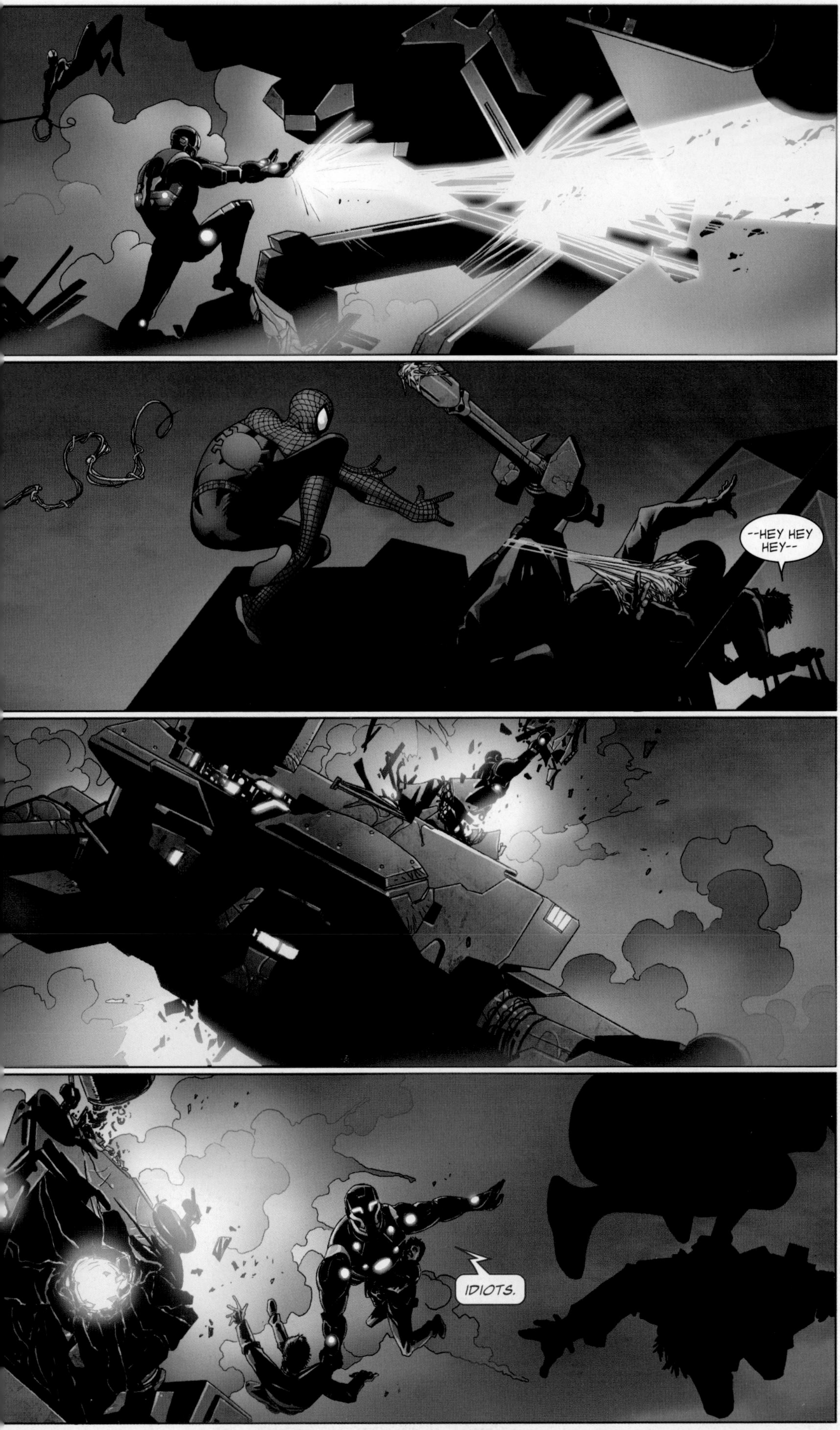
--HEY HEY
HEY--
IDIOTS.

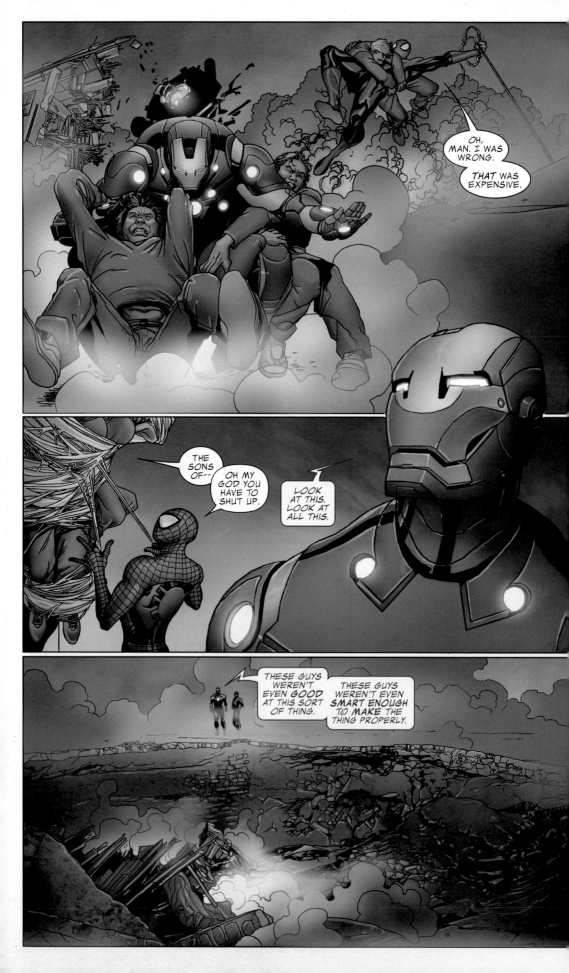

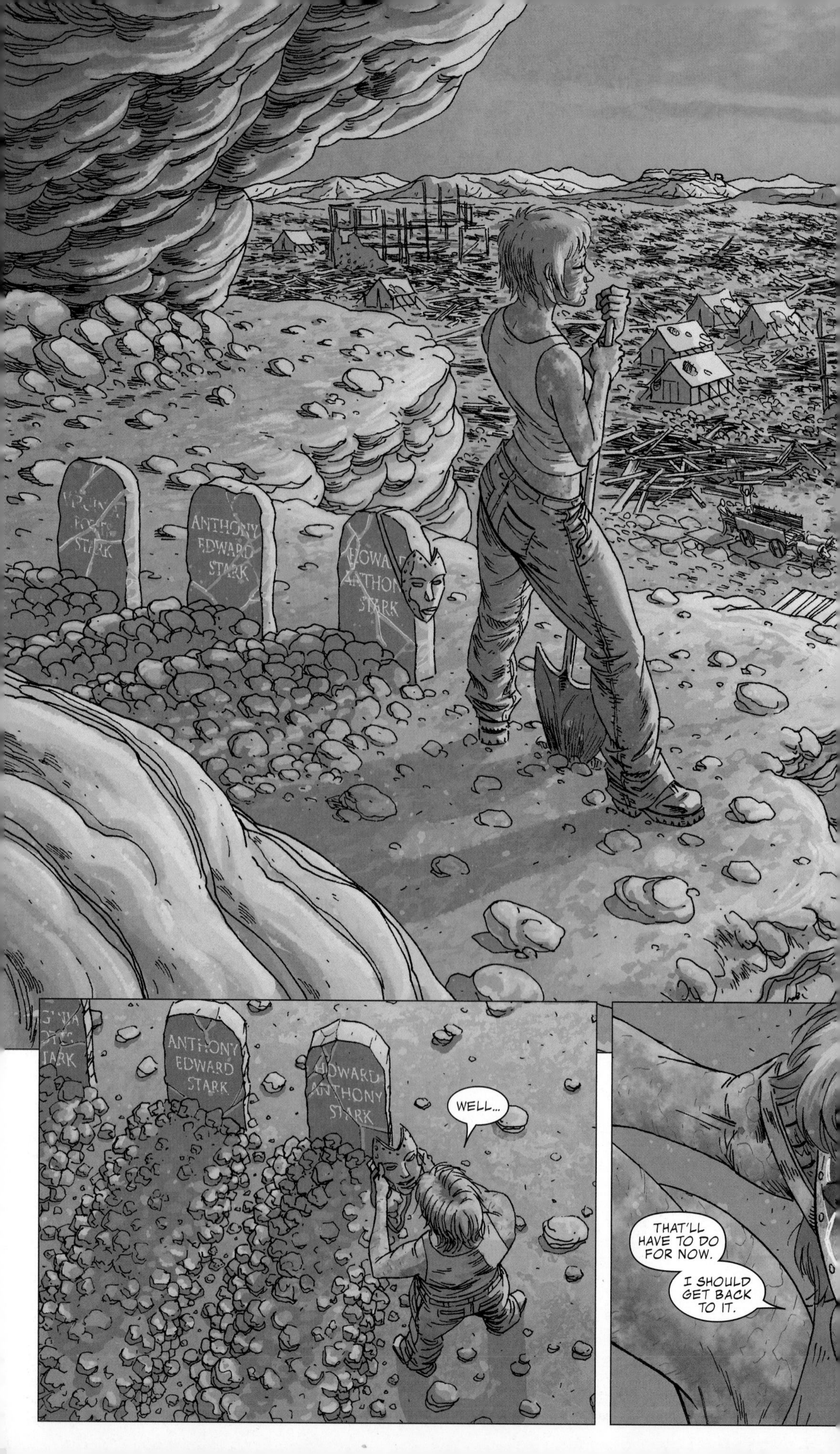
ANTHONY EDWARD STARK
HOWARD ANTHONY STARK
ANTHONY EDWARD STARK
HOWARD ANTHONY STARK
WELL...
THAT'LL HAVE TO DO FOR NOW.
I SHOULD GET BACK TO IT.

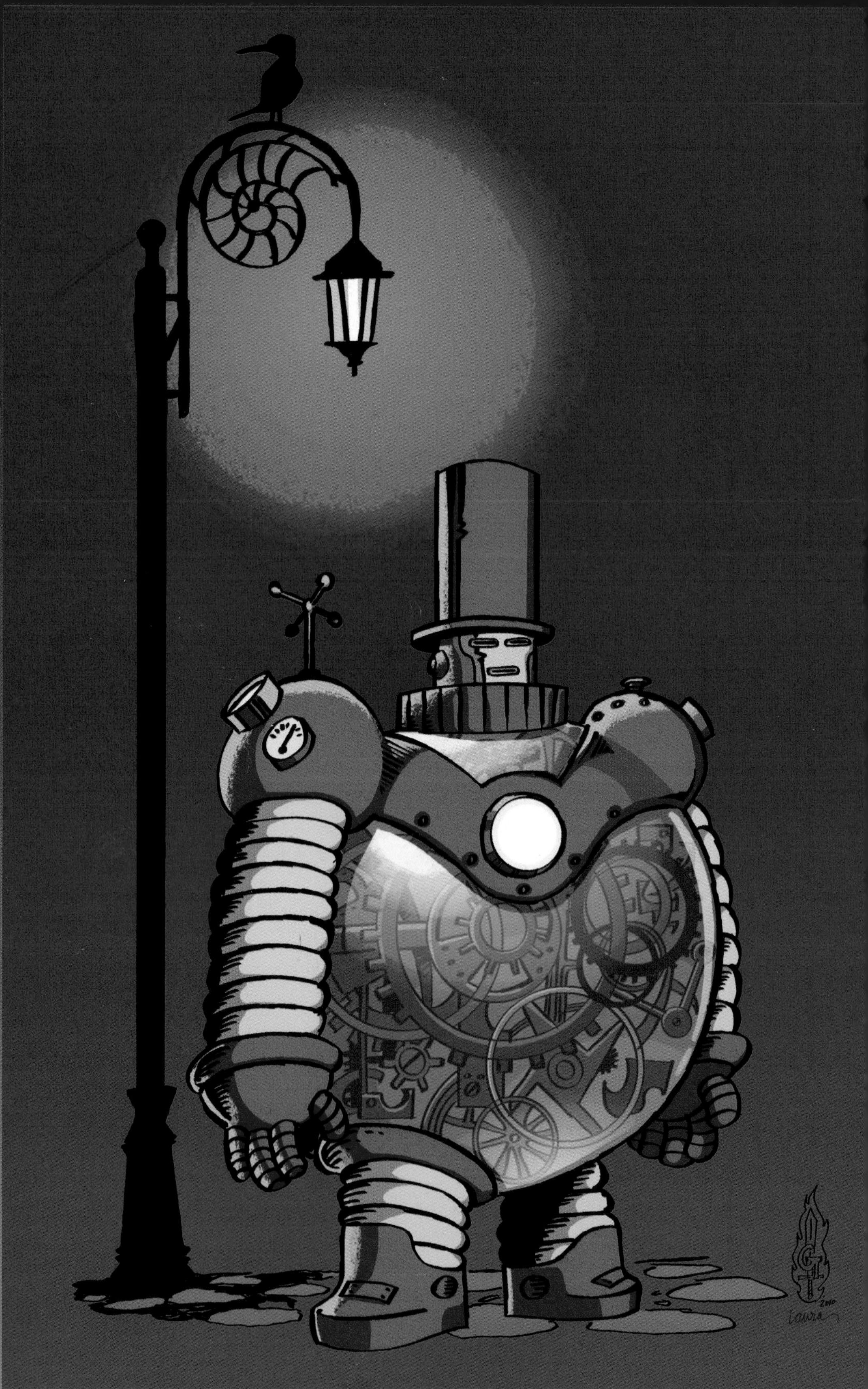

ANNUAL #1 IRON MAN BY DESIGN VARIANT
BY GENNEDY TARTAKOVSKY & LAURA MARTIN

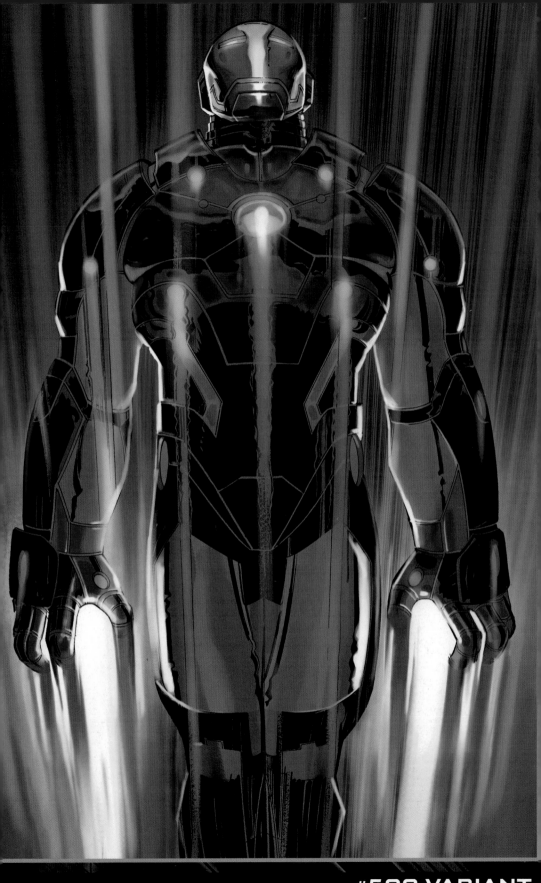

#500 VARIANT
BY JOHN ROMITA JR., KLAUS JANSON & DEAN WHITE

SPEED TEST

SECTOR F

LOG

INPUT

ENTER

LOAD

UPLOAD

RE

PASSWORD :
KEYGEN :

ENTER DATA

STARK RESILIENT R.T.

MARK X

2E46
5HJ8
68L0
VFT5
65JL
BV39
Z10W
VLC2
RGV5
CT57
9803
JGY5
38DF
M7L2
DL80
VTU8

FTX4
N137
004A

Set
01123
Reset

RELAY

00 VARIANT
SALVADOR LARROCA

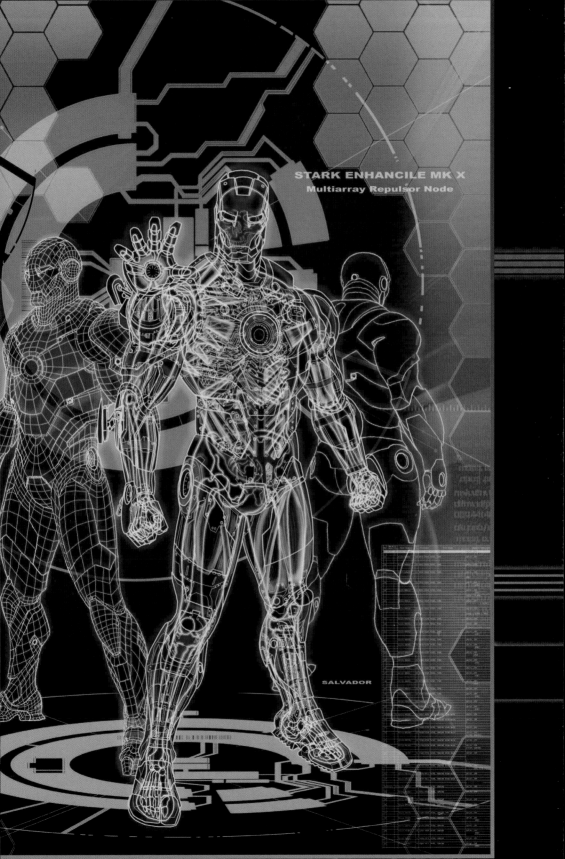

STARK ENHANCILE MK X
Multiarray Repulsor Node

SALVADOR

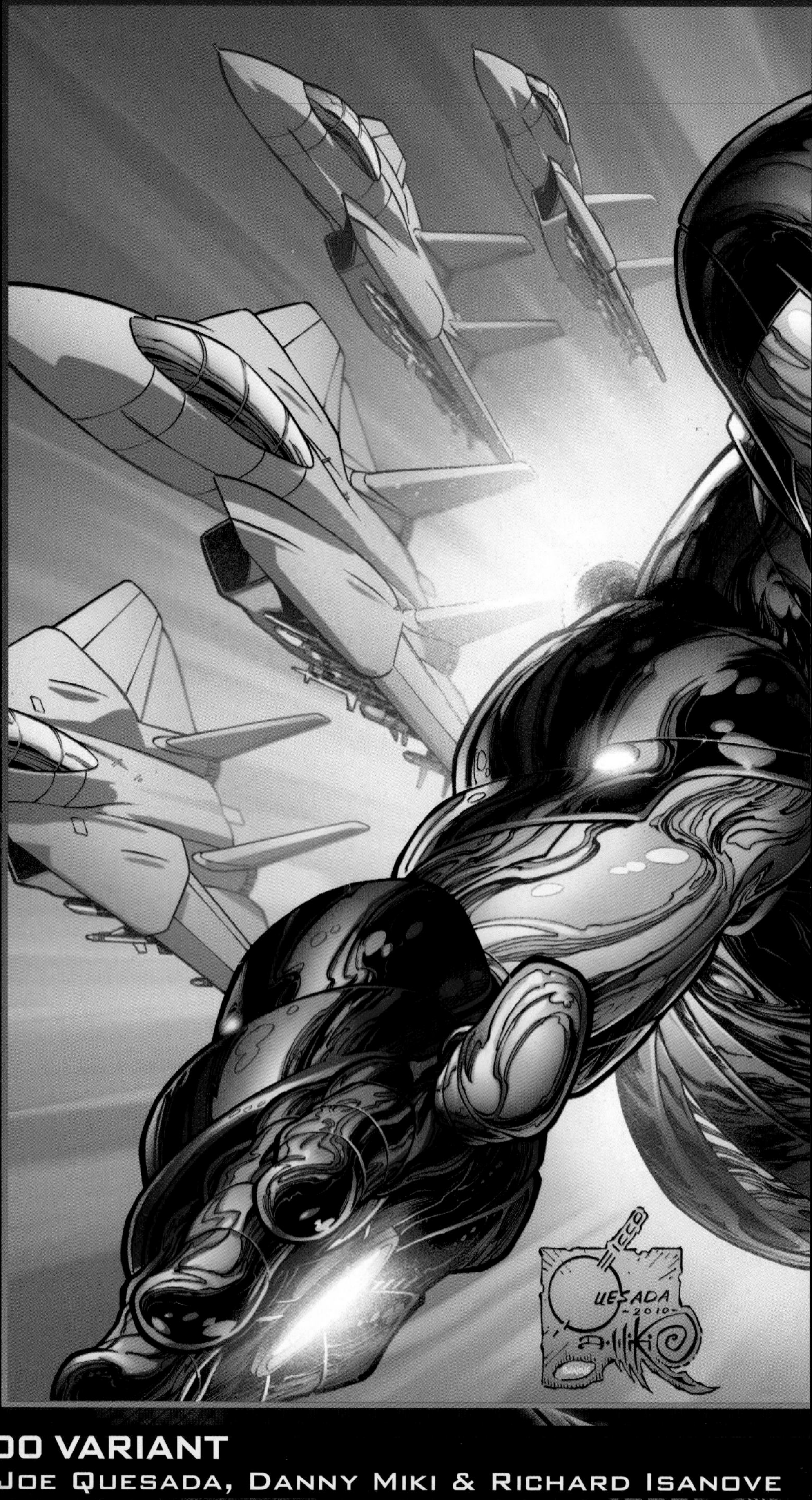
QUESADA
-2010-

#500 VARIANT

BY JOE QUESADA, DANNY MIKI & RICHARD ISANOVE

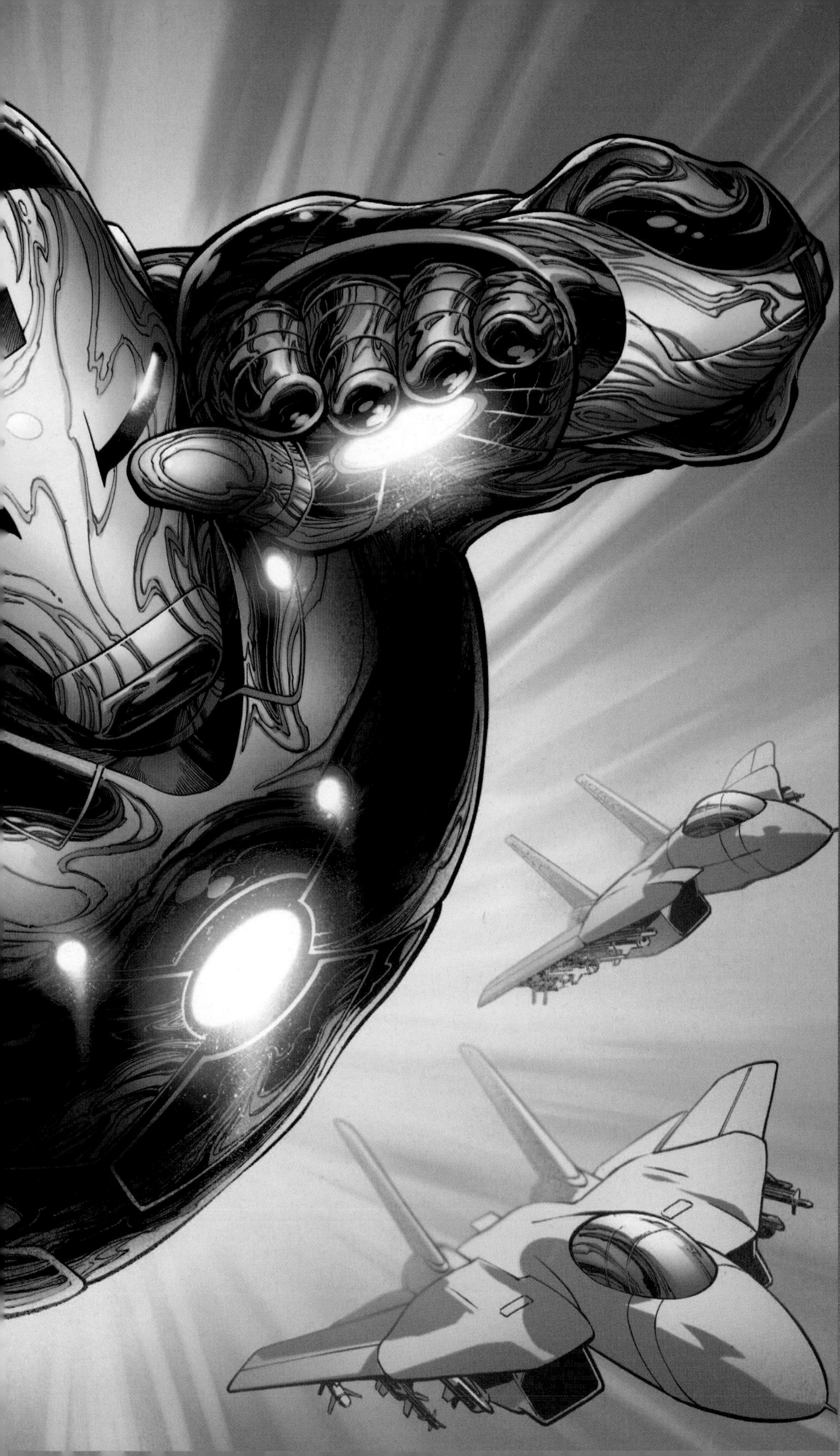

COMBINED VARIANT COVERS
BY MARKO DJURDJEVIC

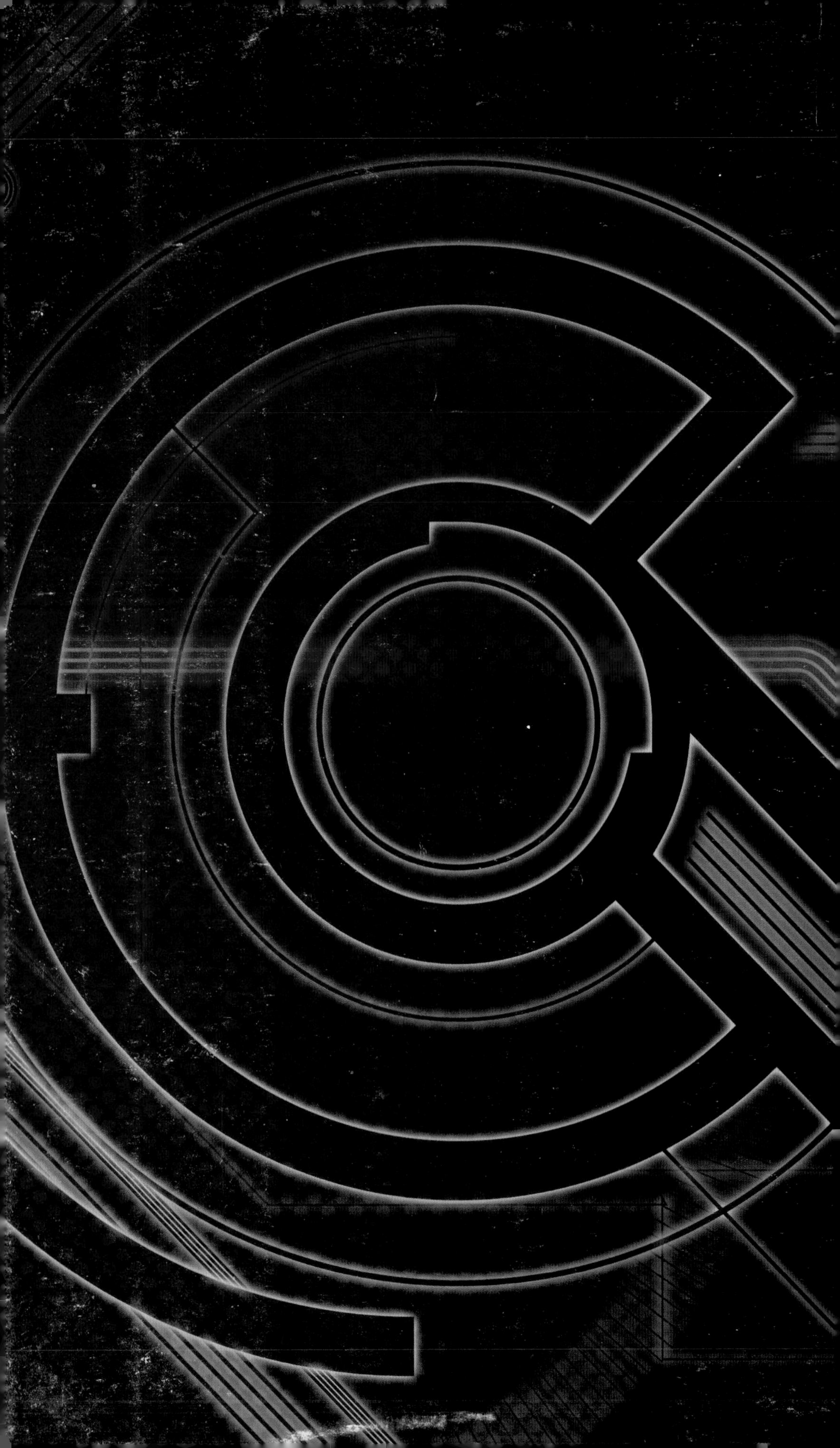